OU
A

OUTDOOR SAFETY AND SURVIVAL

Paul H. Risk
PENNSYLVANIA STATE UNIVERSITY

JOHN WILEY & SONS

New York   Chichester   Brisbane   Toronto   Singapore

COVER PAINTING: Albert Drogin.

Library of Congress Cataloging in Publication Data:

Risk, Paul H.
  Outdoor safety and survival.

  Includes index.
    1. Outdoor recreation—Safety measures.   2. Survival
skills.   3. Survival skills—Psychological aspects.
I. Title.
GV191.625.R57   1983   796.5'028'9   82-23810
ISBN 0-471-03891-1

Printed in the United States of America

10 9 8 7 6 5 4 3 2 1

PREFACE

The principles discussed in this book will be of interest to a wide audience. Both instructors and students in courses related to outdoor safety and survival will find much to enhance their understanding. Those engaging in outdoor recreation also can use this book as a means of gaining skills and understanding to make their outings safer and to prepare them for emergencies. Leaders who take groups into the outdoors under extreme conditions should also find the contents of this book especially important and useful.

Topics are designed to meet the needs of those who travel in any environment of the world. I am well aware that specific areas may require some important variations, but the material presented here can form a good foundation—the specific details of safety and behavior can be modified to meet the occasion.

An important consideration that makes this book different is its emphasis on the psychological aspects of survival. Too often in the past this area has been treated superficially, while the primary focus remained on the acquisition of techniques and skills. Although these are definitely essential, the *attitude* of survival is paramount.

This book is designed to be a single source of outdoor safety and survival information and integrates material from many different publications. It also attempts to update some of these publications, since much of what has been easily available is of World War II vintage, much of which is obsolete. This is especially true with regard to rapidly changing topics such as hypothermia, clothing, and venomous animal bites.

An extensive end-of-book section of Recommended Reading is included. As you study the book, try to read some of the reference material. The newer literature will provide an in-depth extension of the subjects covered and will also enable you to locate sources of additional information through their bibliographies. The older publications are included to allow you to gain a perspective on the origins of the field. Many of the procedures found in them have not changed—what once worked still does. Of special interest are the books and articles by and about those who have gone through actual survival experiences. Through their ordeals, you will gain a clearer appreciation of that all-important *attitude* of survival.

However, no amount of theory bound into a book can entirely prepare you for every eventuality. It is vitally important to use every opportunity for gaining practical experience in the application of this material. As skills are presented, take time to practice them. Work at gaining a degree of ability such that the skills can be performed easily even under the least ideal circumstances. *Do not* assume that by merely reading this book you are adequately prepared. Plan, study, practice. This book is written with only one essential purpose in mind— that you will be a survivor.

I would like to especially thank those who were so important in the inception and development of this book, some of whom must be nameless since their input came through varied courses and readings over many years. Many of the concepts have come from training received through the Los Angeles County Sheriff's Altadena Mountain Rescue Squad and were developed as I presented mountain safety workshops to school groups in Los Angeles County. At least three people from that organization were important in my early training—Paul Spink, Robert Gardner, and Vance Yost. Training and conversations with them planted seeds that germinated into courses I have taught and, finally, these seeds have now reached maturation in this book. Various U.S. Air Force survival instructors have also contributed, as well as personnel from the Air Training Command and Headquarters, U.S. Air Force. My continuing contact with them over the years has flavored much of the material in this book. At Michigan State University, my first Survival Laboratory Technician and ex-Air Force survival instructor, Stan Adams, was a great help both in skill improvement and when the push was necessary to get this effort moving. Paul Petzoldt, Director of the Wilderness Education Association and originator of the National Outdoor Leadership School and Outward Bound in the United States served as a sounding board for concepts as well as a reviewer of the manuscript. H. Morgan Smith, Vice-President of the International Survival Institute, Family Survival, Inc., and former Director of the U.S. Air Force's Arctic, Desert, Tropic Information Center at Maxwell Air Force Base, Alabama, has provided outstanding assistance over the past several years in conceptualizing as well as reviewing the manuscript as the book developed. His words of wisdom have, over time, so engrained themselves that they are not always clearly discernible as separate from my own. I am sure he will read various statements within this book that had their origin with him. His input has been invaluable. Evan Peelle,

Ph.D. President of the Quantum Consulting Group and the International Survival Institute, Family Survival, Inc., is well known for her work in survival psychology, and her involvement in the evaluation and review of this manuscript was gratefully received. My illustrators, Celia Drozdiak and Jan Kolena Cole, worked under very tight deadlines and produced excellence. And, finally, my wife Rosalie has been vitally important in the production of this book. Her moral support and confidence have been vital and she is my strength and support in all difficult tasks. Would that all husbands had such a resource.

Paul H. Risk

CONTENTS

INTRODUCTION

Survival is an attitude. While not always inherited, it is a mental set that may be cultivated. Although emergency preparedness involves training in skills, far more important is the need for calm, considered action under unforeseen, threatening circumstances. Although this book contains many ideas about techniques for coping with environmental extremes, it is the ability to cope with ourselves that is paramount in importance.

This is a book for those who, for any reason, spend time in the outdoors. Hunters, hikers, climbers, picnickers, and others who simply enjoy the outdoors will find information designed to help them pursue their activities more safely.

Within the past ten to fifteen years, recreational use of the outdoors has increased tremendously. It was once easy within a short distance to seek and find solitude and isolation, but we now find many others pursuing the same end. Recreationists, of all varieties, flock to the Mecca of the woods. In fact, it could easily be suggested that outdoor recreation has achieved a position of status. It is the ''in thing'' to do. All types and ages of people participate. A late summer afternoon may see several young people climbing a nearby rock face, while in the woods and fields adjacent those in their fifties, sixties, and even older wend their way through a serpentine orienteering course, competing for accuracy and speed.

Nor does a seasonal change end the race to the outdoors. Fall, as it has for generations, means hunting. But today the rush is on. From every metropolitan area the highways become choked with deerstalkers. And as winter brings snow, we hear the snarl of snowmobiles racing into the backcountry. Cross-country skiers, snowshoers, and winter campers fluff their down in preparation. Groups

1

with varying degrees of organization and experience offer guided instructional trips, ranging from expensive, all-comforts-supplied pack trips to expensive, all-comforts-avoided ordeals. They represent an interesting trend. Some offer relaxed, pleasant recreation in the "dude ranch" style; others offer personal growth through extreme physical and emotional stress. A number of organizations, including colleges and universities, now offer courses that emphasize the acquisition of outdoor skills. While this has been commonplace in Scouting for boys and girls as well as in other youth programs, it has only been in the last few years that climbing, caving, backpacking, and wilderness survival have begun to appear on college campuses.

And along with the more traditional pursuits, experiences designed around contrived stress are growing in popularity. To some extent, the popularity of Outward Bound, National Outdoor Leadership School, and other stress-oriented adventures may reflect a disenchantment with the sedentary opportunities available in the urban environment. The thrill of the unusual and challenging may be the lure.

Yet, the rush of everyday responsibilities and the pace of life produce stresses of their own. Some people are not able to cope with these and seek a means of finding inner strength. The more adventurous activities of climbing and wilderness survival, along with an almost bootcamp atmosphere of physical training, seem to provide an antidote. By finding they are able to handle the diverse and unusual demands of such strenuous pursuits, some find a new overall confidence in themselves. This realization has also spurred the development of programs dealing with the specialized needs of drug abusers, criminals, and mentally disturbed individuals using the outdoors as the setting.

However, all is not well. In growing numbers, the climbers are falling from their lofty perches, the orienteers are becoming disoriented, the hunters are succumbing to self-inflicted gunshots and coronaries, and the skiers are falling victim to hypothermia. In short, people ill-prepared for the adventure they seek find to their dismay that they cannot cope in nature either.

In general, the problems faced by many of the participants are related to a prevailing lifestyle. Almost exclusively urban-oriented and accustomed to the safeguards provided by a society ever more demanding of protection from danger and discomfort, we are simply not ready for nature that can be powerful in the extreme and yet both neutral and random in the distribution of trying conditions. Our development from childhood in an environment where all errors are excusable does not prepare us for an encounter with forces that are absolute and irrevocable. All too frequently we seem to be afflicted by the "Bambi, beauty and bounteous love" effect. Nature is the domain of friendly animals and dew-covered sparkling glades where love and the appreciation of green mountain glories hold sway to the exclusion of all that is unpleasant and hazardous. That *we* may become a statistic on someone's injury or fatality records seems beyond the realm of possibility. In fact, it is a gross unreality that holds us in its grasp. The "macho" (male or female) attitude that seeks to "conquer," after an appropriate "assault," the summits of craggy mountains and to meet nature on her own terms to beat her into submission is not helpful in coping and surviving in a wilderness setting.

In another setting are those unsuspecting individuals who, dressed in street clothes, driving or riding to work meet the fury of sudden storms that may choke off travel and subject them to hypothermia and carbon monoxide poisoning. Homeowners with limited supplies, dependent on utilities to provide power to heat, cook, light, and pump water, also find themselves hanging by a fine thread in the face of blizzards and ice-storms, torrential downpours and floods, tornadoes and hurricanes.

Roderick Nash in his book, *Wilderness and the American Mind*, indicates that, according to our basic definition of it, *wilderness* is chaotic and uncontrollable. When a storm is raging, power fails, and we are on our own, the outlook often appears to be chaotic, disorderly, and uncontrollable. Thus, whether we are in villages, towns, cities, or in the far reaches of the arctic north, we can still be involved in survival.

This book is not designed to teach methods of *defeating* nature by pushing back the forces of the storm. Whenever a hike, a picnic, a climb, or a trip to the supermarket is accomplished in safety it is done so because the participants operated *within* the constraints of nature, modifying their behavior to the demands of the elements. Human beings are among the most adaptable animals on earth, and it is this ability to adapt and to plan ahead that we will examine.

But remember throughout your study and in all your outdoor activities —

SURVIVAL IS AN ATTITUDE.

This book is designed to teach you to develop a survival attitude.

1

PREPARATION
FOR
SURVIVAL

We are natural beings. We are not alien creatures somehow separated from the realities and needs imposed on us by an environment. Our needs are largely the same as those of the rest of the animal kingdom. Any lack of ability to secure necessities from the outdoors is related almost exclusively to a lack of experience and an unfamiliarity with the surroundings. It is the aim of this book to expand your fund of knowledge and provide the basis for an enlarged outdoor experience. This book is designed to help you stay alive. It is also hoped that the reader will develop an increased awareness of and appreciation for the outdoors.

It is virtually impossible to succeed in the presence of overriding fear. Through an understanding of human capabilities and the human capacity to function in new environments, we will enhance our competence. And from this competence will grow a confidence bounded by a realistic appreciation of human limitations and a respect for those things in the outdoors that have the power to threaten our safety and existence.

INCONVENIENCE VERSUS EMERGENCY

A significant percent of the population in developed countries is accustomed only to buffered experiences with the outdoors. Wind is viewed through the window as it causes branches to sway, waves to roll, snow to blow and drift. From the warm, dry comfort of an automobile the traveler gazes at the passing countryside at all seasons of the year. Agencies have been developed to warn us when toys are unsafe, when drugs are questionable, or when vehicles are poorly designed. Thus, accustomed to an existence that is extensively protected and padded, we respond to inconvenience as though it were an emergency.

In general, the average person seldom has to face a real emergency. Simply put, an emergency is an event that has the capacity to threaten our physical well-being or lives. An inconvenience merely interferes with our mental or physical comfort. Although most events are in the nature of inconveniences, they may become emergencies. And what is an inconvenience under one set of circumstances can be an emergency under others. For example, a flat tire in June under sunny skies in central Pennsylvania is generally an inconvenience. It means only that we must get out, change the tire, and be late for an appointment. The same flat tire in February in the middle of a blizzard may easily constitute an emergency. Or a coronary, brought on by the exertion of changing the tire in June, escalates the inconvenience to emergency status. Here are some occurrences that usually are only inconvenient.

1. Being lost on a hunting trip or hike.
2. Being stuck in a mud hole on a dirt road in an automobile.
3. Running out of gas.
4. Getting a flat tire.
5. Having a power failure in the home.
6. Running out of food on an extended backpack trip.

But all of these events have the potential of becoming emergencies. Looking at them one by one, it is evident that being lost in itself means only a delay in returning and perhaps some embarrassment. Stuck cars, running out of gas, and flat tires are also only delays. Home power failures mean it's not possible to watch television, listen to the stereo, run the dishwasher, or use the clothes washer and dryer. Yet these (whatever our initial feelings of deprivation) are still only inconvenient. It is, believe it or not, possible to survive without television, radio, dishwashers, and washing machines! Of course, loss of power in the home may also result in loss of heat. But even this may only mean that we have to don winter clothes and coats indoors. We are still better off than we would be outside. And finally, lack of food, as we will see later, is the least important problem in most survival situations.

The point of all this is that many or most of the everyday, and even out of the ordinary, occurrences that affect or afflict us are too frequently responded to as though they were life-threatening crises. It is of great importance that the proper perspective be maintained and realistic priorities be assigned to the events that we encounter.

WHAT CONSTITUTES A SURVIVAL EXPERIENCE?

When the average person thinks of "survival," the term conjures up scenes of extreme danger of an exotic nature. We tend to think of burning deserts, steaming jungles, and arctic wasteland. In fact, survival situations may *develop* from

PREPARATION FOR SURVIVAL

the most commonplace events. Although this may seem contradictory in view of the previous discussion, it is not. It has already been mentioned that the individual situation dictates whether a particular problem constitutes an emergency. Here are examples of inconveniences that may *develop* into survival situations.

1. A car stuck on a little-used road.
2. A hunter, hiker, or camper lost in the woods.
3. A change in the weather with an increase in wind, rain, or snow, and falling temperatures.
4. A disabled snowmobile.
5. A broken ski or binding.
6. A capsized boat.
7. A severe headache making travel impossible.
8. A minor injury or illness that makes travel unwise or undesirable.

BASIC RULES FOR PREPAREDNESS

Whatever the situation, there are a number of things that may be done to reduce the chances of becoming involved in a survival emergency and that can minimize the severity of the problem. Here are nine rules that ought to be considered each time a trip into the outdoors is planned.

1. Never hike, climb, hunt, fish, ski, camp, or do any outdoor activity, alone.
2. Leave a travel plan behind and stick to it.
3. Dress properly for present and potential conditions.
4. Carry basic equipment—at the very least a knife, a whistle, and matches.
5. Know your personal skill and physical limitations. Abide by them.
6. Know your geographic area.
7. Have a topographic map and compass. Know how to use them.
8. Don't fool around.
9. Don't let your ego kill you.

Now let's look at each of the rules in detail.

1. NEVER HIKE (OR DO ANYTHING DANGEROUS) ALONE

Trouble when it comes is always easier to handle with help. What might have been only an inconvenience often becomes serious when the victim is alone. At the very least, the discomfort factor increases. A sprained ankle when there is someone to assist is very minor. But, when alone, it spells trouble.

Ideally, the *minimum* number of people involved should be three. In the case of injury or illness, one can stay with the victim and the other can go for help.

If only two people are in the party, it then would be necessary for the healthy or uninjured person to leave the victim alone while assistance is sought. Certainly, many people violate this rule; and if an intense solo encounter with the outdoors is the goal, then it is a rule that must be broken. But whenever the decision is made to go it alone, it must be done with full awareness of what this means. You are then totally on your own and must be willing and able to cope with all circumstances without help.

Help can mean more than just assistance in time of injury or illness. A lost person suffers from many anxieties and fears that may be minimized by the company of another. Imagine the conditions as darkness grows. Even when a campfire is burning, there is the feeling that the blackness is endless and that isolation is complete. Uncomfortable and insecure, the lost person listens intently to every rustling leaf, every squeaking branch. Peering into the night, imagination animates the dark with creatures. The crunching and crackling of small rodents in their nocturnal search for food becomes the approach of "Bigfoot." Often total loss of control ensues, with the lost person screaming and running in panic-stricken flight through the woods only to become seriously injured in a fall. A companion at this time may help by calming fears and restoring normal perspective. Of course, there is also the possibility that this helpful soul will be just as frightened.

2. LEAVE A TRAVEL PLAN—AND STICK TO IT

A travel plan should be left with at least two people—one who loves you and one in authority. There is a very good reason for planning this way. Often, rangers and others whose job requires that they be the repository of such information have been so inundated with situations in which hikers and campers have failed to report back on their return that they minimize the seriousness of the situation and wait for more definite indication of problems. If the travel plan is also left with someone who has a stake in your future, he or she will contact the authorities and make certain that something is done immediately. (Of course, it pays to be sure this person *really* cares. They may be simply heaving a sigh of relief.) Generally, rangers and wardens in state and federal forest areas would be the logical people with whom to leave travel information. But local police agencies will also be helpful.

The second part of this rule is to not deviate from the plan after you establish it. A search was once conducted for a climber whose wife gave the search and rescue team the travel plan left by the man as he was leaving. Dispatched to the area, no sign was found that anyone had been there. The search was broadened and a day passed. Other areas where the man was known to climb were investigated and a second day passed. Finally, on the third day after his failure to return, his body was located in an area far from what his travel plan indicated. He had fallen, possibly on the first day of the solo climbing trip. Crawling to a sheltering rock, he managed to build a small fire. From appearances, he had maintained the fire for at least a day and perhaps longer before he had succumbed to injuries.

He had violated two rules. First, he chose to climb alone and, second, he went to a place his travel itinerary did not indicate. No one was there to administer first aid. No one could go for help. And lastly, no one knew where he was. And when time was critically important to his survival, the search team spent fruitless hours searching the wrong area. If a travel plan must be changed, be sure that one or both of the people you left the plan with knows of the modification.

As a last consideration, information may be left attached to your car. However, this also indicates to potential thieves that your vehicle is unattended and gives them all the information they need to work in safety.

3. DRESS PROPERLY FOR CURRENT AND POTENTIAL CONDITIONS

The old saying, "If you don't like the weather, wait a minute," certainly applies to outdoor activities. The difficulty is that it may well get worse before it gets better. In fact, Murphy's Law would indicate that it *will* get worse. If you aren't dressed for what may develop, then carry additional clothing. In one disastrous event a 19-year-old man, his fiancée, and sister commenced a hike along a moderate trail in the mountains of Southern California. The weather in the valley was warm and the man was wearing cut-off jeans, a jersey T-shirt, and tennis shoes. As the trio moved up the trail, two factors began to have effect. First, the trail became shaded and, second, the hikers began to gain elevation. Both resulted in the temperature gradually falling. Soon there were isolated snowbanks under the trees and in the shade of rocks. As they climbed still higher and the temperature became lower, they found patches of snow on the trail. It was not long before the trail was covered with thawing, slippery snow. Instead of the relatively level surface they had been accustomed to, the footing now sloped outward and downward. At one point, the man, whose tennis shoes offered little assistance on the slick trail, slipped down the steep side of the mountain. His fall was arrested by a tree about 50 feet below the trail level. Rising a bit shaken to his feet, he looked up the slope to the trail as both his sister and fiancée urged him to remain where he was while they went for help. Saying he was alright and that he didn't want to cause a lot of trouble, he began to climb up the steep snow-covered slope, kicking at the frozen surface to make steps. But after only a few feet, his tennis shoes slipped out from under him and with a rush he fell once again. This time his fall was not stopped, and he plunged from their sight. The search team's arrival disclosed that he had fallen 1100 feet, striking rocks and partially covered tree stumps before, fatally injured, his fall ended in the stream at the bottom of the canyon. In this case, the first fall was most likely the result of inappropriate footgear. But, the second and fatal fall was caused not only by slippery shoes but by overconfidence (inaccurate assessment of personal skill) and by a desire to save face. Both of these factors will be discussed later.

The literature is filled with survival situations in which victims compounded injury or died of exposure because the clothing in their possession was inadequate to cope with changing weather conditions. This is especially true when falling temperatures combine with rain and wind, creating an insurmountable and rapid loss of body heat that produces a fatal hypothermia.

4. CARRY BASIC EQUIPMENT

Three items ought to comprise the very least amount of equipment carried on any outing. A knife, a whistle, and some matches can often make the difference between life and death. Of course, the list may be expanded; later on we will look at the contents of a survival kit and discuss other suggestions for additional items to take along.

Knife

The knife need not be a huge sheat-type instrument, although a large knife carried on the belt can have a place in the list of items carried. But given the choice of only one, a folding pocketknife with at least two blades will suffice (Figure 1-1). The main blade should taper to a point and be at least $2\frac{1}{2}$ to 3 inches long, and the other should have a straightedge, as illustrated in Figure 1-1. Skinning and preparation of food are accomplished with the long tapering blade, while carving trap triggers and other rough chores are best handled by the second.

Figure 1-1   An ideal design for a survival pocketknife. (Paul H. Risk)

PREPARATION FOR SURVIVAL

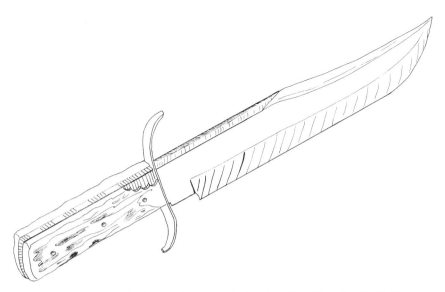

Figure 1-2 A possible design for a good sheath knife. (Rosalie R. Risk)

A large Bowie-type sheath knife can be of great assistance but too frequently is carried for the wrong reasons. These are: (1) to look tough and woodsy, (2) to kill bears, and (3) to chop branches and saplings for shelter material. Those who reason number 1 generally hook their thumb over the handle, walk with a swagger, never smile, and say "howdy" a lot. And frankly, it's hard to separate them from those who plan to grab bears by the scruff of the neck and dispatch them with one swift thrust. Both of the first two reasons are ridiculous. Of course, it is remotely possible in the event of a bear attack that the large knife could be used as an absolutely last ditch defense. But, in general, the best bear defense, if escape is impossible and a rifle is unavailable, is passivity.

The last reason—to chop branches and saplings for shelter material—is reasonable. The knife selected ought to have a significant amount of weight—almost a baby machete. Its blade length should be no less than 9 inches, and the tang or section of the blade that passes through the hilt and into the handle should be the same width and thickness as the rear of the blade itself. (Figure 1-2). In most sheath knives the tang narrows abruptly as it passes into the handle, and in the rough use of chopping or digging it may break off leaving a blade with no handle. Another alternative is a small machete or hatchet. A 14-inch machete is ideal and there is less likelihood of injuring the user than with a small hatchet should the instrument glance off whatever is being chopped.

But it should be held firmly in mind that 99 percent of camp chores can be most easily and efficiently carried out with a pocketknife.

Whistle

A whistle is a signaling device that is not subject to laryngitis. No matter how hard it's blown, it will not get hoarse or stop working. On the other hand, the human voice, subjected to continued harsh use under stressful conditions, may do either or both. In addition, a whistle can be heard farther than someone using only their voice.

In the case of children, the whistle becomes even more important. Each year large numbers of children become separated from families and other groups and unfortunately a few are either never found or are recovered dead. Faced with the fearful situation of isolation from family and friends in an environment they consider hostile, they may, although only a short distance from security, simply crouch in the brush and fail to respond to the calls of searchers they regard as strangers. This is especially true of very small children. In one instance, the author after being involved in a day-long search literally stepped on the 5-year-old girl who was the object of the operation. She was only a few hundred yards from camp. Yet her position made it impossible for her to see camp or be seen by those in her group. As she was taken by the hand and asked if her name was Linda, she nodded but would still not speak. Fear, coupled with strong parental warnings never to speak to strangers, may have caused her silence as the search was carried out throughout the day. If she had been wearing a small, metal police-type whistle with instructions to blow it if she was lost or afraid, the search would never have been initiated.

Metal is preferable to plastic because the sound of metallic whistles is far more shrill. Some have suggested that in winter a metal whistle may become dangerously cold and cause injury to the lips. Those so concerned have most likely never worn a whistle for long periods. If it's free to swing at the end of the cord around the neck, sooner or later it will smack the wearer right in the teeth as they run or engage in other vigorous activity. The moral is to tuck the whistle down the shirt or coat. In this way, it's easy to retrieve but not free to bash you. At the same time, it stays warm.

The whistle should not be worn on a lanyard that will support the weight of the body. In the event that the wearer should catch it on a branch while running, serious injury could result. It would be better to lose the whistle after breaking the lanyard rather than to hang oneself.

If the individual is old enough to understand, be sure he or she is taught to blow the whistle three times if in need of help. Three whistle blasts is an internationally understood emergency signal. The response from others in the party is two blasts. But, in the case of a very young person, it is only necessary that they know to blow and blow loudly. However, it is of extreme importance that nobody blow the whistle just for fun, to experiment or for any other reason than in the case of a real emergency. In my survival courses as well as with my own children, the rule has always been "Never blow your whistle unless

Figure 1-3   Three match containers. The metal one in the upper right is not desirable. (Paul H. Risk)

there's a real emergency. Because if you ever do and there's *not* an emergency, there will be when I get to you!'' Otherwise, like crying ''wolf,'' the signal will become meaningless.

Matches
Preferably, the matches carried should be the common kitchen type, which will strike on almost anything rough. Matches that require a special surface almost guarantee the absence of the necessary striking material when they're needed. They ought to be carried in a waterproof container that is brightly colored and not subject to jamming or leaking. Plastic containers seem to be the best currently available. Although there are metal, threaded match safes, they are hard to use in cold weather, jam easily from dirt, and leak from deformation if they're stepped on or treated roughly (Figure 1-3).

The matches themselves may also be individually waterproofed either by dipping in shellac or melted paraffin.

It's also a good idea to carry one container of matches in the pants pocket and another in the pack. That way, if the pack is lost, this vital item is still available.

5. KNOW YOUR PERSONAL SKILL AND PHYSICAL LIMITATIONS

Abide by them. The 19-year-old hiker mentioned above failed to take into consideration his lack of skill as he tried to climb back to the trail. The result was fatal. Too often we see inexperienced people attempting outdoor ventures that are well beyond their skill. This is especially true in climbing. Over the past few years rock climbing and other mountaineering experiences have become increasingly popular. And with more frequency, we see injuries and death resulting from attempts that are beyond the victim's abilities. Ironically, the activity seems to attract those who are least likely to admit personal limitations. They forge on in the face of odds that would cause a more experienced (or mature) person to turn back.

Some years ago three teenage boys and an adult advisor hiked, against National Park Service advice, to the bottom of Grand Canyon in midsummer on an unmaintained trail. With minimal equipment and insufficient water, the return trip found them off the trail and lost. As the day progressed, park visitors far above heard cries for help from the group. Impatient, the boys and advisor attempted to descend a sheer cliff to get back to the canyon bottom and the relative security of the Colorado River. However, their skill was limited and they had no proper climbing gear. The advisor and one of the boys were killed in a fall of several hundred feet. A second boy died before reaching the river.

In fact, many people today are simply not in the physical condition they think they are in, and the hikes and other outdoor activities they plan are beyond their strength and stamina. At the very least, the experience becomes an ordeal and, at the worst, a cardiac malfunction may result. Intelligent planning and a program to improve physical condition prior to the outdoor experience are very important.

6. KNOW YOUR GEOGRAPHIC AREA

Before you leave, spend some time examining maps of the area. Talk to those who have been there before. Be generally familiar with the lay of the land and the location of roads, streams, ridges, and other landmarks.

7. HAVE A TOPOGRAPHIC MAP AND COMPASS

Know how to use them. This rule is almost a correlary to the one preceding. Having examined maps of the area prior to the trip, don't assume that you can memorize them. Take a good topographic map along. Learn map-reading skills before you leave and carry and be familiar with a good quality compass (Figure 1-4).

8. DON'T FOOL AROUND

Many injuries have resulted from horseplay. Running and throwing rocks are high on the list. In one youth group camp, a young man running through the campsite during twilight failed to see some logs piled near the stove. Tripping, he fell toward the incandescent iron stove top, which was glowing orange in the darkness. In the reflex defensive action of throwing his hands out to stop

14

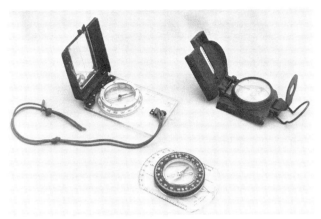

Figure 1-4   Acceptable compass designs. (Paul H. Risk)

the fall, he placed them directly on the searing stove top. Second and third degree burns were the result.

Another youth throwing rocks off the top of a steep canyon struck a mule in a party hundreds of feet below. The mule was killed. Luckily as it sank to its knees it did not roll over the cliff. Instead, it rolled toward the inside of the trail. However, its rider was pinned against the rocks and suffered a broken leg.

Searches have been initiated when yelling and horsing around were thought to be cries for help.

9. DON'T LET YOUR EGO KILL YOU

When the inconvenience imposed by delays impinges on others, we often tend to take unreasonable risks to prevent this awkwardness. Late for an appointment, we speed and endanger ourselves and others. The lost hiker often suffers from a number of concerns. People will be worried. A lot of folks will be inconvenienced if they have to start a search. The person lost will look stupid or silly. Image conscious, we worry about our credibility. People will think I'm a greenhorn—that I don't know what I'm doing in the outdoors. I've got to get to work. My wife, father, mother, brother, sister, etc., will worry. The 19-year-old hiker, worried about what people would think, took a risk that cost him his life.

When an emergency occurs, it is essential that a whole new set of priorities be developed. It no longer is important what people think, how late you are going to be, or how inconvenient it will be for searchers. Planning and action

BASIC RULES FOR PREPAREDNESS   15 must revolve around what is best *under the circumstances*. No amount of concern regarding people or events, which are irrelevant to the current situation, will alter conditions even a slight bit. People will worry and just as certainly be inconvenienced. But they will be far more distraught and inconvenienced if you don't survive.

THE IMMORTALITY SYNDROME

One of the most difficult tasks any survival instructor has is to convince students tht the skills and course information comprise anything beyond mere intellectual exercise. Operating under what might best be described as an immortality syndrome, most people firmly believe that nothing will ever happen to them. Unfortunate occurrences will only happen to the other person. Perhaps this saves us from unnecessary worry and prevents us from stewing and fretting throughout our lives about events that largely don't ever come to pass, but there is another effect of shielding ourselves in this manner. Those who have never conceived that they could ever be involved in a survival emergency tend to respond less well when confronted with the actual situation. They lack a survival attitude.

PREPARATORY INOCULATION

As you progress in your study of survival, play a game with yourself. Rather than considering what you would do *if* you ever found yourself in a survival emergency, plan for what you would do *when* it happened. Such an attitude attaches far more relevance to each of the skills and concepts learned. Plan *now* for your own personal emergency. (You'll be able to get so much more out of it! Otherwise, you might miss something important!) Stop for a moment and consider the training a commercial pilot receives. Do they wait until they have an emergency at 38,000 feet before considering how to handle it? Is the scenario something like this? "Let's see, we have a fire in the starboard outboard engine and the control surfaces in that wing are sluggish. Let's get out the emergency procedures book and review." Meantime there's a resounding boom as a flash of orange flame billows into the sky and pieces of what was once an aircraft rain to the earth. Of course not! Training in emergency preparedness commences long before they even have a chance to get their hands on an aircraft. It progresses in flight simulators that are firmly fastened to the ground where errors are not so costly. Every conceivable situation is thrown at them so that a response, tempered by a lightning ability to modify procedures to fit the circumstances, becomes an integral part of their mental operation. They develop relevant associations in the realization that in the course of a career in flying they will indeed be faced with emergencies of varying severity and not only passengers' lives but their own hang in the balance. This ability to develop relevant associations in thought patterns is critical as you study survival material. It *can* happen to you. And when it does, you are very likely going to be the only person around who knows anything about what to do.

DON'T DEPEND ON OTHERS

It's fine that the plan calls for you to always be with someone else. However, also learn to be self-sufficient. This may sound selfish, but to place reliance in others is to weaken your own resources. In addition, the person you rely on may not be present or functional when the emergency develops. If you are totally self-sufficient, you can be of great assistance not only to yourself but to others with less education in survival preparedness. If, in addition, that person you usually have along on outdoor activities *is* there and *is* functional, so much the better. Then there'll be two people to provide assistance.

A second part of preparatory inoculation deals with participating in experiences that simulate the responses necessary in actual emergencies. This begins by *planning* how to handle your emergency before it happens. The mental set developed tends to prepare you emotionally as well as intellectually to make correct decisions and responses under actual emergency conditions. This preparation is vital. Lacking it, a victim is far less likely to be able to cope effectively when faced with the stress of real situations.

Although planning is important, it is also desirable to participate in field training experiences that simulate as nearly as possible actual conditions that may be encountered during an emergency. Field training should impose as much stress on the trainees as practical, but should also be conducted so that success is experienced by all. However, participants should feel that the possibility for failure is very real. The feeling should remain that they have passed through real danger but, because of skill, knowledge, and training, have done so unscathed. At the very least, especially in the event that intensive and elaborate field training is impossible, the student should take every opportunity to practice the skills discussed in this book.

SUDDENLY IT'S YOU

In spite of planning, care, and good physical condition, it finally happens. You're involved in a personal survival emergency. It could be anything—a plane crash, an auto stranded in a snow drift, or a hiking trip. Really, it doesn't matter. In general, the response pattern is similar. But, let's use disorientation as a case in point. Having put the thought out of mind for an hour or more, the sudden realization strikes that indeed you're lost. A sudden rush of heat seems to emanate from the center of your chest and surges to your finger tips. Immediately the warmth drains away leaving tingling hands and a cold clammy skin. The coldness seems to grip at your heart. Lost! It's finally happened. After all those years of only vaguely considering the possibility, it has really happened. The scenery, so shortly before tranquil and beautiful, now takes on a stark appearance. No, this can't really be happening. Surely you will soon see something familiar. Of course, this is just ridiculous. A return of some calm occurs. But a moment later, the harsh realization returns that you're indeed lost. The adrenaline reaction repeats itself. You may vacillate back and forth several times between unbelief and shocked awareness of the situation. Then comes the moment when no amount of rationalization works and total awareness of the situation sinks in. That moment is probably the most critical time in a survival experience. How you respond within the first few moments after you're willing to admit real involvement in a survival situation may well dictate whether you survive at all.

THE ADMISSION PROFILE

Generally all people, no matter what the emergency, pass through a response sequence that is similar.

1. Undercurrent of concern; marginal awareness of a developing problem.
2. Flash of intense concern; brief intense awareness.
3. Failure to accept evidence; return to stage 1.
4. Flash of intense concern again; intense awareness.
5. Total acceptance and awareness.
6. Panic or control.

PRINCIPLE OF 30

In general, correct action and rational behavior is hardest to maintain during the first 30 seconds or so after complete acknowledgment of the seriousness of the situation. If calm, rational action can be maintained during that period, chances for survival rise greatly. Survivors, some seriously injured during this period, indicate clearly that it was during this phase that panic seized them and their irrational acts seriously compounded their situation. During this initial phase it is most important to control irrational urges. Stop! Sit down if conditions permit. Take a deep breath. Let it out gradually. Do not use it to scream. Do not do anything sudden. Above all, do not run. Remember that nothing has changed in the few seconds of realization. You're not suddenly in more trouble. Use your sense of humor. You're finally lost. It's no longer practice. It's no longer a vicarious exercise of reading survival manuals. It's the real thing.

18

Great! You've been waiting weeks, months, perhaps years since you studied this survival information. Say to yourself, "Wonderful, I'm finally lost and at last I'm going to get the chance to try all those skills I learned from study!" If you can get that kind of grip on your emotions, you're going to survive! You see, it isn't just learning how to build fires in the rain, carve shelters in snowbanks, or snatch fish from a stream with your bare hands that will ultimately keep you alive. It's your attitude. In fact, if you forget *everything* else in this book as well as everything else you ever have studied or heard about survival, you must always remember one thing. SURVIVAL IS AN ATTITUDE.

After the first 30 seconds pass and some degree of calm has been maintained, another sequence takes over. Generally, survivors indicate that having conquered the initial surge of panic is only the first step. After perhaps 30 minutes, having assessed the circumstances, there may be a resurgence of panicky and irrational thought. Once again, it is important to restrain the urge to do anything sudden. There are very few situations in the outdoors that require immediate action in which it is impossible to think first. Rethink your situation. Realize anew that you are still alive and *capable* of thought. That awareness should be heartening. It means that things are not as bad as they might be.

Finally, there is a chance that as time goes on there will be a recurrence of great anxiety coupled with depression. This often happens when survivors expect to be found in a certain amount of time and that limit has been exceeded. Discouraged at the failure of rescuers to arrive at the expected time, imagination takes over and concerns over whether anyone really knows about them begin to affect attitudes. In a number of cases, survivors have indicated a cyclic recurrence of depression at three-day intervals.

CONTROL OF FEAR, PANIC, AND DEPRESSION

Keep busy and act deliberately. Irrational responses to fear are often enhanced by sudden actions. In order to exercise maximum control and thus remain as calm as possible, move and act in as deliberate a manner as conditions permit. Of course, there are situations in which immediate action is necessary. Aboard an airliner following a crash landing in which structural damage occurs, the chances of fire are very high. Delay is often fatal. So, under these conditions it is important to get off the aircraft as fast as you can get to an exit.

Of course, this doesn't mean climbing over other passengers or doing anything else that will interfere with their survival chances. But it *does* mean knowing how to activate exits and leave the plane *fast*. But, in general, such situations are rare. So, take your time. Move more slowly than would be usual. Think things through clearly. Speak slowly and quietly. Make a conscious effort to avoid speaking too loudly or yelling. Incoherent speech will only confuse those who are trying to help and result in delays while they sort out what is being said. And this will only raise your level of frustration and reinforce feelings of helplessness and fear.

Besides acting in a deliberate manner, it is important to keep busy. Be constantly involved in tasks that keep your mind from focusing on depressing aspects of the survival situation. There is always something that can be done to improve the situation. Carve a bowl, collect firewood, improve signals, write a journal. Some survivors who floated for many days at sea say they recited poetry, sang songs, and worked mathematical problems in their heads to keep from dwelling on conditions. Above all, this is not the time to do a physiological inventory. Unless medical conditions make it imperative, avoid concern regarding pulse and respiration rates. Most people have never tried to locate their own pulse. Fumbling around the inside middle of their wrist (where the pulse is *not* located), they are horrified to find that they have none. Obviously, the situation is far worse than they thought! They're in the middle of cardiac arrest! Worse—they must have died and failed to notice! If, by accident, their wandering fingers do locate the pulse near the thumb side of the inner surface of the wrist, they are not likely to be relieved. Since they have just frightened themselves so badly, the rate may be 160 or higher and seem to be irregular. This combination of facts, coming in the midst of a situation the victim isn't particularly enjoying, is no way to maintain calm. In fact, it can ruin your whole outdoor experience!

If respiration rates are observed, the victim often assumes they are breathing too fast. They feel a shortness of breath. Tension and anxiety do the rest. In an effort to get more air, they force themselves to breathe deeper and more rapidly. Hyperventilating, they become dizzy. Supposing dizziness to be incipient heart failure, the anxiety level rises still more. More rapid breaths, more dizziness. The cycle mercifully limits itself when the victim faints. Dissolved oxygen and carbon dioxide levels in the bloodstream then begin to return to normal and consciousness is restored automatically. Of course, hyperventilation can also be treated by breathing into a paper bag or by holding one's breath to bring the oxygen-carbon dioxide ratio back to normal. But, in most emergencies, victims are unlikely to think about this treatment.

20

2

THE
ATTITUDE
OF
SURVIVAL

SURVIVAL STRESSES

Stresses that promote feelings of fear and insecurity as well as those that have a more direct effect on survival ability may be categorized as psychological, physiological, and environmental. However, both physiological and environmental stresses have psychological components. In effect, there is much overlap in the three categories. While environmental stresses such as wind and cold

Psychological

Unfamiliarity	Loneliness	Thirst	Dirtiness
Fear	Depression	Dispair	Lack of Hygiene
Anxiety	Helplessness	Hunger	
Isolation	Boredom		

Physiological

Pain	Thirst	Injury	Sleep Deprivation
Hunger	Illness	Fatigue	

Environmental

Cold	Wind	Snow
Heat	Rain	Presence or absence of dense vegetation
Dryness	Snow	Topographical features
		Animal Hazards
		Plant Hazards

may directly affect survival chances, there is also an indirect relationship since the victim exposed to environmental extremes is aware of the hazard of the situation and may, for example, feel colder than conditions warrant. The physiological stress of an injury or illness may cause symptoms to be felt more intensely as anxiety mounts.

While this list is not an exhaustive one, it does contain most of the significant stresses that either directly or indirectly affect attitudes or the physical condition and thus survival ability.

PSYCHOLOGICAL FACTORS

Although skill is important, nothing is as critical to the survivor's success as the ability to cope with the psychological stresses encountered. Survival is indeed an attitude. It is the ability to "keep your head when everyone around you is losing theirs." It is the ability to assess the situation calmly and deliberately take actions that are life-saving. It is the ability to control fear to a degree necessary to continue functioning effectively. Let's examine some of these factors.

UNFAMILIARITY

Fear is perfectly normal when an individual is faced with unfamiliar or threatening conditions. But the level of fear is dependent on several factors. First, it is well to realize that many fears are unwarranted and learned. They are not innate and neither are our responses to them. Babies are almost devoid of fear. Born afraid only of loud, sudden noises and the sensation of falling, by an early age they have learned completely unrealistic fears of snakes, spiders, dogs, heights, tight places, and "lions and tigers and bears." Even the mere mention of mice sends cold chills down some backs, and the sight of blood (ours or someone elses) may produce instant loss of consciousness. Terror tales and horror films animate the dark hours with unspeakable monsters. Even such seemingly harmless tales as "Little Red Riding Hood" and "Peter and the Wolf" assist in the development of these fears.

Throughout our lives we watch parents and others completely lose their composure at insignificant things. These actions are reinforced while watching television as we observe vacationers who have just lost their travelers checks running pell mell through crowded streets on the verge of hysteria. How ridiculous! Is it any wonder that we develop certain fear-response patterns that are of no assistance in an outdoor emergency?

In general, if we will remember Pogo Possum's comment that "We has met the enemy and they is us," we will be far better off. In fact, there are very few animals in the outdoors that are dengerous. This is especially true in North

America but largely applies in other parts of the world as well. Certainly bear and other attacks do occur. But they fortunately do so infrequently. Literally thousands and thousands of hikers and campers enter bear country every year and most never even see one. However, in Chapter 14 precautions to follow to reduce still further the chances of attack will be presented.

Wolves have been maligned for generations, yet modern information leads us to believe that the chance of attack by a healthy wolf is in the same range of probability as being struck by lightning under a clear blue sky. It is safe to assume that about the only way you could be injured by a wolf would be to back it up in a box canyon, grab it by the hind foot, and try to kill it with your fingernail file! You might be injured in the encounter. But only because the poor beast realized *it* was being attacked by an insane person.

Snakes are always high on the list of fears, yet the chances of encountering a dangerous snake are not as high as our imagination would lead us to believe. And the chances of being bitten are still lower. Given the opportunity, most snakes will attempt to flee at the approach of that entirely unpredictable animal scientifically dubbed *Homo sapiens*.

There are plenty of things to keep your mind occupied in a survival situation without worrying about occurrences that aren't going to happen.

If possible, use fear to your advantage. The increased adrenaline production stimulated by fear is not limited to its involvement in the psychology of anxiety. It also causes increased blood flow to the skeletal muscles, heightened alertness, and greater energy. These combine to enable the survivor to move more quickly, exert more force in tasks requiring physical strength, and make quick decisions. A fatigued person receives a burst of new energy and is capable of functioning long after normal limits would have been reached.

ISOLATION

Most people in today's world have never been completely alone except for short periods of time. A person living alone might dispute this. But isolation in survival situations is far different from self-imposed separation in society. At home we know that we can end our separation any time we choose. Stepping out of the house or apartment onto the street brings us into contact with others. Even under remote living conditions, there exists the comprehension that our isolation is a controlled state both in terms of duration and intensity. Under ordinary conditions, we have constant contact with others. People pass us on the street, in the office, at school, in the market. We are aware at least of the presence of others around us, even if they are at some distance. Family members are there. Radio and TV provide company even if vicariously. The telephone links even very remote areas. Seldom, if ever, are we completely cut off from the company of others and left entirely alone.

There are several reasons isolation seems so threatening. First, and perhaps most important, is that we are then keenly aware of total self-dependency. No longer are there others to assist with tasks or to offer psychological support. Doubts and insecurities leap to the forefront. We become vividly aware of the absence of services and supports that have always been taken for granted and therefore not considered worthy of conscious thought. Police and medical services as well as shelter and food suddenly are absent. Under such conditions, it is important to draw on those times in your life when you *have* succeeded— *have* coped. All of us, to some degree, are self-sufficient. There is no reason to throw in the towel now. Yet there have been times when seemingly experienced people have given up completely when faced with total isolation.

Probably the classic example is that told of a pilot flying over Alaska in the dead of winter. His engine developed a malfunction and stopped. Gliding toward the snow below, he pressed his microphone button and called "Mayday," giving his approximate location and difficulty. Several times this was repeated as he descended, but no response was forthcoming from his receiver. Belly-landing on the snow surface, the aircraft sustained only very minor damage and the pilot was uninjured. But gazing out at the stark, Alaskan landscape filled him with terror. With only very limited survival gear and dressed in relatively light flight clothing, his fears undoubtedly grew rapidly. Again he tried the radio, but to no avail. Apparently deciding that his situation was hopeless—that he was doomed to suffer a lingering death of hunger and exposure— he took out a pistol and killed himself. A short time later a rescue helicopter landed beside him! His radio receiver had not been working. Although his distress call had been received, he was unaware of responses that were sent back. Drawing an incorrect conclusion, he made a decision that was unwarranted. Someone knew he was in the air and sooner or later a search would have been started. At any rate, once he pulled the trigger his options were immediately reduced to zero. Apparently, fear and isolation were more than he could cope with. It is imperative that the victim *always* take the position that things are going to improve. A phrase that has important implications in survival is—"It doesn't matter whether you think you *can* or think you *can't;* you're right!" This is especially true in the negative. If you assume the task is impossible you simply won't try. And that is a guarantee of failure.

Feelings of isolation are enhanced by open vistas of wilderness or simply the awareness of being surrounded by trackless forests or other undeveloped land. The feeling of being closed in by dense forests affects some people adversely. Others are disturbed by great open expanses such as exist in desert country.

In any case, isolation in itself is not a threat to survival.

LONELINESS AND BOREDOM

These often work together. Faced with an overbearing sameness in surroundings and activities and coupled with lack of companionship, the victim may become bored, depressed, and very lonely.

Both conditions can be helped by varying daily activities. Change the routine. Use spare time to improve your situation. Until you have hot and cold running water and a heated bedroom with stereo and TV, there are still things that can be done. Improve the shelter. Enlarge it. Build storage facilities. Get the lumps out of the sleeping area. Clean up the signals. Expand them. Repair clothing. Build cooking utensils. The list is limitless.

HYGIENE PROBLEMS

Accustomed to having neatly brushed hair and a shower twice a day, many survivors find personal hygiene a difficult situation. In conducting advanced survival courses, the author prohibits students from bringing combs, hairbrushes, toothbrushes, toothpaste, soap, and shaving equipment that are so often part of our normal daily routine. Expected to exist in mock survival conditions for two weeks, many of the students find tangled hair, sprouting whiskers (on legs as well as faces), and dirt a real problem.

But most hygiene considerations relate to comfort alone and are not critical. Of course, in extended survival situations, accumulations of dirt on the body, tangled hair, and other hygiene problems may lead to health difficulties. However, with a little improvising, most such needs can be met.

Devise ways to cope. A sassafras or other aromatic twig chewed to a frizzled, fibrous tip will substitute nicely for a toothbrush. Fingernails can be kept clean with a sharpened stick or the tip of a pocketknife. Some plants produce a soapy lather when crushed and make a suitable substitute for commercial cleaning products. If nothing else, water alone or water and sand can be used to wash soiled utensils and even skin.

In the final analysis, there may be situations in which it will be impossible to stay clean. Just remember that body odor and dirt don't kill. Discomfort is merely inconvenient. Plan now to be able to cope with being uncomfortable so that it won't interfere with your ability to survive when it comes in combination with other undesirable conditions.

THIRST AND HUNGER

These are both obviously physiological stresses. However, they have strong emotional ties. Especially for those who have never had to go without a meal (or several), the idea of missing breakfast can cause an unhealthy attitude.

Survivors with limited or exhausted water supplies will be psychologically very involved and concerned. They will usually feel thirstier than dehydration would normally dictate.

Keeping mentally active doing chores will greatly alleviate such concerns. Direct your attention to other things. A more detailed examination of both of these factors may be found under the next large heading, Physiological Stresses. Both thirst and hunger cause irritability, depression, and withdrawal and must be dealt with in a positive manner.

INJURY AND ILLNESS

Malaise, or feeling generally "lousy," can be emotional as well as organic. Again, just knowing that you're sick or hurt is depressing. It is obvious that you are not capable of functioning at the same level as when you are healthy, and that can be very discouraging. Malaise increases with anxiety.

Visible indications of injury or illness such as bleeding, deformities, bruised tissue, or swelling are additional reasons for concern and tend to enhance feelings of worry. Pain, nausea, dizziness, and blurred vision may be present, and these constant reminders can severely reduce the will to live.

Survivors have indicated that it is possible to continue to function even under extreme pain in the presence of serious injury. Do not give up.

A plane carrying a family of five, flying in mountain country, attempted to cross the peaks but, in poor visibility, struck one of the higher ridges; the glancing blow wrecked the aircraft and killed the father and mother. The remainder of the family was made up of a 12-year-old daughter with her 8-year-old brother and 10-year-old sister. The older girl had suffered serious cuts and lacerations as she was thrown clear of the aircraft. In addition, the femur (upper leg bone) was broken with one end protruding through the flesh. In spite of this she took charge, directing her brother and sister to gather baggage and excess clothing together. Pieces of the plane were rounded up and an improvised shelter was constructed. Locating the parents' bodies and realizing that they must continue to do what was necessary, they found a cigarette lighter in their father's pocket that enabled them to kindle a fire.

When the search team arrived two and a half days later after nighttime temperatures had fallen to freezing and below, they found the three alive and in remarkably good condition with the severely injured older girl still firmly in charge and providing the strength and guidance so important under the circumstances.

She had recognized pain as something that could be coped with, made the decision that she could and would, and had taken positive action, deliberately and successfully doing everything that had to be done.

THE ATTITUDE OF SURVIVAL

Some, far older and more experienced, have given up and died under similar conditions.

PHYSIOLOGICAL FACTORS

Physiological stresses are those that directly affect the body's ability to operate normally. Difficulties are created that are organic but have strong emotional ties. In spite of the chemical and structural nature of physiological stresses, much can be done to manage our survival. The will or desire to keep going, to succeed, to survive should never be underestimated. In coping with physiological stresses, it is critical to realize the impact that our perception of the problem has. Just because blood, deformity, or discoloration is present, there need not be an implicit assumption that the condition is life threatening. For example, scalp wounds bleed profusely and spectacularly since the blood may run down the victim's face but are very rarely a serious problem unless underlying damage to the skull or brain has occurred. Even with crude closure, they heal quickly and with few complications. But it's demoralizing to have someone running around making a lot of incoherent noise with blood running off the tip of their nose. Realizing in advance what to expect and developing a proper perspective on the relative seriousness of injuries will be very important in handling the psychological component inherent in such damage to the body. Also, the more you learn about the human body and emergency procedures of first aid, the less likely you are to be unrealistically anxious about problems.

INJURY AND ILLNESS

Both injury and illness impose stress on the body's system of maintenance. Fluid and chemical balances often are disturbed. The body's efficiency is affected. Stamina is lowered.

HUNGER

A specific physiological stress that deserves mention at this point is hunger. Lack of food is usually a consideration that comes to mind immediately when one imagines a survival situation. However, food is generally the *least* important item in the list of needs.

Lack of food produces a series of effects on the body that, if understood, will not be overrated in terms of seriousness.

Symptoms of Starvation
1. Hunger pangs. That feeling of craving for food. Usually, these only last for two or three days.

2. Weakness. Inability to do physical labor that normally would have been easy. Limited stamina.
3. Dizziness and nausea. Often as early as the second day of starvation, the victim will notice dizziness especially on arising from a sitting or lying posture. This may include a minor spinning or vertigo, the sensation of a narrowing visual field (tunnel vision), or even fainting. Caused by the inability of the body to quickly increase blood pressure to compensate for the sudden movement to rise, it usually only lasts a moment. But, if starvation is prolonged, dizziness, lack of coordination, and fainting may pose threats to safety especially around the campfire or near precipices. Nausea may accompany the sensation of vertigo but is usually not severe.
4. Headache. This is usual during the first few days of starvation but usually goes away as time passes.
5. Weight loss. After three to four days, the victim may notice that clothing is getting a bit baggy. However, weight loss is ordinarily gradual and not particularly noticed by those in the survival party.
6. Slowed heart rate.
7. Increased sensitivity to cold.
8. Irritability, depression, nervousness, social withdrawal.

SLEEP DEPRIVATION

For various reasons including biting insects, heat, cold, wind, and other discomfort, usual sleep patterns may be disrupted. Prolonged periods of sleep deprivation increase irritability and nervousness. Victims become argumentative and uncooperative. Small, otherwise inconsequential occurrences may cause arguments.

It is important to catnap whenever possible. Although it may be impossible to sleep a normal 8 hours during nighttime, it is still possible to accumulate enough rest to continue to function normally just from short naps.

Sleep not only restores physical abilities but provides an escape from the concerns of the survival conditions. Provided that such sleep does not compromise important tasks, it is desirable to slumber as much as possible.

FATIGUE

Fatigue, among other things, is characterized by a buildup of lactic acid in muscle tissue as a result of exercise. This substance produces many of the characteristic feelings associated with being physically tired. The body needs rest periods to enable blood circulation to remove lactic acid and other products of exertion from the muscles. Without adequate recuperation time muscle pain, aches, and cramping will result. A severe cramp causes damage to the fibers

THE ATTITUDE OF SURVIVAL

of the muscle and may take several days to heal. During this time the survivor, operating at reduced capacity because of injury, is less able to take the active part necessary in assuring safety. So don't overdo unless conditions absolutely mandate expenditures of energy far beyond ordinary capabilities. For example, in some military situations where escape or evasion is necessary, it may be appropriate to drive the body beyond its normal limits.

3

WHEN
PREVENTION
FAILS

FIVE KEYS TO SURVIVAL

In addition to maintaining your energy and a survival attitude, it is essential that five items or categories of items be available. They might be called the FIVE KEYS TO SURVIVAL. Their order will vary depending on the situation but, in general, the following sequence is often the one recognized.

FIRE, SIGNALS, SHELTER, WATER, AND FOOD

Whatever the conditions, it is safe to say that food is the *least* important item. A healthy human in reasonably good physical condition can live between 30 and 50 days under survival conditions with nothing to eat providing they have adequate water. The need for fire may be the most important factor in most survival situations.

The FIVE KEYS are necessary throughout our lives, and this we share with all living things. It does not matter whether we are in a survival situation or not. Sometimes we call these items something else in everyday life, but they are still necessary.

Fire, for example, may be referred to as warmth. As human beings, we can only exist in a very narrow range of temperatures. We extend that range by adding or subtracting clothing and shelter. We heat our homes and even our vehicles in order to drive back the chill that could become fatal. Let's examine each of the FIVE KEYS in order, looking at rationale and procurement.

Fire

Fire, of course, serves to warm us. But, more importantly, it can also provide a psychological benefit. A person lost in the summer at temperatures in the 80s or 90s might still choose to build a fire before doing anything else. In extreme heat or cold, shelter may be first in importance, but fire will then follow second.

Fire building gives the survivor something constructive to do. While gathering fuel, kindling, and tinder and during the subsequent construction of the fire, there is an opportunity to calm down. The act of gathering and building the fire focuses the mind on something positive. And, when the first flame flickers alight, it is a visible symbol of success. You've done something correct! After perhaps a long and fear-ridden experience, wondering if you've done *anything* correctly, you finally have a fire.

Fire is an almost magical thing. Many of us have sat around campfires or beside fireplaces. Often these past times have been warm, cozy, and filled with pleasant experiences. As soon as that first flame comes to life, our memory of some long-forgotten good feelings is revived. Evenings cooking hot dogs, singing songs, and making "smores" suddenly come back. Many of us have sat entranced around such fires. In the midst of uncertainty and discomfort, a fire can provide a comforting, secure warmth. It might even be said that memories can come to our rescue. The smoke wafts to us on the breeze and its fragrance stirs our imagination. Perhaps you have experienced the aroma of burning leaves in autumn or fresh-cut hay. Or perhaps you recall the marvelous aroma of a breakfast prepared somewhere in your past.

Of course, fire can also cook our food and purify water. These practical uses will be dealt with later.

Lastly, fire may help us make signals. If our plight can be made known early, we won't need to worry about the rest of the FIVE KEYS.

Signals

Signals may be simply thought of as communication. If you doubt that we must communicate in order to survive, try to procure daily necessities without speaking, writing, or using hand signs. You can get very hungry.

Shelter

Shelter includes not just the boxes we build around ourselves and call houses, but also clothing. Our clothing is really added layers of insulation that enable us to function in a broad range of circumstances. Really, everything from the skin out which we use to control and balance heat production and loss might properly come under this heading.

Water

Water is necessary for every living thing. It is one of the prime controls of plant and animal distribution. We need it on a continuing basis.

Food

Food, although nowhere near as important as our emotions would dictate, is certainly necessary for long-term survival whether in the wilderness or the penthouse.

THE SURVIVAL RESPONSE SEQUENCE

Although conditions may vary, and probably will, this generalized sequence of responses to outdoor emergencies can provide a framework for planning. Study it and commit it to memory so that under the stress of an actual emergency, you will be able to proceed in a logical manner. The survival response sequence (SRS) has seven basic components.

1. Acknowledge
2. Relax
3. Evaluate
4. Inventory
5. Stay or travel
6. Organize
7. Action

A little phrase that may help lock the sequence in your mind goes like this: "**A**lligators **R**arely **E**ver **I**gnore **S**our **O**ld **A**nts."

ACKNOWLEDGE

Often the hardest part for an adult in an emergency is to fully accept the fact that they are in trouble. As discussed previously, vacillation may occur numerous times before the victim is finally willing to recognize and accept the facts of the situation and say, "Ok, I'm lost." Until this occurs, nothing constructive can take place. So stop wishing things were different! Acknowledge full involvement and move to the next step in the SRS.

RELAX

Stop. Don't run. Don't scream. Stay where you are. Sit down, take a deep breath, and get yourself under control—especially when you're lost. In one instance, a search team tracked a hunter two days and three nights by the gear he was throwing away as he ran through the woods in panic-stricken flight. Finally located at the bottom of a canyon, the team approached. From about 50 yards away, one of the searchers called out his name. He turned with a frightened expression and ran away as fast as he could go on frost-bitten feet. He had succumbed to panic almost immediately after acknowledgment of the situation, and this continued off and on for the entire search period.

In another instance, a 12-year-old boy in his flight actually crossed a paved highway in the mountains. He came down the slope, crossed the highway, and went right up the other side and back into the mountains without pausing—so engrossed was he to keep moving in an effort to find his way "out."

EVALUATE

While sitting and relaxing, the victim can easily, calmly, and systematically evaluate the situation. How serious is the problem? This will vary depending on proximity to civilization, the terrain, the weather, injuries, illness, and other considerations. Age and the condition of others in the party are also important. What are the mental attitudes of those in the group? Was a travel plan left with appropriate individuals? When will others expect you back? For example, if the projected trip was 14 days and the emergency developed on day 2, nobody will be concerned for at least another 12 to 13 days.

Be as dispassionate as possible in the evaluation phase. Here is where preparatory inoculation (PI), advance planning, and experience in the outdoors will pay off. If you've successfully weathered stressful situations before (PI), you will likely cope better with this one. Competence in outdoor skills and experience in dealing with the requirements of the outdoors foster confidence and calm. And you'll be better able to evaluate appropriately and accurately.

Now relax again. Sometimes an evaluation of the situation produces the feeling that things are *worse* than first thought. Fear, anxiety, and depression can descend on the victim again, and there is a real danger of irrational action once more.

INVENTORY

This step actually begins during the evaluation phase. At this point, determine what is available to reduce the severity of the problem. Check to see what people have in their pockets, are wearing, have in their packs, and in their heads. You may have a medical doctor, nurse, Special Forces member, paramedic, or other specialist or resource person in the group. Ordinary items can be modified and used in creative ways. A partial list of possibilities is given here.

Lipstick
This cosmetic can be used to prevent chapped lips or as a sunburn preventative. It is also a soothing treatment for minor scratches and abrasions. And it can even serve as a direction marker if traveling.

Comb
This is a morale booster. Keeping hair neat gives a feeling of the routine of daily life back home. It can also become a musical instrument with paper. Its teeth may be sharpened and used as improvised needles for sewing. Emergency medical instruments may be made from its sharpened teeth.

Small Sewing Kit
Sometimes found in a purse, this item can be invaluable in mending and maintaining clothing and equipment.

Keys
These can become fishing lures in a pinch. Sharpened by rubbing on a rough stone surface, the key can also become a cutting instrument or scraper.

Key Rings
These can provide the wire or metal parts for various construction projects, including triggers for traps and snares or holders for cooking utensils.

Coins
Those as large as a quarter or fifty-cent piece may be sharpened for use as a cutter or scraper. Smaller ones may be used as fishing lures.

Pant Cuffs, Shirt Tails, and Similar Excess Material
These pieces of clothing may be unraveled for thread. The thread may be used for sewing or twisted together to form heavier cord for other projects.

Belts
Military or scout web belts when unraveled produce yards of very strong and useful cord. Belt buckles may be sharpened as tools. Leather belts may be carefully cut to produce several feet of leather thong or lacing (see Figure 3-1).

Shoe Laces
In general, these probably are best used for the purpose for which they were designed. However, under critical circumstances, they might be temporarily used for something else.

Figure 3-1   Slicing leather for lacing. (Ceila Drozdiak)

Shoes
In a pinch, shoes or boots may be used as a water container or carrier, but should be carefully dried after such use. The contributor of the boot or shoe should not wander around barefoot. A foot injury almost always brings the injured party to a complete halt.

Makeup Mirror
This is an important signaling device. Its use is detailed in Chapter 5.

Magnifying Glass
Older people or others with reduced vision sometimes carry reading glasses that can converge the sun's rays to a burning point for fire building. This is also discussed in Chapter 5. (Prescription glasses seldom do this.)

Rain Gear
A means for collecting rainwater or a way of protecting oneself from the sun.

The list could go on and on. The only limitation on the use of objects commonly in our possession is our own ability to improvise. Periodically go through your pockets before you are in a survival emergency and see what you can think of.

If your emergency involves a vehicle (auto, plane, boat, etc.), parts of it may be pressed into service. Headlights, landing lights, or flashers make good signals. Shiny metal panels also reflect the sun and can be used to identify your position. Rear and sideview mirrors may be removed for the same purpose. Control cables in aircraft as well as electrical cables and wires can be used in shelter construction. Upholstery may provide needed insulation.

STAY OR TRAVEL

Generally don't! As a rule of thumb, travel is almost never a desirable alternative. On the other hand, it is probably wise in considering a survival situation to "never say never."

There are several reasons why travel is usually unwise. Travel may take you out of the area being searched. Especially in a situation where you are lost, you are likely nearest to where you ought to be when you first acknowledge the problem. If travel is continued, it is very likely that you will only wander farther and farther away from where the searchers expect you to be and thus reduce your chances of being found. But the temptation to keep moving in the hope of finding something familiar is very strong. Don't yield! Stop. Locate a suitable campsite nearby and establish yourself in one spot. Wait to be found.

Travel saps energy. Perhaps existing on reduced or nonexistent rations and operating under great stress, you will burn up energy reserves that are necessary for survival.

Exceptions

The only general exception to the prohibition on travel occurs in tropical rain forests. Habitation there normally occurs only along waterways, and the survivor would have to travel to and along such waterways until help was located. Also, visibility from the air is almost nil in dense vegetation, and thus search aircraft would not be able to see the survivor or most ground-air signals.

However, travel may apply in other situations as well. A hiker or traveler who has left no indications of route or plans and for whom a search is not likely to be started may have to travel in order to survive.

In most temperate areas travel, if it must be undertaken, ought not to follow streams. The old idea that streams will sooner or later lead to civilization is simply not true. The only definite fact is that streams are always located in the lowest part of the terrain and are usually choked with vegetation. Following a stream places survivors in tangled vegetation where it is almost impossible to see or hear them. The stream itself does not necessarily lead to civilization but may well flow into swamps, marshes, or simply farther into the wilderness. If you are following a stream, you may be compounding your difficulties. If possible, the route should be selected to keep to the high ground. This does not mean to go from summit to summit in mountainous terrain. A travel mode ought to be selected that remains well above drainage patterns and that, at the same time, provides a view of the surroundings and increases the chances of being seen by searchers on foot or in the air.

If you are with a vehicle, stay with it. An automobile, plane, snowmobile, or boat is far easier to see than a lone individual, and the chances of being found are greatly increased.

Finally, if travel is the decision, head for the closest point where rescue is likely. A map or knowledge of the area will make such decisions easier. Set a pace that can be maintained for long periods. Generally, this means a pace that seems too slow at the start. As fatigue sets in, it will probably be about right. There is no rush. No matter how tired or ill or injured, a slow pace with frequent rests may enable you to complete the journey.

ORGANIZE

Before doing *anything*, a plan should be developed. Think through each of the preceding steps. If the decision has been to travel, a route must be planned. If you are going to stay, camp must be established and basics procured.

Delegate to various members of the group those tasks that must be accomplished. Be sure everyone has something to do and can feel useful. Don't try to do everything yourself. If you are the only person in the group trained in survival, let this be known and assume a leadership position. This is easiest to do at the outset. A leaderless group wastes energy and resources.

If you are alone, a clear plan is just as necessary, with priorities established for the various tasks that must be done.

ACTION

Take action. Do something! The best plans don't mean a thing if nothing is done. Once a conclusion has been drawn, don't vacillate. Get moving. Don't go back to the drawing boards the first time things appear to not work as well as designed. Many times it will take several tries before you have success. Unless the plan is conclusively shown to be in error, stick to it. Too many survivors, faced with less than perfect results the first time, have jumped from plan to plan to plan, wasting precious time and energy.

4

FIRE

Only a few years ago, most people could easily build a fire. Wood heating and cook stoves were a part of most people's lives. And until very recently, the campfire was an integral part of any outing. Fire-cooked food, homes warmed by stoves, and enlivened evenings in camp, all were part of most people's experiences. But all that is changing with the advent of our mass migration to the cities. Even more recently, the emergence of low-impact camping, coupled with regulations in many state and federal lands that prohibit open fires, has resulted in masses of people who no longer can build even the most rudimentary fire. As a National Park Ranger, the author has witnessed numerous attempts that might only be described as ludicrous. In one instance, a large log was placed flat on the ground while one by one matches were applied to the end. As a twisted heap of blackened, burned-out matches accumulated under the end of the log and no reassuring glow of fire grew, the camper's ire rose. Finally in utter frustration, the builder kicked log and burned matches across the campsite.

This might be humorous except for the fact that, when outdoor emergencies occur, the ability to build and maintain fires often means the difference between life and death. The simple truth is that today most people cannot be depended on to construct a fire. In our society, it is not necessary in day-to-day activities. There is no opportunity to learn how.

The benefits of fire are both physical and psychological. Physically the fire can warm us, cook our food, and purify our water. It can also become a signal to notify others of our plight. Psychologically, fire can lift out spirits—providing a kind of companionship—an island of calm and security amidst the stress and turmoil of the emergency situation. In many cultures the coffee or tea break has become deeply ingrained. In a stressful frame of mind, a beverage (or just hot water) heated over the fire and consumed may lift the spirits. This accustomed tie to the relaxation of the worktime break period may be an important means to calming frayed nerves. The few moments of quietly watching the fire, holding a warm cup, and feeling the warm liquid enter the stomach may be used to plan subsequent action to improve the situation.

Do not wait until necessity dictates fire building. The stress of an outdoor emergency will reduce chances of success. Nervousness and shaky hands are not much assistance. Take the time now to develop competence. Practice over and over until you are secure in the knowledge of how to build a fire even under the most trying of circumstances.

THE FIRE TRIANGLE

Three things are necessary for a fire to burn. They are heat, oxygen, and fuel. The triangle in Figure 4-1 shows the necessary relationships.

HEAT

Heat for igniting a fire is usually provided by matches. For use in the outdoors, use matches that will strike on any surface. The common ''kitchen'' match is

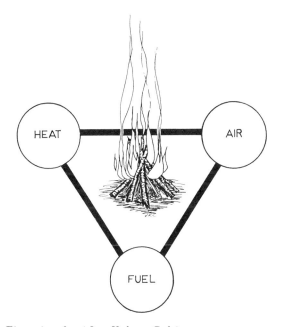

Figure 4-1   Fire triangle. (Jan Kolena Cole)

easily obtainable in most areas. Those that require special surfaces for striking are simply impractical and most likely the specialized surface won't be available. Some people carry a piece of fine sandpaper on which to strike their matches. This is a good idea as long as it isn't *necessary*. The sandpaper may be used for other purposes as well.

So-called windproof matches may also be helpful. These are sold by several suppliers and burn intensely when struck, making them nearly impossible to blow out in the wind.

Some matches are available that are both windproof and waterproof. Coated with a varnishlike substance, they often come in a small box. They ought to be transferred to a waterproof match container since the manufacturer's container provides no protection when the matches are exposed to continuous dampness.

Homemade Waterproof Matches
If you wish to prepare your own waterproof matches, it is easy to do. Using wooden kitchen-type matches, carefully dip the entire match into shellac, varnish, or melted paraffin. Allow them to dry and place them into a waterproof match container.

Note
If you are going to use paraffin, be sure to melt in a double boiler. Paraffin is flammable and heating it directly on a stove burner or over an open flame is hazardous. The temperature is difficult to control and the wax may reach its flash point and burst into flame. Also be careful with water near melted wax. Water droplets may flash into steam if accidently splashed into the melted wax, which may cause hot paraffin to be thrown onto the skin, resulting in serious burns.

Other Methods of Igniting a Fire
Flint and Steel
A technique used far back in history is that of striking a steel or iron against a rock of greater hardness. The stone used has usually been flint, quartz, or other material that when broken forms sharp edges and is harder than the metal. The metal is struck down against the sharp edge of the rock, causing minute flakes to be scraped from the steel. The pressure and heat generated by the two striking together allow the fine metal flakes to ignite as sparks. If the striking motion of the metal against the stone is angled properly downward, the resulting sparks can be carried into the waiting tinder.

Tinder of various sorts has been used. Shredded or thoroughly pounded bark such as cedar, hemlock, and birch may be used. Linen or cotton cloth may be charred by burning in reduced oxygen. This is often done by lighting the cloth

Figure 4-2   Preparing tinder by charring. (Paul H. Risk)

Figure 4-3   Tinder "nest" of fine twigs and cattail fuzz. (Paul H. Risk)

THE FIRE TRIANGLE

in the air and dropping the flaming material into a small metal can, replacing the lid to smother it (see Figure 4-2). The charred pieces of cloth will catch a spark and may then be fanned into a flame. Paper may be charred in the same manner.

If the charred material is placed in the center of a nest of fine material, such as cattail fuzz or milkweed down, the growing spark as it is fanned into flame will move into this and the whole will burst into flame (Figure 4-3).

A piece of an old metal file may be used as a steel igniter. Experiment with various kinds of rock until the best combination of steel and rock is found. When everything is working well, there should be little difficulty in creating a burst of sparks at each strike.

It is well to realize, though, that there are far better ways to make a fire. Flint and steel can be and often are very, very frustrating. For a skill competition, such a technique is fine. But, in a real emergency, it is well to have a better method. Nevertheless, practice this procedure so that you can understand the principle. Then, if everything else fails, you would be able to use it. And watch your knuckles! They are extremely easy to hit.

Fire by Friction
Fire Drill
A lot of jokes have been made about rubbing two sticks together to make a fire. But the technique is even older than flint and steel. There are several variations on the theme, but perhaps the fire drill is easiest to master.

To start you need a fire board cut as illustrated in Figure 4-4, a drill, a palm piece, a thong, a base board, and tinder. Wood selection for the drill and fire board are very important. Not all wood types are equally well suited for the job. Some ideal woods are: *cottonwood, yucca, willow, elm, and nonresinous pine*. In my experience it is best to make the drill and the fire board from the same wood. But there are those who recommend that the drill be harder than the fire board. The key is the development of the fine, charred dust around the point of the drill. It is this dust, heated to the combustion point by the friction between the drill and the board, that ignites. It comes from the drill or the board actually being ground away. Try several different types of wood from your locality. But whatever you use, it must be dry and preferably well seasoned. Select material for the drill from lower, dead branches of trees that have not been lying on the ground. Fire boards split from the heart of a seasoned log or tree will be best.

The arms are braced against the legs, as shown in Figure 4-5, and the bow pushed to and fro with smooth, rapid strokes. At the same time, heavy pressure is exerted with the palm piece to increase friction between the drill and the fire board. Almost immediately, smoke will begin to rise from the junction between the drill and the fire board. (Success to *this* point is almost guaranteed and

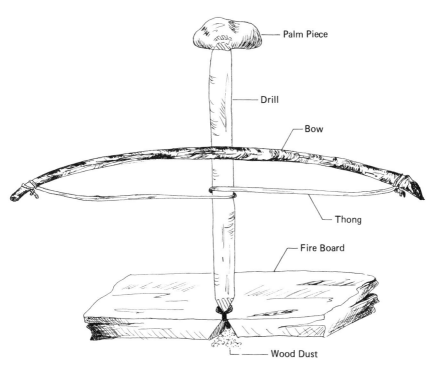

Palm Piece

Drill

Bow

Thong

Fire Board

Wood Dust

Figure 4-4   Fire drill. (Celia Drozdiak)

should be very easy to accomplish.) If everything is progressing well, the density of the smoke will increase. A deep brown to black powder will begin to accumulate in the depression of the fire board around the point of the drill. More and more smoke will pour from the spinning drill point as the heat of friction rises. Soon sufficient heat will be generated so that a coal will ignite in the charred dust in the depression. Quickly stop drilling and, while carefully cupping the tinder nest in the hands, wave the hands up and down to increase the flow of air through the embryonic fire. If everything is ideal, the smoking, smoldering mass will burst into flame. Place this burning material rapidly into the fire's tinder base and fan the whole to flames, while gradually adding larger and larger tinder kindling and fuel.

All this seems quite simple. But in actual fact, while smoke is easy to obtain, fire is not. A great deal of skill and practice, coupled with the right wood and considerable energy (some have suggested divine intervention), are required to obtain a fire. One thing is certain. Whether you get a fire or not you *will* stay warm. In fact, by the time you are finished, sweat may be dripping off the end of your nose and your arms may be about to drop off. In the last fifteen years of teaching survival courses, I have seen only 3 to 8 percent success rate for

Figure 4-5   Fire drill in use. (Paul H. Risk)

students on their first try. This information is not provided to be discouraging, but merely to encourage you to bring matches. But practice. One of my lab technicians was able to routinely produce a flame in 30 to 45 seconds. Perhaps you will too.

The Fire Saw

Fire saws are ideally suited to areas in which bamboo grows. But it is possible to experiment by buying bamboo from a furniture company even if it's not native to your area. While it may never be necessary to build a fire using bamboo, it is still a good idea to be prepared.

After splitting the bamboo, as shown in Figure 4-6, a groove is cut in the convex (curved toward you) side of one half. Tinder is placed in the concave side opposite. It may be held firmly with a piece of bark. The saw is the remaining half of the split piece of bamboo. After placing the edge of the saw

44

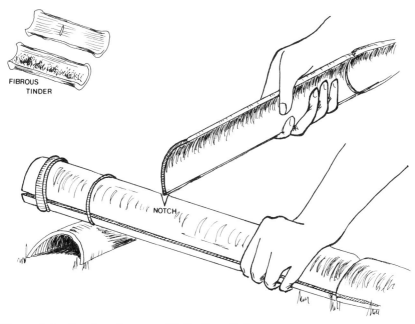

FIBROUS
TINDER

NOTCH

Figure 4-6   Bamboo fire saw. (Celia Drozdiak)

in the groove, apply firm pressure, and smoothly and rapidly saw back and forth.

The best tinder to use for this process is fine bamboo fiber secured from the material you are working with. Bamboo used for either the saw or fire board or for tinder must be completely dry for best success. However, even bamboo that is a tiny bit damp will work with perseverance. To secure tinder, apply a knife at 90 degrees to the cut edge of the bamboo and scrape, as shown in Figure 4-7. Very fine dust and fibers will be shaved off. The knife should *not* be at such an angle as to actually *cut* the fibers off. This is a scraping process.

In contrast to the fire drill, even neophytes will find fire building by this method relatively easy.

Metal-Match®

This composition metallic rod (shown in Figure 4-8) when scraped with a knife blade or the included steel strip produces very hot sparks. Experience shows that the little piece of steel included with the Metal-Match doesn't do as good a job as a knife blade.

As in scraping bamboo fiber, the knife is about 90 degrees to the Metal-Match. Don't try to cut into the rod. Just scrape. If the tinder is not bone dry or is too coarse, carefully scrape some filings from the rod into a pocket of

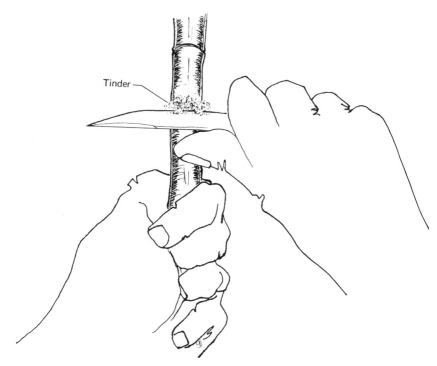

Tinder

Figure 4-7 Scraping tinder from bamboo. (Celia Drozdiak)

the tinder. If pressure is gently applied and the scraping action slow enough, the resulting filings will not ignite. After a dusting of the Metal-Match filings has accumulated, strike a spark into them. They will flare up and often provide the added boost to get the tinder to burn.

Figure 4-8 Spark-producing devices. Metal-Match® is in the upper right. (Paul H. Risk)

46

Figure 4-9   Cutting shotshell to obtain powder. (Paul H. Risk)

Metal-Matches may be carried in the pocket without fear of spontaneous ignition. But prolonged storage in humid areas may degrade them. They appear to develop a whitish powder on their surface and, over time, the rod disintegrates. The author carries one that has been used to start numerous campfires for over ten years. Although it is thinner than when purchased, it still has years of service left. This is a highly recommended item.

Gunpowder

Smokeless powder obtained by opening shotgun, rifle, or pistol shells may be used to assist in fire ignition. However, *black powder* burns much more rapidly and quantities of it may explode. In either case, a small quantity of the gunpowder is sprinkled on the tinder or piled beside it. A spark or a match may then be used to ignite the powder. KEEP YOUR FACE OUT OF THE WAY! Whether black or smokeless, the powder burns suddenly and if you are working over it may flare up in the face.

Figure 4-9 shows the proper method of opening a shotgun shell to obtain powder. As with all shells, be careful not to subject the percussion cap in the shell base to any impact. Damage to the cap may result in the shell exploding.

Figure 4-10 shows how to remove the projectile from a metal rifle or pistol cartridge. The percussion-sensitive chemical in centerfire cartridges is located in the cap in the center of the base. Rim-fire cartridges (usually .22 caliber) have this compound in the rim of the base. Pressure, a crushing motion, or any impact may cause detonation.

Automobile Cigarette Lighter and Pocket Lighters

While it might seem obvious, emergencies have occurred where the victims forgot about their lighter as a means for starting a fire. It will ignite tissue paper, writing paper, fine tinder, and many other things that may be used to start your fire.

Figure 4-10   Prying a projectile out of a rifle cartridge. (Paul H. Risk)

Batteries

The electrical system in a vehicle offers still another avenue in fire starting. Especially where the batteries supplying power are capable of large current flow, any short will result in a very hot, somewhat spectacular, spark. This means that battery cables briefly touched together, wires attached to the battery specifically for this purpose, or any other live wire in the vehicle shorted against the frame may be used to provide a spark. However, a word of caution is in order. Auto, truck, and aircraft batteries as well as those in snowmobiles and many other applications are generally of the wet-cell variety. They rely on the action of acid on metal or chemical plates to provide current. The chemical action of the traditional lead-acid battery also generates hydrogen gas. Hydrogen gas when combined with air can create an explosive mixture. Any spark in the immediate vicinity of the battery may cause the battery to explode, throwing fragments and acid over a wide range. So be sure that any attempt to draw a spark is done some distance from the battery and in a well-ventilated area.

Even the batteries in a flashlight may be used to ignite tinder. If the batteries are fresh, merely unscrew the bulb end of the flashlight. Furniture-grade steel wool forced across the contacts causes a short. The shorted current will over-heat the tiny metal fibers, and you will almost instantly see a glowing spark (or several) form in the steel wool. Quickly remove the steel wool from the flashlight. Place it near the tinder and blow on it. With a roar, the glow will become intense. The steel wool will be somewhat melted by the heat generated. This method will work even if the steel wool is wet, providing the excess water has been removed. This may be done either by pressing the steel wool between layers of dry cloth or by slinging it rapidly to throw off the moisture.

The steel wool may also be ignited easily with a Metal-Match, flint and steel, a match, or a cigarette lighter.

When drawing sparks from vehicle batteries, slap the wires together quickly and for only the briefest moment. Otherwise there is danger of welding the wires together.

Current flow at the time of the intentional short may also rapidly heat the wires and burns may result. It is best to wear gloves to protect the hands.

Of course, almost anything that burns may be used as a part of the fire-building process.

Highway Flares

When their use as a fire starter exceeds their value as signals, highway warning flares (sometimes called fusees) may be used to start fires. They are usually ignited by striking a starter compound at one end against a special surface on the cap. But be careful. Flares drop pieces of burning or semi-molten material that are capable of inflicting serious burns and starting unwanted fires.

Gasoline

If an automobile is available, gasoline to soak a cloth as a fire starter may be easily obtained. Remove the air cleaner and stuff the end of a rag or handker-chief down the throat of the carburetor. Pumping the accelerator pedal or quickly manipulating the throttle linkage will cause gasoline to squirt into the rag. It may then be taken to the fire site and used for tinder. If necessary, larger quantities of fuel may be obtained by siphoning from the tank or removing a fuel line.

If there is a critical need for gasoline in large quantities and you are sure that you will not again need to drive, a hole may be stabbed in the fuel tank with a sturdy knife. Unless a large container is available to catch the gasoline, quantities of it will be lost and may pose a serious safety hazard as fumes or liquid fuel leak out.

Gasoline-Oil Mixture

A more controllable source of fire is a 50/50 mix of gasoline and oil. The danger of ignition from fumes is reduced, and it tends to burn longer than pure gasoline.

SOME THINGS TO AVOID

Sometimes in fictional literature or movies, we hear of someone firing a rifle, pistol, or shotgun into tinder to start a fire. Some literature has recommended stuffing a rag tightly into the muzzle of a weapon and firing a cartridge from which the projectile(s) has been removed. In theory, the rag should be ejected from the muzzle smoldering. Similar antics have been recommended for use with muzzle-loading weapons.

None of these procedures are recommended. While they may on occasion work, they also may leave you with a weapon clogged with a rag or at worst result in a damaged firearm and personal injuries.

OXYGEN

A major reason for the difficulty in building a fire is the lack of sufficient ventilation. Materials are placed directly on the ground with no opportunity for air to circulate through them. Figure 4-11 shows a way to facilitate this process. A heavier stick is supported at an angle, while tinder and kindling are leaned against it and placed underneath. In this way, the tinder will catch quickly,

Figure 4-11   Using a heavy stick as support to promote ventilation in fire building. (Paul H. Risk)

igniting the kindling. After the fire is burning well, larger pieces of fuel may be cautiously added. But care ought to be exercised. Too often, large pieces of wood are added too quickly and suffocate the fire.

FUEL

The third element of the fire triangle is fuel. It may be divided into two other categories—tinder and kindling. Easily ignited with a minimum of heat, good tinder provides a critical element in successful fires; it is normally very fine, dry, and highly flammable. Collect it while it is dry and keep it that way. It is often said that a good outdoor person ought to be able to make fire in a downpour. But it is wise to recall the old pioneer axiom—"Keep your tinder dry." A small plastic bag from the survival kit may be used for this purpose.

The following can be used as natural tinder:

Cattail fuzz	Shredded cedar bark
Milkweed down	Birch bark
Wild carrot tops	Pine needles
Goldenrod tops	Pitch pine splinters
Bird and mouse nests	Dry grass

Of course, plant material used for tinder should be collected when it is dry. This means gathering dead material. Even during summer, such material can include vegetation that grew the previous season. It will be seen standing among the new growth and its brown coloration will help in locating it.

In many moist parts of the world, tinder collected from the ground will be too damp to be useful. But in areas where conifers (evergreens such as pine, spruce, and fir) grow, there often will be considerable quantities of dead needles caught in the tree branches. These will be dry and make very good tinder. Broadleafed trees seldom have accumulations of dead leaves in their branches unless they are part of squirrel or other animal nests.

Once the tinder problem is solved, the next step is to obtain a sufficient quantity of larger fuel for kindling. In general, kindling is wood (such as twigs and very small branches) that measures up to about twice the diameter of a wooden pencil. The same precautions should be observed regarding dampness. Kindling found on the ground will usually be damp. But in most areas dead branches on the lower part of trees and shrubs will supply an adequate supply of kindling. It should be carefully leaned against the fire support to permit ventilation so that the burning tinder beneath can easily ignite it.

Larger fuel for sustaining the fire, especially for cooking and signaling, should also be collected and may be obtained from a wide variety of sources. While it would be possible to produce a list of various woods together with their

Figure 4-12   Keyhole fire. (Jan Kolena Cole)

burning characteristics, it is unlikely to be of much help. Most people are not expert enough to be able to recognize the different woods in their dead state. So it is best to merely remember that the harder woods produce hotter, smokeless fires that leave minimal ash. Softer woods are smokier and produce more ash. Therefore, maple, oak, and ash would be best for producing coals on which to cook.

THE FIRE

All materials—tinder, kindling, and fuel—having been gathered, you are now in a position to ignite them in an attempt to build a fire. Do not get in a hurry and ignite tinder or kindling until *all* materials are at hand. If you do, the tinder or kindling will likely burn up while you are rushing around to find fuel. Especially where materials are in limited supply, this can be very discouraging and dangerous. When you have just used your only tinder and rush back into camp with a load of fuel only to see a trickle of smoke from the dead fire slowly rising into the air—you are in trouble!

Outdoor publications are filled with varied configurations for building cooking and warming fires. I urge the reader to look at them; however, only one will be discussed here. It has the advantage of being both a warming and cooking fire. It is called a *keyhole fire,* and the diagram in Figure 4-12 clearly shows why. The circular end of the keyhole is used to maintain the flames of the fire and to produce the coals. The coals are then raked out into the trench end of the fire, where cooking can be more easily done. The trench should only be a few inches deep and may be quite narrow.

5

ATTRACTING ATTENTION: SIGNALS

CONTRAST—THE KEY TO SUCCESSFUL SIGNALS

Unless planning to homestead, signals are critical for a rapid identification of your situation in the case of emergency. And the key factor in signals is *contrast*. The signal must stand out against its background. Sound against silence; movement against stillness; light against dark, or the reverse; sharp angles against curves; one color against a contrasting one.

THREES—THE INTERNATIONAL DISTRESS SIGNAL

In addition to contrast, a signal shown or sounded in threes is known throughout the world as a signal of distress. Three shots, three fires, three flares spell trouble. All these should tell an onlooker or searcher that you need help.

SOUND

Shots

One of the most often used signals by hunters is a pattern of three shots. However, during hunting season "bang, bang, bang" in close sequence is unlikely to excite much interest. Anyone hearing three closely spaced shots at this time of year is likely to assume you merely missed whatever you were shooting at the first two times. It is important that a *pattern* be perceived by the hearer. So space the shots at regular intervals, say 3 to 5 seconds apart. If the shots are separated by any less time, no one will take notice. Much longer between shots and the hearer will forget they heard the first by the time the last is fired. The result will be the loss of a perceptible pattern of three. Perhaps the best time to fire a weapon to attract attention is after dark during deer season. Since it is illegal to hunt then, the ears of most hunters (and game officers) will be alert to such activities. When the enforcement people come, you may be able to convince them you are lost.

Whistles, Horns, and Other Sound-Emitting Devices

A shrill police-type whistle preferably of metal has already been discussed. Its piercing sound contrasted against the relative silence of night will carry long distances. The whistle should be part of the survival trio—knife, whistle, and matches—that is always included when traveling in the outdoors.

Boaters may also have a freon or compressed air horn useful both in case of emergency and in fog. These devices (Figure 5-1) emit a powerful sound that can be heard much farther than a whistle.

There are also personal protection devices that shriek at the push of a button. Originally designed to discourage a potential rapist or mugger, they also work well in an outdoor emergency. However, any device powered by compressed gases is limited. Once the material producing the sound is exhausted, the signal is no longer of any use.

An automobile horn can also be used in an emergency to signal for help. The same pattern of three may be used. And in the case of any of the noise-producing devices, it is not necessary to pause for 3 to 5 seconds between

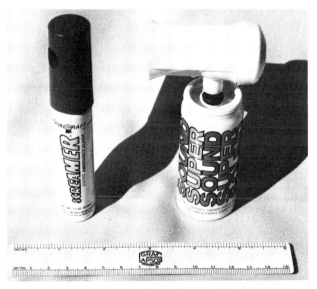

Figure 5-1   Two types of compressed gas horns. (Paul H. Risk)

signals. Three quick blasts from the device will easily be recognized as something out of the ordinary and will be investigated.

LIGHT AND FIRE

Headlights or landing lights may be flashed in patterns of three. A flashlight may be used in the same manner. Intensely brilliant, landing lights may be seen as far away as 85 miles under ideal circumstances.

Light may be obtained in at least three ways. It may be from a *self-contained* source, such as a flashlight or part of the standard equipment of a vehicle as in the case of headlights, spotlights, landing lights, or warning flashers.

It may also be *reflected light,* generally sunlight. Special signal mirrors with built-in sights are available. Easy to use, they are an excellent signal that may be visible up to 15 miles on clear, sunny days. However, lacking this, a pocket mirror, rear or side mirror from a vehicle, piece of broken glass, shiny metal, or even ice may be pressed into service. If the reflective surface in use does not have a sight, shine the reflected spot on some nearby object or the ground. Place the thumb in the light so that a corner of the reflector and the thumb are lined up (see Figure 5-2). Then manipulate the mirror to keep the thumb illuminated as the beam is directed toward a search plane. When the corner of the reflector, thumb, and aircraft are all lined up, the pilot can see the flash.

To improvise a mirror, use aluminum foil or foil from food wrappers flattened on a book, board, or other rigid material, and follow the same instructions to aim the reflected light.

Both landing lights and headlights may be removed from their mountings. Leave the attached wiring. Then direct the beam where it will be of greatest assistance.

A single campfire may be used as an emergency signal, but ideally *three* is a better number. Figure 5-3 helps visualize the concept.

The first fire in the triangle is the campfire, which is probably burning most of the time. Beside it place a large (4 feet high by 4 feet wide) pile of slightly green or damp vegetation. Construct a torch, as illustrated in Figure 5-4. Fire 2 is constructed approximately 20 or more yards away. Use the basic signal-fire design with a relatively small fire base. Perhaps 80 percent of the fuel should be damp or green high-density, smoke-producing material. The completed fire should be at least 4 feet high and 5 feet across. Place another torch near it. Complete the triangle of fires by building fire 3 to the same specifications. Neither fire 2 or 3 should be ignited until search aircraft are visible or some other condition indicates that searchers will see the signal. The reserve smoke material beside fire 1 (the campfire) must not be used until the same situations exist.

Practice the procedure for igniting the three fires. Pretend to throw the smoky

Figure 5-2   Signaling plane with mirror. Note that corner of mirror, thumb, and plane are lined up. Thumb is illuminated by reflected sunlight. (Jan Kolena Cole)

material on fire 1 and simulate lighting its torch. Run to fire 2 with the first torch, and simulate lighting it and its torch. Then with torch 2, make a mock run to fire 3 and pretend to ignite it. Determine whether there are any problems. Is there a hole to avoid, a branch that is in the way?

After practicing over and over, you should be able to handle a real situation effectively. However, there is one question. There is a torch at each of the

*Figure 5-3   Layout for three signal fires. The nearest fire is the basecamp fire.
Note reserve fuel piles at each fire. (Jan Kolena Cole)*

three fires. Why is this? If you run from fire 1 to 2 to 3, there is no obvious
reason to have the third torch. And it isn't for waving back and forth. You
may set the whole forest on fire by that procedure. No, the third torch is to
cover Murphy's law. Although all the practice runs have been in the sequence
1, 2, 3, it may be assumed with some surety that under the stress of actual
need you will forget and run backward. If there were no torch there, you would
have trouble igniting fire 2.

58

Figure 5-4   Torch for ignition of signal fires. (Jan Kolena Cole)

SMOKE VERSUS FIRE

Almost without exception, civilian air searches cease at dark. The main use of a signal fire is in the daytime, so smoke is more useful than flame. On a clear day white smoke is best. Dark smoke shows up best against an overcast sky.

This is all well and good. But the fact is that it is difficult to locate material that will produce dark smoke when burned. Generally, vegetation and woody material produce white smoke. (Actually, the white is largely steam.)

If dark smoke is desirable, there are several things that will produce it. Oil, diesel fuel, jet fuel, kerosene (which is basically the same as jet fuel), gasoline, rubber, some plastics, and synthetic fabrics as well as some desert and tropical plants burn with an intense black smoke. Although the smoke may be toxic when burning plastics and other synthetics, this should pose no threat to you in the outdoors, providing you do not stand downwind and let the smoke cover you.

So, remember:

CLEAR SKY—WHITE SMOKE
OVERCAST SKY—BLACK SMOKE

White smoke is easily produced by piling cattails, ferns, reeds, sedges, grass, or aquatic and marine vegetation on the fire. Just be careful to allow enough ventilation so that the fire base is not smothered.

HOW TO BE SEEN FROM THE AIR

As a search plane flies over, it is often fighting crosswinds. It may actually be being blown sideways as it flies. To compound this difficulty, people on the ground are very difficult to see unless they take steps to increase their visibility.

Wearing bright colors will help greatly. Movement can be very helpful. A search pilot working for the Michigan Department of Natural Resources recounted the experience of looking for an elderly hunter in the state's wild and primitive Upper Peninsula. As he flew over a clearing, he just happened to look toward one side where a stump remained from a logging operation. Thinking he saw something unusual, he flew back. Sure enough, a figure could be seen sitting on the stump watching the aircraft fly over. But the person seemed so unconcerned about the plane that the pilot wasn't sure it was the man they were looking for. Nevertheless, he directed a ground party to the location. The lost hunter was found.

Why didn't he move? The hunter had no explanation except the fact that he was depressed and discouraged. Remember, wild animals "freeze" into immobile statues to *avoid* discovery. If you want to be found, don't be a statue. The pilot said he normally would not have seen the man in such an unmoving posture.

Since the plane may be in a crosswind, it is difficult to retrace a flight path. Be sure that the signal fires have sufficient fuel on them *and* in reserve to permit dense smoke production for 10 to 15 minutes at a minimum. The pilot needs the smoke to be able to find you after the first sighting. The first glimpse of smoke which then dies out may produce nothing but frustration for both the victim and the pilot.

TORCH TREES

Only a safe procedure when the tree is very isolated, it nevertheless has the potential of very high visibility. Build a "rat's nest" in the lower branches of an isolated tree using flammable tinder and kindling. When an aircraft is visible, the ignited tree can be seen for several miles. But poorly placed, it may ignite the entire forest. Of course, in a "forever situation" the danger of a forest fire may be outweighed by the victim's despair. (A "forever situation" refers to a survival condition when all hope is about exhausted and anything goes.)

PYROTECHNIC DEVICES
RAILROAD OR HIGHWAY FLARES

Best at night, these burn with a brilliant red glare. Hold them away from the body. As they burn at extremely high temperatures, molten material drips from them. Hold the flare steadily or move it back and forth carefully. Rapid waving will only increase the chances of burns from the falling hot material.

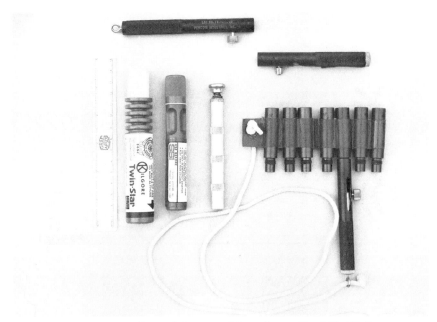

Figure 5-5   Six types of aerial flares and launchers. (Paul H. Rick)

AERIAL FLARES

Also called pocket flares, marine distress flares, and pen flares, these are small devices that shoot a bright, burning star burst into the air about 150 to 300 feet. Some of the more elaborate types fire a parachute-suspended flare that drifts slowly to the ground. Several types are shown in Figure 5-5.

The parachute types ordinarily should be used only over water, since they are likely to descend to the ground while still burning. Although the small, hand-held flares without a parachute are supposed to be out before they get to the ground, the author has seen several strike the ground while still burning intensely.

In some states these devices are banned or tightly controlled. Since they fire a projectile, they are considered by some to be a firearm and come under the same restrictive control as handguns. Check your state's regulations.

In all cases, when the device is fired, hold it well above the head and do not look at it while it is fired. If it explodes or discharges through the side of the launcher, your face should be protected to avoid serious injury.

At any rate, these are very useful. Although they are more visible at night, they still are very effective during the day. A victim under dense tree cover is

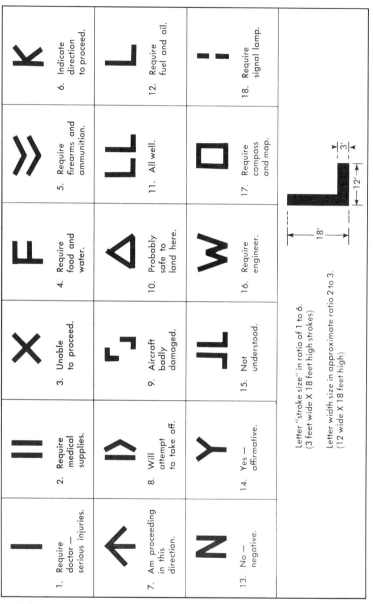

Figure 5-6a Ground-air Signals; Part A. (Courtesy of United States Air Force)

ATTRACTING ATTENTION: SIGNALS

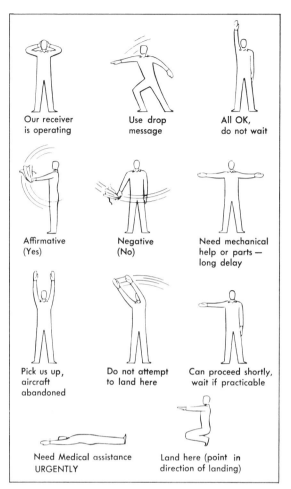

Figure 5-6b Ground-air Signals; Part B (Courtesy of United States Air Force).

often virtually invisible. But the hand-held flare can be fired through a small opening in the forest to attract attention.

SMOKE DEVICES

Often the same companies that manufacture flares also sell chemical smoke signals. They may be purchased in a variety of colors, including white, orange, red, purple, and green. The best general smoke signal is probably orange.

It is the easiest to obtain and will do the job under most conditions. However, pilots report that it tends to blend into the background during autumn when the leaves become red and orange.

GROUND-AIR SIGNALS

Figures 5-6a & b shows a series of of signals designed to assist you in communicating your situation to a pilot. In reality, many pilots are not familiar with all of these signals. However, most do recognize the X signal. Anywhere in the world, the X signifies trouble. Especially when you are overdue and a search has been launched, the X will be sufficient. It is not necessary to laboriously create a huge SOS or anything else. Although if your attitude will be improved and you have sufficient energy, you may go ahead and place an SOS.

CREATE A PATTERN CONTRAST

All signals should be angular. Where possible, right angles should be used. The sharp angles contrast with the natural curves of the terrain and make them easier to see. And, of course, make them as large as practical.

The signals may be done by scraping away vegetation to permit soil to show through. Vegetation may be heaped up on a beach or on snow. Or signals may be tramped in the snow. The indented surface of the tramped snow will appear darker from the air. Such signals show up well. To increase the contrast, vegetation may be piled into the indentations or sea dye marker may be sprinkled over the snow surface.

Signals may also be made using clothing, pieces of fabric, or fragments of a vehicle to form the necessary patterns. In one training exercise, the author had students lie down in an X in the snow and wave their coats. The pilot said the X appeared to be flickering or squirming and immediately caught his eye.

64

6

WATER PROCUREMENT AND TREATMENT

THE BODY'S WATER REQUIREMENTS

Under normal conditions in a temperate environment, the human body daily requires about 2 quarts of water. Half usually is obtained from food and half by drinking. However, this changes markedly under conditions of environmental or physiological stress. In desert conditions, the body may be able to utilize a gallon of drinking water a day.

Water is vitally important to normal body functioning. Since our bodies are literally walking chemical reactions, it is imperative that enough water be present to enable these life-sustaining reactions to continue. When water is lacking, the efficiency with which we operate is strikingly affected. For example, water loss resulting in a 2.5 percent (about 1.5 to 2 quarts) reduction in body weight would cause a reduction in efficiency of about 50 percent. In very hot weather, the body may lose up to 2 quarts of perspiration per hour.

Eating also increases water utilization. Many people have experienced the feeling of thirst after a heavy meal. And, ingesting salty foods increases water need still more. If water is a critical problem, DON'T EAT.

REMEMBER: IF YOU HAVE NO WATER—DON'T EAT.

Water is not only used as a lubricant to assist the food in passing through the alimentary canal, it also dilutes food materials. The digestion process itself requires water in the chemical breakdown of food.

In general, it may be said that a human may survive 4 to 6 days with no water. But this is dependent on conditions. In extreme heat, life expectancy may be reduced to a single day without drinking water, especially if energy is

65

Figure 6-1 Survival time in the desert. (Courtesy of United States Air Force and by permission of Dr. E. F. Adolph)

MAXIMUM DAILY TEMPERATURE (°F) IN SHADE ▶	AVAILABLE WATER PER MAN, U.S. QUARTS					
	0	1 Qt	2 Qts	4 Qts	10 Qts	20 Qts
	DAYS OF EXPECTED SURVIVAL					
120°	2	2	2	2.5	3	4.5
110	3	3	3.5	4	5	7
100	5	5.5	6	7	9.5	13.5
90	7	8	9	10.5	15	23
80	9	10	11	13	19	29
70	10	11	12	14	20.5	32
60	10	11	12	14	21	32
50	10	11	12	14.5	21	32

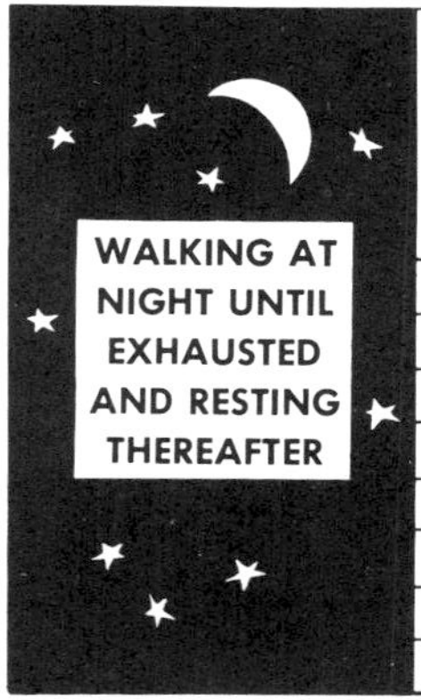

NO WALKING AT ALL

MAXIMUM DAILY TEMPERATURE (°F) IN SHADE ▶	AVAILABLE WATER PER MAN, U. S. QUARTS					
	0	1 Qt	2 Qts	4 Qts	10 Qts	20 Qts
	DAYS OF EXPECTED SURVIVAL					
120°	1	2	2	2.5	3	
110	2	2	2.5	3	3.5	
100	3	3.5	3.5	4.5	5.5	
90	5	5.5	5.5	6.5	8	
80	7	7.5	8	9.5	11.5	
70	7.5	8	9	10.5	13.5	
60	8	8.5	9	11	14	
50	8	8.5	9	11	14	

WALKING AT NIGHT UNTIL EXHAUSTED AND RESTING THEREAFTER

WATER PROCUREMENT AND TREATMENT

being expended rapidly. Yet there have been recorded instances at sea of survival as long as 17 days with no water. Figure 6-1 graphically illustrates the expected survival rate under desert conditions.

PHYSIOLOGICAL VERSUS PSYCHOLOGICAL THIRST

The realization that water is unavailable focuses thought processes on the problem. Where a moment before no sensation of thirst existed, intense feelings of a need for water may suddenly be present. The sensation of thirst is accentuated by exercise—by both the body's need for increased water supplies as energy is expended and by dryness of the mouth, nose, and throat. To conserve energy and to prevent dryness, keep exercise levels low enough so that breathing through the mouth is unnecessary. Mouth breathing rapidly dries the membranes of the tongue, mouth, and throat and quickly reminds the victim of the lack of water.

Although the pebble in the mouth technique does not increase actual water supply, it will stimulate salivation and thus assist in keeping the mouth moist. Chewing gum will accomplish the same thing and give an additional lift in mood because of the refreshing taste.

While there may be pure sources of water in the outdoors, it is safest to assume that all water is contaminated. Regardless of whether you have drunk from a particular source a hundred times with no ill effects, do not assume it to be safe under survival conditions. It is one thing to develop gastrointestinal problems when you can merely pack up and drive home. It is entirely another when you are stranded.

A FEW THINGS TO CONSIDER

1. Water does *not* necessarily purify itself as it flows along a gravelly stream bottom in full sunlight. Various tales have been told that streams automatically purify themselves every mile or so due to the action of sunlight (the ultraviolet component) and oxygenation from flowing over the riffles. Although ultraviolet light and oxygen do tend to kill certain disease organisms, this is not a certainty. If there are organisms of typhoid or amoebic dysentery upstream, you can be assured they are also downstream even if in reduced numbers. And if one or two of them gets into your system, you will ultimately be just as sick as if the drink of water were teeming with them.

2. Springs are *not* a guaranteed source of pure water. While the water may be crystal clear and cold, it still may harbor extremely dangerous disease organisms. The idea that the filtration from passing through sand and rock strains out microorganisms is false. Actually, there is so much room between grains of sand, even in very fine types, that virtual armies of bacteria could march through abreast and not touch the sides.

3. Mountain streams are *not* always safe. Microbial contamination danger-ous to humans generally comes from human waste entering the water, although other sources may be responsible. It may percolate in from poorly placed out houses, run directly in from sewage discharge pipes, or result from urination or defecation into or very near the water. Other possible disease sources may be animal droppings, as in the case of moose or dead animals in or near the stream. Once while hiking in California's Sierra country, the author, having on past trips drunk from the pristine streams of the high country, filled his canteen and drank his fill from a beautiful, rapidly racing brook. A short time later and only a few hundred yards upstream from the drink, we came upon the very ripe, bloated, decomposing, and oozing carcass of a horse lying directly in the stream. Although we did not become ill, I've never felt the same about drink-ing from streams when I couldn't see their source. Especially today, as increas-ing numbers of relatively inexperienced hikers take to the outdoors, we need to exercise caution. Too often human waste is ignorantly disposed of and can seriously contaminate water supplies.

4. Stagnant water is *not* always unsafe. Although green with algae and swarming with insects and their larvae, a stagnant pond may be safer than running water since it may have no connection with contamination. Simply strain out the creatures through your T-shirt or some other closely woven ma-terial, and purify. In a pinch the critters swimming around may be made into quite a nutritious soup!

WATER SUBSTITUTES

There really is no substitute for water. But under dry conditions many strange fluids have been tried. They include fuels such as gasoline and kerosene, as well as urine and blood. As dehydration becomes extreme, the mind can focus on nothing except the intense craving for water and the sloshing sound of other liquids can drive a person to ridiculous lengths. Fuels not only contain no water, they are very poisonous. Urine, by virtue of the body's need to remove waste and the action of the kidneys, is actually more concentrated than the body's fluids. If it is drunk, the body has to relinquish water to dilute it and then reclaim it after it leaves the body again. In addition, dissolved substances contained in the urine may prove to be toxic. Depending on the animal it is from, blood will be at least as salty as your body's fluids and perhaps more so. While there have been recorded instances of survivors claiming to have lived because they drank blood, it is really doubtful. They probably lived in spite of the blood and not because of it.

Under no circumstances may seawater be drunk. Although there have been instances where it has been attempted either in pure form or diluted with fresh-water, the evidence still strongly discourages the practice. Drinking it will generally cause serious physiological disturbances including kidney failure. The victim will typically hallucinate, go into convulsions, and die.

Alcoholic beverages contain various amounts of water. Beer contains the greatest amount of water, followed by wine, with hard liquors containing so little as to be of no use whatsoever. Also the ingestion of alcoholic beverages causes increased urine production—they are distinctly diuretic So the benefit of their intake is distinctly lacking. Moreover, hard liquor such as whiskey, vodka, brandy, and so on, may actually cause dehydration. Water is drawn from the body to assist in assimilation of the alcohol.

WHERE TO LOOK FOR WATER

Streams, rivers, lakes, and springs are all likely and usual places to look for water during warm weather. Such water accumulations occur where the land surface lies below the zone of saturation called the *water table* (Figure 6-2). As Figure 6-2 clearly shows, water is closest to the surface in low areas. Since this is the case, a dry streambed may be a successful spot to dig for water. Digging on the *outside* of a bend is best. The current of the stream is most rapid at the outside of the curve, with eddies and backcurrents allowing sand and other sediment to accumulate on the inside of the curve. The result is that the bed is deepest and therefore closest to the water table where the scouring action of the current was greatest. Since this is also the most depressed area, it is the last area to hold water as the stream receded. There may be residual water quite near the surface. If digging uncovers damp sand, keep it up until water begins to trickle into the hole. Allow it to fill, carefully scoop it out, and purify it.

Note: Water that smells bad is *not* necessarily unsafe.

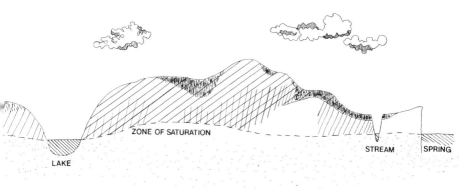

Figure 6-2   Water table. (Celia Drozdiak)

Often water obtained in the above manner has an objectionable aroma, as does water from swamps. The odor is usually from minerals dissolved in the water or from gases of decomposing vegetation; although it is unpleasant it is not harmful. If the smell or taste is unpleasant, pinch your nose when you drink. You will neither be able to smell nor taste. Running it through crushed charcoal from the fire will help to decolorize and deodorize it.

Since cliffs often intersect the water table, springs or seeps may be found there. Often identified in desert country by the obviously greener vegetation growing there, these moist oases may be visible several miles distant. Disappointingly, these spots may only be damp on close examination. Dig back into the wet area. The flow may be increased or at least encouraged to drip occasionally. Place a container under the drips and you will be surprised to see how quickly the water accumulates. And, if the only thing you have to catch the water in is your dirty old sweaty boot or shoe, remember "Beggars can't be choosers." Use it anyway. With a serious water shortage, thirst is probably far more important than an incipient case of athlete's mouth. (Use water purifying chemicals in your shoe.)

Rainwater that has collected in depressions in rock surfaces should be pure since it has not normally contacted human disease organisms. Still, it is recommended that it be purified to be absolutely certain. But in a "forever situation," this source is one of the least likely to be contaminated.

Another source of pure water is rain trapped in hollow portions of vegetation. In tropical areas, bamboo sections may contain water. They can be heard to slosh if the bamboo is shaken. Plants with cylindrically arranged leaves such as bromeliads often trap rainwater also. In both cases, even if there are mosquito larvae swimming in the water, it should be safe to drink. (Mosquitos are only a health hazard when they bite, not when you eat them!)

REMEMBER: TRAPPED RAINWATER IS USUALLY SAFE.

SOME UNUSUAL SOURCES

Dew and Condensation

As temperatures fall during the evening, condensation in the form of dew may form on cool surfaces such as car tops and hoods, aircraft surfaces, and even on vegetation. This may be mopped up with clothing and wrung out into a container. Surprising quantities may be obtained in this manner. Anyone who has been soaked by walking through high dew-covered grass will intuitively realize the potential of dew as a water source. A student once asked how much water could be obtained this way before the car stopped releasing moisture. He apparently was concerned that the water was coming from the vehicle and, once it dried out, it would mean the end of the supply. Keep in mind that the

Figure 6-3   Collecting rain with a sloping plastic sheet. (Paul H. Risk)

water is coming from the air. Water vapor condenses out of the air because the surface of the metal or vegetation is at a lower temperature. Because of this, the air at the cool surface reaches its "dew point" and moisture begins to appear as visible drops. Generally, the air mass represents a huge supply of water and, even though you may mop up all night, as long as the temperature differential between the air and the surface is great enough, the dew will continue to form. The same principal is at work when moisture forms on the outside of a glass of an iced drink. The source of the condensation is not the glass but the air.

Rain itself may provide a significant source of pure water. Especially in intense downpours, it is possible to collect several gallons of water. Try to increase the collecting surface. A raincoat, poncho, or even an ordinary shirt or coat may be arranged to permit *runoff*—the funneling of the accumulating rain into a container. If the material is not waterproof or repellant, it will still act to sluice off the water if it is arranged at a steep angle (Figure 6-3).

Fruit or Berries
Juicy fruit or berries can assist in providing needed water. Their sugar content will also be helpful in providing energy.

WHERE TO LOOK FOR WATER   71

Vines

In North America, wild grape vines can provide a useful source of pure water. In tropical areas, many jungle vines or lianas will do the same. As a rule, if the sap of the vine is clear, watery, and tastes good, it is safe to use.

Reach as high up the vine as possible and cut it off. Then cut lower down. Never make the lower cut first. If you do, transpirational and translocational forces moving fluid through the plant will draw the water up the stem and you may not be able to get anything. By making the high cut first, you break this water column. However, in some jungle vines, the water flow is sudden when the second cut is made. To prevent loss of valuable water, tip the vine to the horizontal before the second cut is made.

Water obtained in this manner is absolutely safe from microorganisms. In order for it to get into the plant, it was necessary for the water to pass directly through cell walls. Disease organisms cannot traverse this barrier. In effect, the water has been filtered by a special microbial filter that has removed any hazard completely.

Barrel Cactus

In some desert areas, the barrel cactus may be a source of potable water. The top is carefully cut out, exposing the internal white pulp (Figure 6-4). The exterior of the cactus is very tough and covered with overlapping long sharp spines, so that a stout knife with a blade at least 4 inches long will be a great help. Or a hatchet will do nicely.

Figure 6-4   Barrel cactus with top cut open. (Paul H. Risk)

WATER PROCUREMENT AND TREATMENT

The pulp is the plant's water reservoir. It may be placed in a piece of thin cloth and crushed to remove water. Or the pulp may be pounded down inside the cactus itself to permit water to accumulate. However, the easiest way is to simply cut out chunks of the pulp, chew them, suck out the water, and spit out the remaining fibrous mass.

The taste will vary from location to location. But the author's experience is that it is much like gritty, diluted aspirin tablets. The grit may be from microscopic cell inclusions called crystoliths. A bit like sand, they are distracting but not harmful. A large cactus may produce two quarts of water.

It takes up to 200 years for a barrel cactus to mature. It is recommended that they be disturbed only in an emergency. In fact, several western states have strict laws protecting most cacti. At any rate, conservation dictates preservation of cacti except when necessary.

Ice and Snow

First, it is important to realize that freezing does not necessarily kill microorganisms. Water obtained from contaminated lake or stream ice may be seriously contaminated. On the other hand, snow is distilled water and, unless animal or human waste has been in contact with it, it will be pure.

Under cold conditions, the only source of water may be snow or ice. The most efficient method is melting ice. Thawing snow can be very discouraging since very little water is obtained from each container full of snow. If you realize that 10 inches of snow is the equivalent of only 1 inch of rain, it is easy to understand the problem. A cup of snow will yield only about a tenth of a cup of water. This will vary slightly, depending on the moisture content of the snow, its crystal structure, and how tightly packed it is. But ice yields water essentially at a 1:1 ratio. So a cup of ice would yield a cup of water.

If you must melt snow, place a small amount in the bottom of the container. As it melts, carefully sprinkle more in, gradually adding more. If the container is filled with snow and placed on the heat, there is danger of burning a hole in the bottom of the vessel. A thin layer of snow at the bottom melts, which leaves an air pocket. The tiny amount of moisture resulting quickly evaporates into steam and is absorbed by the porous snow in the upper part of the vessel, leaving the bottom dry. In the absence of cooling water, the container bottom quickly overheats and burns through.

If you are determined to melt snow in large quantities, be sure to constantly poke it down with a stick or other implement to assure contact with the container bottom until sufficient water accumulates to eliminate concern.

In the absence of a fire, try to avoid eating ice or snow directly. The chilling effect may increase the chances of hypothermia. At the very least, hold the frozen material in your mouth until it melts and approaches body temperature before swallowing. Or place the snow or ice in a plastic bag or other container and suspend it between layers of your clothing so that body heat can melt it slowly. Then consume the water only after it has approached body temperature.

It has been said by some that eating snow actually dehydrates the body. This is *not* true. That is like saying if you drink water, it will dry you out. What happens has more to do with psychological thirst. Since such a small quantity of water results from the melted snow, it is quite discouraging. Thirst is hardly assuaged at all. Even this effect may be done away with if the snow is first melted in a container and the water drunk directly.

If a functioning vehicle is available, snow or ice may be placed in a container and melted near the engine. And on sunny days, a dark garment or plastic sheet may warm up enough to assist in melting snow or ice through solar energy.

Radiator Water

This was purposely *not* referred to as radiator *coolant*. Today most motor vehicles use a permanent coolant/antifreeze that is quite poisonous. However, in the event your radiator is filled only with water, it represents a container of pure water holding perhaps 4 to 6 or more gallons. The heating, cooling, and reheating of the water will have effectively purified it and it may be used safely for drinking.

However, DO NOT use this water if you have ever had to use *any* chemicals in it to prevent rust or stop leaks. And NEVER ATTEMPT TO DRINK PERMANENT AUTOMOBILE ANTIFREEZE even if it is partially mixed with water.

Stills and Desalinating Devices

Large life rafts aboard ocean-going vessels and transoceanic flights contain stills and desalinating devices. The solar still looks like a large balloon when ready for use. Figure 6-5 shows how it functions. Sunlight heats the interior much like a greenhouse. Water vapor rises to the relatively cool upper surfaces where the water condenses and trickles down the sides to the collector and from there into the freshwater container. The stills are ordinarily charged with seawater and then allowed to float on the water, attached to the raft by a lanyard. They continue to work as long as the sun shines.

Desalinating devices are simply ion-exchange columns of reduced size. Their capacity is limited and listed on the device. After they have removed the salt from the amount of seawater listed, they may not be reused (Figure 6-6).

Desert Still

Having once asked a survival class during an examination to describe how to make a desert still, the mind boggling response came back from one student who had missed several lectures that he supposed deserts were usually rather quiet!

74

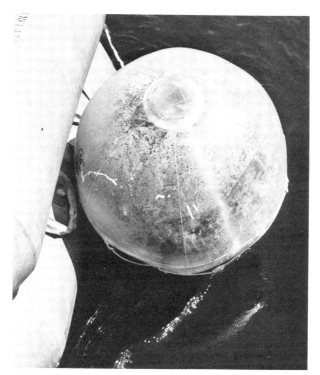

Figure 6-5   Marine still. (Courtesy of United States Air Force)

A desert still is a device for obtaining water directly from the soil or from chopped vegetation. Two designs are shown in Figure 6-7.

The first and more traditional pit type still may, under ideal conditions, yield as much as a half gallon of water in a day. A more usual quantity is a quart. If this were the only source of water, it would be necessary to construct more than one still to supply the amounts of water needed in summer desert temperatures.

The still pit should be about 3 feet in diameter and 2 feet deep. If the hole in the ground is dug in a sandy area where moisture is fairly high, such as a stream bed, the results will be much better. It takes about 2 hours or slightly more for the still to begin producing. Once it is sealed around the edges, it should not be opened until the end of the day or until water production stops. Opening the device causes a loss of moisture and heat, and the startup time of 2 hours again must be dealt with.

The action may be enhanced somewhat by the addition of chopped vegetation. This may be cactus, shrubs, or grasses. However, some plants contain toxic substances that are volatile enough to be carried into the distilled water

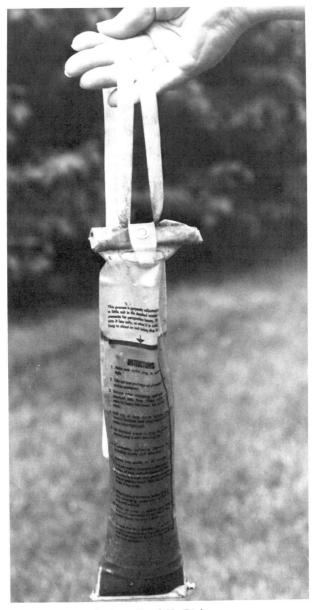

Figure 6-6   Desalinating device. (Paul H. Risk)

WATER PROCUREMENT AND TREATMENT

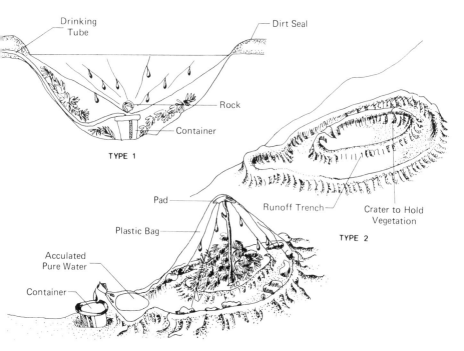

Figure 6-7   Pit type desert still (Type 1); plastic bag still (Type 2). Adapted by Celia Drozdirk from a design by Gene Fear in Wilderness Emergency.

and ruin it for drinking. If you are unsure whether the plants in your area are safe, leave them out.

The plastic sheet used should ideally be clear, but lightly tinted plastic works too. Black or other opaque plastic will not do the job.

As the sun shines on the still, the interior temperature climbs rapidly, vaporizing moisture trapped in the sand or vegetation. This vapor rises to the relatively cool inner surface of the plastic where it condenses as droplets of distilled water. Because of the slope of the plastic, these droplets tend to run together and drip off the bottom of the cone and into the container. The tube enables removal of the water without opening the still. Water not drunk immediately may be sucked into the mouth and transferred to a storage vessel. If a group of people will be using this, it is wise to add water-purifying chemicals to avoid spreading disease of even a minor nature through the group.

The plastic-bag still is from a design by Gene Fear, which is described in Robert Stoffel's *Emergency Preparedness Today,* published by the State of Washington (1976). Its principle is the same as the still discussed above, but the source of moisture is vegetation. Water condenses on the upper part of the plastic, trickles to the outer crater, and from there into the depression at the lower end of the bag. It may then be removed for use by untwisting the end of the plastic bag. The same warning about toxic vegetation would hold for this device as for the above still.

WATER PURIFICATION

Water may be made safe to drink by heat, chemicals, or specific filtration methods. The best method is boiling, since all disease organisms are killed this way, although the newer filtration methods should also successfully remove bacteria and even some viruses.

BOILING

Water should be brought to a rolling boil for at least 2 minutes and preferably 10. Add 1 minute for every thousand feet above sea level. So, at 5000 feet elevation, the water should be boiled 2 minutes for the basic treatment plus 5 minutes for altitude compensation. The total boiling time would then be a minimum of 7 or a maximum of 15 minutes.

CHEMICAL PURIFICATION

Halazone tablets [P-(N, N Dichlorosulfamoyl) benzoic acid], iodine tablets (tetraglycine hydroperiodide), tincture of iodine, and bleach, all can effectively purify water. However, in tropical areas where amoebic dysentery is found the only guaranteed methods are boiling and special filters. The organism that causes this form of dysentery (*Endamoeba hystolytica*) can, when conditions are unfavorable for its development, take an encysted form. It develops a hardened, waterproof wall around itself and waits until conditions improve. Then, the wall breaks down and the amoeba starts its destructive activities again. The encysted form is not successfully attacked by any of the chemical purification methods.

Halazone tablets work by releasing chlorine-based substances into the water. They are effective but recent research casts some concern over their action spectrum. Some organisms are not effectively killed. Also, the tablets tend to decompose readily when exposed to dampness or sunlight. They also lose their effectiveness with age. Chances are, if you have some that have been kicking around your car or pack for the last several seasons, they are no longer effective and ought to be replaced. Water treated with Halazone tastes distinctly "chlorinated."

Iodine-based water-purifying tablets have a broader action spectrum and tend to be less affected by dampness, light, or age. They tend to discolor the water, turning it a pale brownish yellow and impart a distinct taste.

Both types of tablets are used in the same manner. Placed in the canteen or other water container, according to the manufacturer's recommended dosage, they should be allowed to dissolve before starting to count elapsed time. Most manufacturers recommend 20 to 30 minutes before using the water.

If iodine purification tablets are not available, ordinary tincture of iodine may be used. Most first aid kits used to have iodine. However, it has been determined that iodine has very few acceptable uses, often causing more tissue damage and slower healing. So, fewer and fewer first aid kits contain it.

The usual strength is $2\frac{1}{2}$ percent although veterinary strength is usually 6 percent. If you are using $2\frac{1}{2}$ percent iodine, 4 drops per quart of clear water should be sufficient. If the water is cloudy with suspended material, use 8 drops. Veterinary strength iodine (6 percent) may be used at the rate of 2 drops per quart in clear water and 4 drops in cloudy. The water will turn the same brownish yellow as when using iodine tablets and will acquire a strong iodine flavor. Wait 30 minutes before use.

Still another method for water purification uses iodine crystals. A small quantity (4 to 8 grams) of USP-grade resublimed iodine is placed into a 1-ounce glass bottle. When it is necessary to purify water, the bottle is filled from the contaminated source and shaken well. Iodine does not dissolve well in water. But a nearly saturated solution will be formed. The concentration of dissolved iodine will depend on the water temperature. Since this is the case, more iodine solution must be used for colder water. Or the contact time may be increased by allowing the treated water to stand longer before drinking. At 77°F (25°C) 12.5 milliliters of the solution, which results after the iodine crystals that remain have settled, is added to 1 liter of contaminated water and allowed to stand for 15 minutes. Water at a temperature of 68°F (20°C) requires 13 milliliters of iodine solution. At 37°F (3°C) use 20 milliliters of solution. An article by Frederick H. Kahn and Barbara R. Visscher in *Backpacker* (No. 26) will give more details on this procedure. But, use *caution* if this treatment is used. IODINE IS POISONOUS! *Never* allow any of the iodine crystals to get into the drinking water in solid form.

Bleach such as Clorox or Purex may also be used to purify water. Generally, bleach solutions such as these have $5\frac{1}{4}$ percent sodium hypochlorite as the active ingredient. If anything else has been added as a cleaning aid, do not use the bleach for this purpose. It may be harmful if taken internally. After the bleach is added, wait 30 minutes before using.

So you've followed the instructions to the letter. After filling your water bottle from the stream, you have added the required amount of chemical purifier, waited for it to dissolve, shaken the container well, waited 30 minutes, and slaked your thirst. Some hours later you are as sick as a dog from water-borne bacteria. What happened?

One small concern is usually omitted in instructions on water purification.

Figure 6-8   Flushing threads of water container to remove contaminated water. (Paul H. Risk)

Trapped in the threads of the container cap and neck is contaminated water that has not been exposed to the chemical purification agent. Since it only takes a drop of contaminated water to make you ill, you are now sick. To avoid this after the chemical has dissolved, invert the container (Figure 6-8). Loosen the cap just enough to allow treated water to well up and flush the threads of both container neck and cap. Then immediately tighten. You will lose only a few drops of water. But after the required amount of time has passed not only the water in the bottle but that in the threads will have been purified.

FILTERS

Several filters are now on the market that purport to remove all disease organisms from water (Figure 6-9). They usually function by passing the water through activated charcoal, special membranes, iodine or silver compounds, or a combination of these methods. Caution should be exercised in their use. Read

Figure 6-9 Two types of water purifiers that combine chemical and filtration techniques. (Paul H. Risk)

the manufacturer's specifications carefully. A number of the filters do not completely remove or destroy disease organisms and are only completely effective if additional treatment is carried out. In general, those using iodine-based substances are best.

7

SHELTER

For the purposes of this book, *shelter* will refer to anything that extends the body's comfort or safety. Therefore, all clothing as well as enclosed structures—vehicles, tents, sleeping bags, and improvised shelters such as lean-tos and snow caves—will be considered.

The naked, resting human body is comfortable in only a very narrow range of temperatures. A good estimate, taking into consideration variations in individual metabolism, would be from 80 to 90°F. Cooler or warmer, and discomfort results. However, appropriate clothing and shelter can extend the range of comfort or safety many degrees.

Heat is necessary to maintain the body temperature in a range at which the vital life-supporting chemical reactions may continue. Generally, the body's core is held at a fairly constant 99 to 100°F. Even minor changes in this temperature signify cause for concern.

Heat is supplied internally by oxidation of food materials. In a sense, a slow fire burns within us continuously releasing heat. Of course, there are no flames or even a glow. The process is more akin to the rusting of iron. Nevertheless, on a constant basis we chemically convert food and produce heat. If the air around us is warm or cool enough, our heat production is exactly balanced by heat loss to the external environment.

If conditions shift slightly in a cooler direction, the body's metabolism may increase a bit to supply more heat. However, this capability is very limited. Blood vessels near the skin surface (the peripheral circulation) constrict, keeping a larger percentage of the blood in the deeper areas of the body away from the cool surface. We begin to feel chilly. Shivering may develop as the body attempts to supply more heat through involuntary exercise. We put on more clothes, apply external heat, come inside, or try all three.

If conditions shift slightly in a warmer direction, the body attempts to increase heat loss. Peripheral circulation increases to bring greater amounts of warm blood close to the surface, so that heat may escape more rapidly. Our automatic evaporative cooling system goes into action. Sweat glands begin to function—at first insensibly and then noticeably to provide a thin layer of water (perspiration) that, as it evaporates, carries away large amounts of heat. Under extremely hot conditions the body may release copious quantities of sweat.

Heat production is (1) *internal,* resulting from food oxidation, shivering, and exercise, and (2) *external,* resulting from solar radiation, fire, or heating devices, warm foods, or beverages.

Heat loss occurs from radiation, conduction, convection, evaporation, and respiration.

HEAT LOSS

In *radiation* losses, heat passes directly from the body to the surrounding environment. Radiation in cold weather from the head alone may result in the loss of as much as 75 percent of the body's production of heat.

Conduction is a process of direct contact. In contact with cold water, snow, ice, metal, chilled fuel, and so on, heat is lost from the body at a much greater rate than in air. For example, a person in an air temperature of 40°F would not be in serious immediate danger. However, the same person immersed in water of 40°F may die within an hour or less. From a practical standpoint, falling into cold water, handling snow or very cold metal equipment without gloves, sitting or sleeping on the ground with inadequate insulation beneath you, or spilling fuel on the body can result in serious conductive heat loss.

Convection and *air movement* cause heat to be carried away from the body by removing the warmed layer of air in close proximity to the surface of the body and by replacing it with air at a lower temperature. Basically the same process by which a radiator works, this may be a source of great heat loss.

Evaporative loss may occur from perspiration. Also, rain-soaked clothing and melting snow or ice may also increase evaporative heat loss. Wet clothing also drains heat through conduction.

RESPIRATION

Most of us do not think about the heat that is lost as we breathe. But respiration brings cool air into warm lungs where heat is lost from the lung tissue and circulating blood. This is then exhaled, carrying away heat, and then replaced with cool air as we inspire, and the process starts all over again.

The methods to control our comfort and safety are varied. But the principles are constant. Although means for staying cool are also important, this section will deal largely with staying warm. Reversing the process in many cases will accomplish cooling.

CLOTHING AND INSULATION

The key to successful insulation is dead or very slowly exchanging air space. Heat from the body in effect becomes trapped in the air held in the clothing. Because of this, it is virtually impossible to be chic and fashionable in cold weather unless you are slowly crystalizing at the same time. A key concept in the selection of effective warm clothing is BIG, BAGGY, AND UGLY (BBU). Remember, tight ski pants are designed only for speed, usually in racing downhill or in getting into trouble. They simply don't do the job when you're lying on the ski slope with a broken leg waiting for the Ski Patrol. If you doubt this, simply sit down in the snow in a pair of tight ski pants and time how long it takes for your posterior to solidify!

CLOTHING AND MATERIALS
NATURAL FIBERS AND DOWN

Wool and cotton are two materials often encountered in outdoor clothing. They both have particular advantages and disadvantages.

Cotton breathes well, is lightweight, and comfortable against the skin. It may be reasonably warm, especially when layered. However, wet cotton loses virtually all its insulating characteristics. In addition, cotton wicks moisture readily. This means that, if you fall in the water so that you are immersed to the waist, the water will continue to be drawn up into your cotton shirt until the entire shirt is soaked, in spite of the fact that it never was dipped in the water entirely.

Wool, on the other hand, does not wick to any marked degree. Water will only creep up a slight amount above the point of immersion. It is available from very coarse to very soft, so that it need not scratch although worn directly against the skin. Because of its fiber structure, it is an excellent insulator even when wet. Wool may be wrung out and tends to bounce back, restoring much of the insulation capability even while damp. Raw wool contains an oily substance called lanolin which makes it water repellant. Where possible, use wool.

For years down or a combination of down and feathers has been used in winter clothing. Very light and with excellent insulating qualities, pure goose or duck down provides ample warmth. It does, however, have an irritating habit of escaping through minute holes where the seams are stitched. In general, this does not result in significant loss. But down is only effective if it is dry and clean. Wet down is worse than useless. It is a serious hazard. The fluff immediately packs together losing nearly 100 percent of its loft and, therefore,

84

its insulating capability. And, it is nearly impossible to dry in the field. Water-soaked down, holding as it does great quantities of water, becomes very heavy. It is quite possible to lift a soaked down sleeping bag in such manner as to have the wet down tear out several or most of the fabric dividers as it mushes its way to the lowest part of the bag. The result is a completely ruined bag.

SYNTHETICS

In an effort to improve on nature, several synthetic fibers have been developed. Each of them has its own particular advantages. However, down still seems to come out on top when cost, resistance to wear, weight, and comfort are all considered. Its major weakness is loss of insulating capacity when wet.

Components of clothing have three distinct functions: transmission of liquid and vaporous water, insulation, wind and water proofing.

Moisture Transmission

Both socks and underwear are now being manufactured from polypropylene fibers. This material wicks moisture away from the skin 5 to 6 times faster than wool. The result is a reduction in conductive heat loss and a feeling of dry warmth. When perspiration is allowed to build up in underwear next to the skin, a chilly, clammy feeling results. Polyproplyene material is available in several thicknesses.

Insulation

Polyester fiber is used in an increasing variety of garments. DuPont's Hollofil® or Hollofil II® (also sold as Hollobond®) is a material made of hollow, chopped fibers. The individual fibers are approximately 2.5 inches long and average 23 microns (0.0009 inch) in diameter. Their short length requires that the material be quilted to prevent shifting of the fibers. As with most of the synthetics, the material when wet can be wrung out and field dried easily. Its low compressibility helps maintain its loft even when soaked. In addition, the hollow center of the fibers acts as an increased insulation, similar to that possessed by caribou hair, polar bear fur, and harp seal fur.

A Celanese Fortrel fiber called PolarGuard® is formed of crimped, continuous filament polyester fiber with a diameter of about 24 microns. Its crimped structure increases dead air space, and the continuous fiber enables it to be used without quilting. It too does not retain moisture well, bounces back to original loft when wrung out, and is easily field dried.

One of the newer materials, manufactured by 3M Company, is called Thinsulate.® From a blend of polyester and polyolefin fibers, the material is 40 percent heavier than the same thickness of down. But its minute fiber diameters (38 microns for the polyester and a mere 1 to 3 microns for the polyolefin components) make it almost twice as warm as an equal thickness of down according to 3M Company. U.S. Army tests indicate the same insulating capacity as down per unit thickness. Because it maintains most of its insulation quality even when wet and is easily dried in the field, it is an excellent material.

Also recently, a pile manufactured from a single-fiber synthetic or a blend has come on the market. Woven on a scrim backing, pile has excellent insulating qualities. It is, however, rather bulky. Absorbing approximately 1 percent of its weight in water, it becomes far less wet than wool. A type of pile called Borglite® made of DuPont dacron Hollofil is, according to Bryant in the October/November 1981 issue of *Backpacker* magazine, 40 percent warmer than nylon pile and 5 percent warmer than polyester pile.

Summary of Insulation Properties for Synthetics
PolarGuard, Hollofil, and Other Similar Synthetics

Cost: Less than down.
Insulating capacity: About one-third heavier than down for equal insulation; less insulation per unit thickness than down.
Wet characteristics: Does not flatten out when wet; field driable
Flexibility: Somewhat stiff when compared to down.
Compressibility: Harder to compress than down.
Weight: Heavier unit for unit than down for same insulation.
Migration: Hollofil migrates if not quilted, but far less than down would. Continuous fibers do not spill from tears as down does.

Thinsulate®

Cost: More expensive than other synthetics.
Insulating capacity: Same insulation as down per unit weight; manufacturer says almost twice (1.8) per unit thickness (U.S. Army data indicates same as down per unit thickness). Twice as warm as other synthetics per unit thickness.
Wet characteristics: Does not flatten when wet; field driable.
Flexibility: Stiffer than down and polyesters; tends not to fill cavities between body contours and garment as well as down and polyesters.
Compressibility: Not as compressible as down or synthetics.
Weight: Heavier than down.
Migration: Does not migrate or spill from tears.

Protection

Insulation by itself can be relatively useless. Without protection from wind and water, a fabric becomes soaked or is easily penetrated.

Wind protection is often integrated with the insulation, forming a covering

86

or outer layer on the insulating garment of a tightly woven nylon or nylon/cotton blend. A common blend is 60/40 cloth, which is approximately 60 percent cotton and 40 percent nylon.

In years past, rain protection was largely provided by coated nylon parkas, ponchos, and cagoules (an ankle length poncho). More recently, a synthetic film chemically known as PTFE (polytetrafluoroethylene) was developed by W. L. Gore and Associates. Their material is called Gore-Tex® and has the interesting characteristic of easily passing water in vapor form but not as a liquid—the fabric's pore spaces are too small for liquid water molecules but large enough to pass water vapor molecules. Gore-Tex is usually sandwiched between layers of other fabric, such as nylon, and thus has the dual capability of protecting from both wind and water. Although quite expensive, the material is very effective and an increasing number of these protective garments are coming onto the market. The result is clothing that prevents sweat buildup yet still provides ample rain resistance.

EFFECTIVE USE OF CLOTHING

Stores are filled with various types of cold weather clothing. Ads in outdoor publications show intrepid adventurers sporting masses of bloated arctic-grade outfits, braving the polar blasts of the photographer's studio.

At the same time, college and university campuses abound in students dressed for a summit assault on Mount Everest. There has developed a certain pressure to *look* like an outdoor person. But a person can *look* like the ads and be intensely cold or drenched in sweat. In short, there is more to clothing selection and use than merely observing a slick ad.

Before making extensive clothing purchases, it is wise to realize that people vary widely in their need for clothing. This is related to their physical condition, the amount of adipose tissue (fat) under their skin, and their general metabolism. As a result, what is sufficient for one person may leave another chilled to the bone. And what is too warm for me, may be just right for you. If possible, talk the storekeeper into permitting return privileges. Your clothing must be tailored to your needs in more than style.

Remember the principle of BBU (Big, Baggy, and Ugly)? Combine this with the *layer principle* and be warm. For general survival, perhaps the poorest design is the typical snowmobile suit. A one-piece garment, it is designed for one purpose—sitting in one place in cold weather with a high wind. Yes, the snowmobile is racing around the terrain, but the driver or passenger is doing very little exercise. And the wind may be very high, generated largely by the machine thundering along at high speed. In the case described, it is important to maximize heat retention and windproofing. But what happens when the snow machine bends or breaks a vital part of its anatomy or is strangled by some impure fuel, leaving the driver and passenger stranded? If they are traveling alone (rule violation #1) and have not left a travel plan (rule violation #2), the only way they will get home is by shanks mare. This means exertion. Exertion means greatly increased heat production inside a suit designed to be comfortable under less stressful conditions. Perspiration is the result. Although some of these suits can be unzipped down the front, up to the elbows and knees, and down much of the trunk, upper arms and legs are still encased in too much clothing. At the least, sweating under these conditions means damp clothing. Dampness means loss of insulation and a creeping chill.

Under extreme cold conditions ice may actually form in the clothing. Sweat accumulating on the skin surface soaks into the clothing and begins to migrate toward the drier outer surface. Some of the perspiration evaporates (taking a significant amount of heat in the process), and this vapor begins to migrate toward the outer layer of the clothing. Reaching the outer level of the clothing, the vapor cools enough to condense and soak the cloth and other insulation. Some of it may actually freeze. Some may wick its way back toward the skin, reaching a temperature enabling it to re-evaporate (more heat loss), migrate as vapor toward the cool outside air, cool, condense, wick, and start the cycle all over again. In addition, a tiny bit more ice may form in the outer portion of the clothing. This thermal game of ping-pong continues with the result that heat loss becomes extreme and life threatening.

The answer to the problem is the *layer principle*. Several lightweight layers of clothing in increasing sizes, to avoid compression of the under layers, is the best way to stay warm. When inactivity or falling temperatures brings about a need for more warmth, simply add more layers. As activity increases or temperatures rise, these layers may be removed to keep the wearer comfortable. Remember—it is very difficult to take a snowmobile suit or heavy down parka off in layers without seriously affecting its resale value!

A GENERALIZED MODEL

To provide an idea of what is being described, let's start with a bare body and work out.

There are those who recommend starting with wool underwear, and if the wool is soft enough, there is certainly no need to worry about scratchiness. Therefore, this is one alternative. But whatever type is chosen, it is better if it is made as separate top and bottom. This provides more control, allowing part to be worn without the other half.

Fishnet underwear, also called Norwegian fishnet underwear, is favored by some. Looking like long underwear made of minnow net, it is more holes than substance. However, it is often misused. For greatest warmth, first don the net underwear and then a layer of snug but not tight-fitting wool or cotton underwear. The holes in the net material are then capped and provide the dead air space necessary in good insulation. By itself, covered only by a loose-fitting pair of trousers and shirt, the insulating characteristics are largely missing. Although the material does provide excellent ventilation.

Fishnet underwear tends to be rather nonelastic. As a result, it may be binding—too tight across the shoulders or around the legs. Any such restriction not only interferes with ease of movement but also may impede blood circulation and thus promote chilling.

Any of the winter-grade two-piece long underwear brands may be substituted according to personal preferences. Thermal underwear, often called waffle-weave, combines the effect of the net and the covering.

Polypropylene underwear may also be used. More expensive than the more traditional types, it provides good insulation while not retaining moisture. Perspiration tends to pass through quickly, thus eliminating the feeling of dampness or clamminess associated with other underwear.

Over the underwear, pull on a pair of loose (BBU) wool trousers. If going into extreme conditions is contemplated, they ought to be held up with suspenders rather than a belt to allow air movement and reduce interference with circulation. The author prefers a medium-weight wool turtleneck sweater over the underwear on the top of the body. The turtleneck protects the major heat loss areas associated with the throat and neck. Then a loose-fitting long-sleeved wool shirt.

From this point on, a lot of individual needs and preferences ought to be considered. I generally prefer a light down parka (sometimes called a down sweater) covered with a 60/40 cloth parka shell. The down sweater as well as the 60/40 parka both have hoods. But, if I contemplate a long period of relative inactivity in very cold weather, I use a heavy down parka.

Down pants are also available for very cold environments. But, for general hiking and backpacking and even winter camping, a pair of windpants of unlined nylon may be pulled on over the wool trousers. These should have closures—Velcro or elastic at the ankles.

Perhaps a few comments about specialized clothing are in order. Cross-country skiers frequently wear knickers with knee-length stockings. Hikers in an effort to loose excess body heat may even wear shorts. These are both fine where rapid release of generated heat is the goal. But a problem develops when reduced activity or dropping temperatures require more covering. If determined to wear either type of clothing, it is wise to carry additional changes for those times when you rest or establish camp. Also, shorts and knickers provide virtually no protection from thorns, briars, or brush which will become painfully evident if it becomes necessary to leave the trail. And remember, it is not possible to extend the length of a pair of shorts.

Feet, head, and hands remain. Most hikers wear two pairs of socks both for insulation and prevention of blisters. The socks can slide against each other and minimize friction against the foot. Again, it is appropriate that personal choice determine the type of socks worn. I generally wear a medium-weight athletic sock, followed by a heavy wool pair. Socks are also available that purport to wick perspiration away from the feet to increase comfort, and many swear by them.

Footgear of many types is available. Probably the best type would be Eskimo mukluks. But these are not easily available. If warmth alone is the consideration, snowmobile boots with rubber bottoms, nylon uppers, and a felt inner boot are probably the best on the market. They are very comfortable and breathe (release water vapor) rapidly enough to minimize moisture accumulation around the foot. However, they are rather soft and, as a result, are not as comfortable when wearing snowshoes. Also because of their softness, they give only minimal lateral support in the handling of the snowshoes. A few years ago, snowmobile boots came with nontreated nylon uppers. Now they are almost always treated with a waterproofing compound. While this may be helpful under melting snow conditions, it severely reduces the passage of water vapor from inside the boot.

Several varieties of boots with felt inner liners, rubber bottoms, and leather or leatherlike uppers are now on the market. However, they breathe very poorly, causing socks and felt liners to become soaked with perspiration. As soon as this soaking takes place, the feet begin to get chilled. This is especially pronounced and rapid if inactivity follows exercise. I have had the experience of ice forming in the boot, freezing the felt to the boot bottom and the socks to the felt. If this type of boot is used, it is vitally important to change the felt liners at least once during the day.

Leather climbing or hiking boots may be appropriate under some conditions. But in winter they generally do not provide sufficient insulation and hardly breathe at all. In addition, climbing boots usually have a steel shank that runs most of the length from sole to heel to prevent or minimize flexing during climbing. This metal stiffener also acts as a very effective heat sink, rapidly drawing warmth away from the foot. Winter hikers or climbers who plan to be exposed to long periods of very cold weather should also have expedition down or synthetic-filled overboots.

Boots with Ensolite or other closed-cell insulation between the leather layers are warm but do not breathe at all. Once the feet become wet from sweat, they are not warm enough and the boots may well become a liability.

Soles that are cleated are a great help on footgear. Vibram (Figure 7-1) or Vibram-like soles and heels are highly recommended. They are a headache in sticky, high-clay content mud. But most anything else is too. And, under any other conditions they are superb.

Once the temperature goes below 10 to 15°F, it is impossible for gloves or mittens to keep hands warm for more than 2 to 3 hours during periods of

Figure 7-1   Vibram soled boots. (Paul H. Risk)

inactivity. The only exception to this would be electrically heated mits or hand protection with pocket warmers. Circulation to the hands is not sufficient to maintain their warmth under very cold conditions. Nevertheless, the best combination is a pair of wool gloves, followed by either a wind shell mit (no lining or filler) or a down or synthetic-filled mit. Gloves allow the fingers to function but increase the surface area and reduce heat retention. Mittens by enclosing the fingers in one compartment are more effective in limiting heat loss by reducing surface area. But, if everything fails and your hands are getting dangerously cold, pull your arms up inside your parka and place your hands under your armpits. (If you can't do this because your clothing is too tight, you have just flunked the BBU test. Remember—Big, Baggy, and Ugly. Whatever the case, the sleeves of your parka should pull down snugly over the cuffs of your gloves, both to reduce cold air entry and keep snow out.

The *head* is a very important area. At 40°F, the uncovered head loses up to 50 percent of the heat the body is producing. And this jumps to a staggering 75 percent at 5°F. Of course, a great deal depends on the texture, thickness, and style of the hair. A bald head is a great radiator, while an Afro hair style would maximize insulation and thus slow heat loss from the highly vascular scalp.

Knit wool stocking caps, balaclava helmets, and ski masks are all possibilities. Headgear should be selected to allow it to be rolled down over the ears when necessary. A wool stocking cap, covered by the parka hood, will adequately protect the head. The hood should, when zipped, cover the chin.

RAINGEAR

Pants and parkas are available with Gore-Tex. This is probably the most broadly useful way to go. But hip-length rain parkas with rain chaps or pants of treated nylon are excellent. Protection from rain is vitally important in preventing hypothermia. Ponchos tend to flap in the wind, allowing rain underneath. There are full-length anoraks that will also cover a pack.

IMPROVISED INSULATION

It is usually not well-equipped and clothed persons who find themselves in trouble in the outdoors. Frequently, they are persons who planned for a pleasant day only to have conditions suddenly change. With inadequate clothing at their disposal, they are in serious trouble.

Dry plant material may be pressed into service under such conditions. Milkweed fluff and cattail fuzz both make excellent insulation. Stuffed between layers of clothing, it is quite possible to improve your dress markedly. Dry grass and leaves may also be used in this way. Yes, a few small insects and tiny spiders may be picked up in the process, but this minor concern is far outweighed by the need for additional clothing.

Upholstering from a vehicle may be ripped open to get at the stuffing and this may be placed in the clothing. Seat covering or automobile headlining may be cut with a knife and sewn into improvised clothes, using a needle made from wire or part of a key ring. Anything that can be sharpened—paper clips, hair pins, broach pins or parts from other jewelry, a spring from a wrist watch expansion band—all represent possible sources for a needle. Improvisation is entirely related to our ability to imagine unique procedures and new uses for commonplace items.

HOUSING

Since the term *shelter* has been used for any covering from the skin out, I will use housing for any structure or similar thing that is used to get out of the weather.

First, it is important to realize that all survival books illustrate and discuss numerous kinds of improvised housing. And it is fine if you are able to construct a perfectly symmetrical and aesthetically pleasing lean-to, A-frame, or other structure. But it isn't at all necessary. The aim is to stay warm and dry, out of the wind, snow, or rain. If you can do this under an overhanging rock, beneath a fallen tree, or in a hollow log, then do it. Some survival victims spent a miserable time simply because they had firmly locked in their minds the idea that they did not know how to construct housing. So they went along, passing up many opportunities for natural shelter.

Whatever you do, take utmost advantage of naturally available shelter and materials. If necessary, add to them but try to minimize labor.

Housing protects us from extremes of:

Heat
Cold
Wet
Wind
Discomfort

What follows deals with general guidelines and some shelters applicable in a variety of conditions. More specific information on special-purpose housing can be found in the sections on particular environments or seasons.

BASIC SHELTER TYPES

Probably the most widely known shelter is the lean-to. It is basically a single ridgepole against which a sloping roof leans. Open in the front in the simplest form, it is not the warmest house in cold weather. However, it may be modified into an A-frame by placing a second sloping roof on the opposite side from the first one. (See Figures 7-2 and 7-3.)

Lean-tos should be constructed so that the prevailing wind approaches from a back corner (Figure 7-4). Wind striking the back of the shelter tends to eddy and form turbulance as it comes over the top; this can make smoke from the campfire a more or less constant problem. (Of course, the smoky atmosphere will discourage mosquitos, but you may develop emphysema. See Figure 7-5.)

Roofing for the lean-to may be made from sheets of bark, bundles of grass, reeds, cattails, or evergreen boughs (Figure 7-6). In any case, start at the bot-

Figure 7-2   Lean-to shelter. Since light is still visible through the thatching, the shelter is not yet complete. (Paul H. Risk)

Figure 7-3   A-frame shelter, using bark as covering. (Paul H. Risk)

tom, laying a single row. Then, overlap the next row, as shown in Figure 7-2, and so on until the shelter is complete. The angle of the roof should usually not be less than 60 degrees to promote drainage. The boughs should be placed with the cut ends toward the top of the shelter and their natural curvature toward the ground.

Often an examination from within will disclose thin spots in the thatching. Simply add more material at those points or, if maximum protection from rain is sought, add a complete second layer over the first, once again starting at the ground and row by row layering up to the ridgepole.

The ends should also be thatched closed, as shown in Figure 7-7.

If a bough bed is desired, it is recommended that on snow or cold ground you will need a minimum of 6 inches of insulation under you. This translates into almost *3 feet* (!) before you lie down. The boughs are placed in basically the same manner as though you were making a roof. But the cut ends go into the snow or ground. If the ground surface is too hard to permit insertion of the bough ends, don't worry. Just proceed as though they were stuck in (Figure 7-8). If several days pass before you are rescued, it will be necessary to add more springy material to help the bed maintain its insulating qualities.

With a fire placed in front, the shelter can be very pleasant. If your survival kit also contains a couple of aluminized Space Blankets® or anything else with a shiny, reflective surface, it is possible to turn the lean-to into a veritable

94   SHELTER

Figure 7-4 Proper orientation of a lean-to. The wind flows smoothly around as it strikes the rear corner of the shelter. (Jan Kolena Cole)

Figure 7-5 Improper orientation of a lean-to. The wind produces turbulence and draws smoke into the shelter when it comes directly from the back of the shelter. (Jan Kolena Cole)

reflector oven. Hang one Space Blanket with the shiny side toward the fire along the inside of the shelter back. Then arrange a frame to suspend one at a angle behind the fire, with the reflective surface toward the shelter. The author spent a very toasty night in just such a shelter when the outside temperatures dropped to 5 below zero. We were quite comfortable sitting and talking in our shirt sleeves! (See Figure 7-9).

Figure 7-6   Placement of boughs for thatching of a lean-to. (Jan Kolena Cole)

Of course, the Space Blankets may be used to construct a shelter without boughs. They are waterproof and the multilayer types are very strong with grommets at the corners to facilitate lashing in place.

In desert conditions, a double layer will provide improved protection from the sun (Figure 7-10).

SHELTER

Figure 7-7 Proper placement of boughs for end closure of a lean-to. (Jan Kolena Cole)

Lean-tos may also be built in pairs facing each other. With a Space Blanket hanging in the rear of each and a fire between, a cozy situation results.

Trees that have been blown over can also provide the basis for good housing. Or a tree may be cut and arranged so that it rests on its own base, as shown in Figure 7-11. All that remains is to stabilize it so that there is no chance of it shifting seriously when it is occupied. By working under the trunk and cutting off branches, an opening results a similar shelter can be constructed around the base of a standing evergreen tree (Figure 7-12). Add additional thatching on the outside and arrange other branches to help shed moisture. Branches along the upper side of the felled tree may be cut off and used as roofing material.

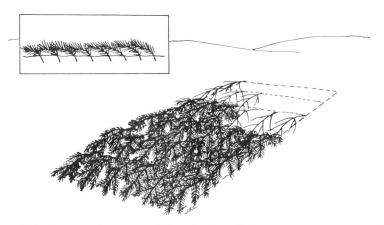

Figure 7-8   Proper placement of boughs for a bed or mattress. (Jan Kolena Cole)

Figure 7-9   A double lean-to with aluminized Space Blankets® hanging along the back wall as reflectors. (Jan Kolena Cole)

CAMPSITE SELECTION

The site should provide easy access to building materials. Since it is important to conserve energy, it is unwise to haul housing materials long distances. Dead saplings for poles, boughs for roofing, and bedding material should be near at hand.

Figure 7-10   Desert shelter using a double layer of material to improve insulation. The same technique may be used in cold weather. (Jan Kolena Cole)

Fuel should be abundant for the same reason. Especially in cold weather when it may be necessary to maintain a fire 24 hours a day, it will quickly become apparent that great amounts of wood are necessary. One of the more humbling experiences in primitive camping (or more recently, home heating with wood-burning stoves) is the huge quantities of wood that are necessary.

Similarly, water ought to be near at hand. However, don't sacrifice a mos-

Figure 7-11 A lopped tree shelter. (Jan Kolena Cole)

quito-free area just to be near water. In the long run, the avoidance of biting insects can be helpful both in terms of rest and relaxation as well as health. High ground is more likely to have a breeze and be freer of these creatures. Of course, in winter these areas will also be windswept and cold. Since mosquitos won't be a problem this time of year, your camp could be in a lower, more protected area.

A spot should be selected that will give you a good view of the sky or the valley through which searchers may approach. This will also enable you to be

100

Figure 7-12   Tree well shelter. (Jan Kolena Cole)

camped close to your signal fires and facilitate their ignition when the time comes. And, of course, safety should be considered. Avalanches, flash floods, tides, and surf—all pose potential problems if the campsite is in an inappropriate place. There are other considerations, but they are discussed in some detail in the chapters dealing with specialized conditions.

8

HOW
TO
PROCURE
AND
PREPARE
MEAT,
FOWL,
AND
FISH

Although food is the least important consideration in most survival situations, it is nevertheless especially important in maintaining a positive attitude. And, in long-term survival situations, food becomes increasingly important.

Conservation and protection of wildlife both have their place. Wanton killing of game or other animal species is not justified. But, in survival, it must be realized that sportsmanship and "giving the edge" to the prey have no place. The aim is to do everything possible to maximize the chances of a full stomach for the survivor. This chapter discusses a number of techniques that are neither sporting nor "fair" from the animal's standpoint. In fact, a majority are not even legal. They must not be practiced except under special permit from the state or federal agency that controls utilization and protection of the particular species or under actual emergency conditions.

Some of what is presented may be repugnant. But remember, only our cultural heritage dictates our diet. Raised eating hamburgers, we enjoy hamburgers. Raised eating giant white bark beetle larvae or grubs, we would enjoy grubs. The important thing to consider is whether you can modify your particular food prejudices to permit eating foods that are alien to your habits.

In teaching survival, it has been interesting to observe a wide variety of students as they attempt to cope with exotic foods.

From private pilots to forest rangers, park rangers and university students, there were always a few who were undaunted by anything. Without a flicker of emotion they tried fried Junebug grubs, snakes, and partially digested material from birds' crops. A substantial number of others were very reticent to deviate from established dietary patterns. And, a few could neither be urged nor coerced to try even some *not* very exotic fare.

During both the Korean and Viet Nam conflicts there were soldier prisoners who accepted death rather than eat the same nutritious but unfamiliar food their guards were served. With this knowledge, the oft-heard statement from survival students that—"If I *had* to I could, but I'm just not hungry enough"—simply doesn't stand up. For some, no amount of need would be enough.

Begin *now* to prepare psychologically to eat whatever is available. There are two basic rules in animal food utilization.

1. If it moves you can eat it.
2. Cook it.

Rule #1 has several exceptions that will be presented both in this chapter and others dealing with specific environments. Some of the exceptions are critical. For example, eating the flesh of certain fish living in coral atoll areas of the South Pacific Ocean will bring about very serious illness and often death. As with all new information, it is important to learn not only the basics and rules of thumb, but the exceptions. In most cases, it is easier to start with the exceptions since they are fewer.

Rule #2 is close to inviolable. While there are a few animals that may safely be eaten raw, there are some that contain dangerous parasites. Trichinosis from incompletely cooked pork or bear and liver flukes from raw fish are only two examples.

And, the nice part is that most animal food is quite good tasting. That can't be said about plant food. But this brings up another point. There is a difference between *edible* and *palatable*. If something is edible, it can be eaten without illness or death. If it is palatable, it can be eaten, enjoyed, and will stay down! Palatability is very subjective and strongly influenced by the power of our own minds. Most people think snake meat is delicious—until they find out what they are eating! Then it is suddenly terrible. The average person could be served domestic cat and dumplings any Sunday and believe it was chicken. Delicious! But imagine what their response would be as soon as it was identified for them.

Remember, the only thing preventing you from having some really shocking gastronomic experiences is your geographic location. If your survival situation is the result of a round-the-world plane flight, you could come down anywhere. For that matter, with hijackings what they are you can never really be sure what you'll be having for dinner at the end of a *local* flight!

HOW TO BEGIN

Start small with animals that require no special skill or equipment. In general, all *smooth insect larvae* are edible. Fuzzy catepillars sometimes have stinging hairs. And, whether they do or not they ought to be avoided. It is hard to get rid of the fuzz and the tiny hairs may be irritating to the mouth, throat, or the rest of the alimentary canal.

Requiring no traps, insect larvae are also slow. Even if you are completely exhausted you should be able to outrun a grub! They are also very nutritious. Some larvae may be almost 50 percent protein. Most are no lower than 30 percent. Good beef is only about 15 percent. Insects may also have a substantial fat content.

Look for them under the bark of dead trees, under rocks and logs, at the base of grass roots, in galls, and in streams and lakes.

The outer covering of *adult insects,* which is their skeleton, is made of a substance called chitin which is indigestible for humans. However, all the internal anatomy is easily digested and the somewhat crunchy outside will just add fiber.

While *bee and wasp larvae* are edible and have a pleasant nutlike flavor, they are also usually well defended. Approach them only as a last resort. A massive attack by the adults may leave even a nonsensitive human sick or dying.

It is possible to fire their nests with a well-placed torch. Their wings are very fragile and will shrivel with the slightest touch of flame. However, if the heat is not intense enough, they will not be killed and will merely fall to the ground where they will run all over. And, their stinging apparatus will still be fully operational.

Smoke may be used to tranquilize or even kill bees in a hollow tree. But, unless you know what you are doing be extra cautious.

Grasshoppers and crickets are not only nutritious but quite tasty. They may be roasted on a thin stick over coals or toasted on a hot rock. It is recommended that you take their long hind legs off before they are eaten to minimize scratchiness when you swallow.

Large beetles or *moths* may fly toward or into the flicker of an evening campfire. There is little of substance to moth wings so discard them and eat what remains. Some are very large with well filled-out bodies. The beetles may also be roasted, toasted, or fried.

With a little more imagination, adult insects or their immature stages may also be added to soups and stews. In general, I have never developed a real liking for boiled insect larvae by themselves. Although they are delicious roasted or in stews.

Snails are another example of a truly slow-moving prey. All snails are edible whether marine, aquatic, or terrestrial. However, there are some tropical types that possess a sharp, barbed shaft with a poison apparatus. When handled, they extrude the pointed barb through one end of the shell and inject a powerful venom. Nevertheless, even these if cooked are edible and tasty.

Slugs are sometimes referred to as snails without shells. While they do pos-

Figure 8-1   A large slug. (Paul H. Risk)

sess a tiny vestigial internal shell, they appear to be completely naked. Varying in length from an inch or less, they may in some areas such as tropical rain forests and the Pacific Northwest (Figure 8-1), reach a length of several inches. Large ones on the Olympic Peninsula or in Washington state are called banana slugs both because of their size and color.

Slugs and snails may be boiled or roasted. However, when they are boiled, a slimy material rises to the top of the cooking container. If it is too disgusting, skim it off. When well cooked, the snail may be slipped out of the shell with the tip of a pocketknife or a long splinter. They are generally more tender when boiled. Roasted on a stick, they are in texture a bit like eating a piece of chopped garden hose. But their flavor is excellent. The same may be said of slugs. No, it is unnecessary to "clean" them first. Eat the whole animal.

Now on to *snakes*. Especially in areas where venomous snakes are found, it is wise to kill the snake before picking it up. There are few good reasons for *ever* handling a live poisonous snake. It may be said that most people who feel they must do it are only trying in a foolish manner to impress others.

Snakes are easily demobilized. A blow anywhere on their back with a stick will fracture their spine. The result is loss of control of the half below the break. The snake will cease to be able to move forward. However, the blow should be delivered with a blunt instrument. Striking it with the cutting edge of a machete or other sharp tool will leave only the rear portion, while the front of the snake disappears into the brush.

The old idea of catching snakes with a forked stick really doesn't work very well. Often the surface of the ground is rocky or simply too hard to penetrate, and the snake slithers through the fork like a ball through a croquet wicket

Figure 8-2   Trying to catch a snake with a forked stick. (Celia Drozdiak)

(Figure 8-2). A long stick laid across the snake behind the head will work far better (Figure 8-3).

While the reptile is pinned down, cut the head off. If it is a venomous snake, bury the head. This is not for any mythical reason—just so you don't forget where you put it and sit on it. Slit the skin down the belly and peel it off. It should slip off easily. The entrails are easily removed from small- to medium-sized snakes simply by running the thumb down through the body cavity. What is left, although it is very likely still squirming, is delicious if properly prepared. Fried or roasted over the coals will likely produce the best-tasting product. Boiled snake tends to lose its firmness and fall apart, leaving a potful of tiny bones with fragments of rather unpalatable flesh. Large snakes may be cut transversely into steaks after the skin has been removed.

All *lizards* are edible and pleasant to eat. Small- to medium-sized lizards may be stoned, shot with an improvised slingshot, or easily snared with improvised nooses. Make a slip noose with any available cordage. It may be fishline, parachute suspension core lines, or fibers from grass or other vegetation (Figure

HOW TO PROCURE AND PREPARE MEAT, FOWL, AND FISH

Figure 8-3   An effective method of catching a snake using a straight stick. (Rosalie R. Risk)

8-4). This is then afixed to a long pole. Strange as it may seem, lizards basking on rocks will frequently remain still while the noose is carefully maneuvered over their heads. I have actually bumped a lizard's face on numerous occasions and had it only move a tiny bit to one side as I finally slipped the cord around its neck and lifted it from the rock. The woman shown in Figure 8-5 had no trouble in catching all the Fence Lizards shown—and it took only about an hour.

Lizards should be skinned by slitting down the belly. The skin will pull off the legs with no additional cuts. Remove the internal organs and roast the lizard. But, like snakes, it is not recommended that lizards be boiled. They lose too many of their taste-tantalizing qualities.

Wherever they are found, birds' *eggs* can lend real variety to the survival menu. And it does not matter what stage of development they are in. Drop them in the cook pot and boil them up. They may also be cooked by placing them near the coals and carefully rotating them after first punching a small hole in the end to allow the release of steam. Or, carefully run a thin twig through the egg and improvise a small rotisserie.

Eggs may be found in nests in trees as well as on the ground. But be careful about climbing trees. A broken leg will not improve chances for survival. And, reaching into a bird nest into which you cannot see may only turn up a scorpion or snake in the warmer states or tropical areas.

Figure 8-4   Using a long stick and cord to catch a lizard. (Jan Kolena Cole)

Turtle eggs as well as snake and lizard eggs are edible and may be found buried in sandbanks along streams or other areas frequented by the adults. Turtle eggs when boiled have a strange characteristic. The yolks congeal but the whites do not. The result is a slightly runny egg—a lot of solid yolks looking like yellow grapes in clear jelly. The whites do congeal in a more expected manner when the eggs are fried.

Immature mammals such as squirrels, mice, chipmunks, and rabbits may be found by investigating their nests. But the adults generally require special

Figure 8-5   Lizards caught by using the stick-and-noose technique. (Paul H. Risk)

equipment to catch. If caught, these young animals are excellent eating when they are roasted, fried, baked, or mixed into soups and stews.

Around water it may be possible to find *crayfish* (Figure 8-6), freshwater clams, or frogs. An improvised spear helps in catching crayfish. But they may also be scooped up with a net formed from a forked stick and a shred of T-shirt material. If you decide to catch them with your hands, remember that

Figure 8-6   Cooked crayfish, snails, and frog legs. (Paul H. Risk)

their pincers can make quite an impression. When boiled or steamed, crayfish (also called crawdads) turn red much like lobster. The meat in the tail is the easiest to obtain. That in the claws and legs is also edible. It is white and of essentially the same texture and taste as shrimp and lobster. If boiling is not possible, the animal may be baked with other food in a pit under the coals or roasted.

Freshwater *clams* and *mussels* may be dug in the sand of shallow water and also steamed or cooked on the coals. When they open they are done.

Frogs may be shot with a .22 caliber weapon or slingshot. But one of the best and easiest ways to catch them is spearing at night with a light. A bright flashlight is best, although an improvised torch will also do well. Build a spear (Figure 8-7) and walk quietly along the bank of a stream or pond during the summer months. The frogs' eyes will shine as they stare fixedly into the light. Do *not* throw the spear! Carefully lower it down as close to the frog as you can without getting it between the light and your target. Often it is possible to bring it within a few inches. A quick thrust and you are well on your way to a fine meal.

> **Warning:** Some toads and frogs, especially from desert or tropical areas, secrete a toxic substance from glands in their skin. Because of this, it is best to carefully skin them, washing the meat and your hands before preparation for food. As a general rule, avoid eating toads at all.

There are some salamanders and newts that may also be poisonous. These are amphibians frequently found along waterways and under fallen logs. While lizards have scales, salamanders and newts have skin and usually feel moist to the touch (Figure 8-8).

Avoid fuzzy caterpillars. Caterpillars are the larvae of moths and butterflies. Some, such as the Io moth-caterpillar, have a stinging apparatus. One, called commonly an Asp in Texas (but not related to the snake by the same name), can cause intense pain as a result of its sting. Whether they sting or not, the fuzz may be irritating to the mouth, throat, stomach, and intestinal tract.

Marine shellfish during certain seasons may be extremely toxic. This is usually during warmer months and corresponds with the ingestion of microscopic organisms by the shellfish. This is discussed in more depth in Chapter 12, *Survival in Marine Environments*.

FIREARMS IN FOOD PROCUREMENT

Chances for obtaining a meal are greatly increased if firearms are available. Most survival situations will require the use of whatever weapons are in possession at the time. But pilots and others contemplating travel in potentially

HOW TO PROCURE AND PREPARE MEAT, FOWL, AND FISH

Figure 8-7   Improvised spear. (*Jan Kolena Cole*)

hazardous areas may want to consider selecting a firearm that is the most useful.

TYPES OF FIREARMS

Handguns

Handguns, except in the hands of an expert, are probably not the best choice. Their short sight radius (the distance from the rear to the front sight) makes them far harder to fire accurately. Also, it is quite difficult to hold a pistol

Figure 8-8   Salamander (top) and newt (bottom). (Paul H. Risk)

steadily enough to hit the target. But, if this is to be your choice, select one with at least a six-inch barrel to maximize the sight radius as well as one with a .38, .44, or .45 caliber. My personal preference would be .44 or .45 since they are large enough to effectively stop larger game such as deer. Both shotshells and hollow point or other expanding projectile ammunition should be kept with the pistol. Shotshells may be hard to find but can be obtained from someone who does their own handloading. Any sporting goods store and many hardware stores should have the more usual types of ammunition. The shotshells can be used to kill small game such as squirrels and rabbits. But do not waste ammunition by shooting snakes. They are far easier to kill with a stick, as we have discussed. Fire either from a sitting position (Figure 8-9) or with the pistol firmly braced against a tree or rock (Figure 8-10). Use a two-handed grip whenever possible to increase stability.

HOW TO PROCURE AND PREPARE MEAT, FOWL, AND FISH

Figure 8-9   Firing a pistol from the sitting position. (Paul H. Risk)

Figure 8-10   Firing a pistol with a hand braced against a tree. (Paul H. Risk)

FIREARMS IN FOOD PROCUREMENT   113

Figure 8-11   A rifle/shotgun combination. (Paul H. Risk)

Shoulder Weapons

Rifles and shotguns are best suited for the use of a survivor. Probably the best weapon would be a combination rifle/shotgun. These are manufactured in various calibers and gauges. Usually the shotgun is the bottom barrel with the rifle above. A .22 Hornet/.410 shotgun is a very useful combination, although .30 caliber/20 gauge would also be good (Figure 8-11).

If a single shoulder weapon is to be selected, first choice would be the over/under rifle/shotgun combination, second would be a shotgun alone, and third would be a rifle alone. The shotgun (of .410 or 20 gauge) should be provided with both shotshell and slug ammunition. In this way you can have most of the advantages of the rifle and the shotgun.

If a rifle is the only weapon, pick a smaller caliber weapon such as a .22 or .22 Hornet, since most of the procured food will be small game and a larger caliber would tend to destroy too much meat. In any case, the shoulder weapons should be fired from the most stable position possible. The best positions for firing a weapon are prone, sitting, or resting the weapon on a tree or rock (Figure 8-12).

Sport has nothing to do with survival hunting. The only object in survival is to get a meal. So do not attempt to hit game that is running or flying. Wait until the animal is motionless; then fire from a stable position. Waterfowl paddling around the water are easy targets. Quail and other birds often feed on the

Figure 8-12a   Firing a rifle from the prone position. (Paul H. Risk)

Figure 8-12b   Firing a rifle from the sitting position. (Paul H. Risk)

Figure 8-12c   Firing a rifle that is braced against a tree. (Paul H. Risk)

ground or perch in trees and are much easier to hit there. Most small birds will be killed or disabled by a hit anywhere in the body. The same is true of squirrels, rabbits, or other game in this size range. Where there is a choice, aim for the chest. A hit there is almost always fatal. Hunting literature seems to be full of the exploits of hunters who take pride in shooting the heads off small game so as to leave the meat unblemished. This is an excellent technique on the pages of sporting magazines and other literature. In fact, such is the rare exception. You will not have ammunition to waste in survival and should shoot for the largest part of the animal.

Where possible, larger game such as deer, elk, pig, fox, and similar animals ought to be shot in the chest. The target really is the heart, and a hit in the areas indicated in Figure 8-13 will usually hit either this vital organ or the lungs, causing serious and rapid blood loss. BUT, DO *NOT* SHOOT LARGE POTENTIALLY DANGEROUS GAME WITH A SMALL CALIBER WEAPON. While it is possible to kill large animals with a shot in the eye from a small caliber weapon, it is also possible to miss completely or just wound. If one misses, only ammunition has been wasted. However, in the latter case, life may be threatened by an angry, wounded animal.

Here are some general guidelines.

1. Be careful with the weapon.
   a. Keep it in working order. Carefully clean dirt and grime from the mechanism.
   b. Be sure that the barrel does not become clogged with dirt, snow, or mud. A blocked barrel is likely to cause serious damage to the weapon and may explode. Such an explosion often occurs a short distance in front of the chamber and can result in serious injury or death to the user.
2. Forget everything about being sporting.
   a. Get as close to the game as possible. Increase the chances of a fatal shot the first time.
   b. Fire only when the animal is motionless.
3. Never rapid fire. The first shot should do it.
   Especially in the case of a novice, a running animal is unlikely to be hit. Unless it stops running, do not fire a second time.
4. Fire from the steadiest position possible.
5. Don't immediately chase a wounded animal.
   a. Wait 15 to 20 minutes. Often, if an animal thinks it is not being pursued, it will stop and lie down. It is not unusual for a fatally wounded animal to run a considerable distance before collapsing.
   b. Never pursue a large potentially dangerous animal such as a bear or water buffalo into dense vegetation. The role of the hunted and hunter may reverse when it is least desirable.
6. Look for blood.
   a. Before you squeeze off the shot, carefully observe the animal's sur-

In rut, buck drags feet

Buck points toes outward, seems to strut

Doe points toes straight ahead in a lady-like fashion

2"

DEER

BUCK

DOE

ANTELOPE

"Rubber heels"

WILD PIG

2½"

Dew claws

FOX

Tail mark

2¼"

Fore

Hind

Figure 8-13   Typical vital areas in mammals. (Courtesy of United States Air Force)

roundings. As soon as the shot is fired, mentally note the animal's immediate environment. It will be harder to recognize after the animal is gone.

b. After the waiting period of 15 to 20 minutes, walk to the spot where the animal was standing and carefully examine ground, grass, leaves, and plants for evidence of blood. This may take some time. Be thorough.

c. Then follow the animal's escape route, looking for more blood, tracks, crushed or disturbed vegetation, or broken branches.

7. Be cautious.

Even though the animal is down and apparently dead, it may only be stunned or semiconscious. An animal such as a deer may suddenly rear up and strike out with its front hoofs inflicting serious injury. If there is any uncertainty, shoot the animal again in the head. BE SURE THE ANIMAL IS DEAD BEFORE HANDLING IT.

HUNTING

Stalking may yield success for an experienced hunter but still-hunting is generally better for a beginner.

Find a spot where animals are active. This may be a trail, a watering hole, or a feeding area. Trails will appear as worn, beaten-down paths. Animal tracks may or may not be present, depending on the softness of the ground. In a heavily traveled trail, grass may be worn completely away. Animal droppings may also be found and, if some are relatively solid and moist, they indicate recent use. Droppings may also be found that are older and thus dry and crumbly. Both will be found on an active trail. A less used trail or one in heavy grass may merely appear as a depressed area in the grass. Or the grass may have been pushed aside, leaving a clearly seen path. Especially in the case of rabbit runs, it may help to squat down to grass-blade height to better visualize the travel areas.

All animals need water and seem to have favorite locations for obtaining it. Examination of streams, rivers, lakes, and other bodies of water may reveal many tracks. Hiding adjacent to such an area may be very productive.

Feeding areas are not always as easy to determine. Browsing sites of deer are often found in the edge areas where forest meets clearing. Sitting quietly downwind from such a location may disclose animals feeding.

Effective Still-Hunting Tips

1. Locate a game feeding, traveling, or sleeping location.
2. Hide downwind. Many animals do not see well, but their sense of smell largely makes up for that. Be sure that the wind is blowing *toward* you from the area you are watching.

3. Break your silhouette. Something as simple as putting your back against a tree will cause you to better blend into the surroundings. An unfamiliar outline may cause an animal to avoid normally frequented areas.
4. Hunt from a tree if possible. Animals such as deer seldom look above eye level. The result is that hunting from tree stands can be far more productive than any other method. However, it is also very easy to overshoot when firing a weapon from a tree. Aiming slightly lower than would otherwise be natural should help to offset this tendency.
5. Don't move. Although a deer or other animal may lack visual acuity, they do perceive movement very quickly. Any movement no matter how slight may be enough to spook the animal. So, do not wiggle around, scratch, or slap mosquitos.

Hunting at Night

Many animals will stare fixedly at a bright light at night and may be approached closely. A reflective surface in their eyes will make them highly visible. Anyone who has ever shined a flashlight into their dog's eyes has experienced this somewhat startling effect. The reflected light may be yellow, orange, red, or green depending on the kind of animal.

A flashlight or spotlight may be used to great advantage. It may be fastened alongside the gun barrel to allow proper aiming and still keep the eyes illuminated.

In the absence of electric light, a torch may be improvised by using a pine knot, or similar pitchy wood, or a bundle of grass. Native Americans used this technique long before flashlights were invented. In fact, it may be possible even without a gun to approach an animal upwind with a torch or other light and kill it with a spear or club.

TRAPS AND SNARES

To read about primitive traps, snares, and other entrapment devices promotes a feeling that all such devices properly constructed will yield a bounteous harvest. It looks easy. But looks can be and are often deceiving. First, the trap must be properly constructed. Second, it must be correctly placed. Third, an animal must come along and either blunder into it or be attracted to bait. At the same time, nothing about the trap location, presence, or smell can give the animal warning. What this all means is that it is not necessarily easy to trap or snare game. Often, the success ratio is as high as 15:1. Fifteen set traps will yield one success. Or, to put it another way, to get a meal a day per person, four people should have 60 traps set; five people should have 75; and so on.

REMEMBER: SET 15 TRAPS FOR EACH MEMBER OF THE PARTY.

And be sure to *use simple traps*. Complicated ones require more time and energy in their construction and may not be as good as they look.

As in hunting, it is not reasonable to expect to find animals thick as dog hair throughout the wilderness. Traps should be placed along trails or in areas where animals feed, water, or travel.

Learn animal habits. Become familiar with their activities. Don't wait until an emergency to suddenly develop an interest in wildlife biology.

Animals need the same things you and I do. They must have food, water, shelter, and protection from predators. Open areas deprive them of cover and protection, so they tend to limit their time to certain locations, feeding or traveling close to an escape route. Edge areas where they have easy access to both food and cover are favorites.

> **Note:** The techniques discussed in this section are illegal in most areas. Special permits may or may not be available from departments of wildlife or natural resources for survival training. Check with the proper authority before practicing.

Probably, the best advice that can be given to a novice is not to be overconfident. Trapping and snaring is a specialized business. The more knowledge that can be acquired about the habits and habitat of the animals sought, the greater the success rate. Students are often very disappointed at their lack of success. As a result of this known high-failure rate, some states are very cooperative with survival courses sponsored by reputable agencies and issue a special survival trapping permit.

The diagrams and ideas in survival books make trapping look simple. And, it is easy to construct the devices. The trouble comes when the animals simply avoid them. Or, even more frustrating, spring them but are not caught.

TRAP PLACEMENT

Observe the area carefully. Animals are creatures of habit and often travel along well-defined trails. Squat down in grassy or briar-covered areas and look at grass-top level for beaten areas of rabbit trails. Deer also travel well-defined trails, especially during winter. These trails and other frequented areas can be identified by a number of clues.

1. **Tracks.** These are especially easy to find around pond edges or other moist areas. All animals need water, and a watering hole may be located by looking for tracks. Snares may be constructed at the edge of such watering holes.
2. **Droppings.** Droppings along a trail can give much information on how recently animals have used it as well as what they were. They should be moist if they are fresh and will therefore be darker in color. By breaking

droppings open, one can disclose what the animals have been eating and give clues as to their feeding areas.

3. **Hair.**   Animals in passing through briars, fences, or trees often leave tufts of hair caught there. This can assist in locating a good trap location. An animal, accustomed to brushing against a particular object, loses wariness and is more likely to enter a trap or snare at the same location.

4. **Food Remnants.**   Browse lines in areas where there are high animal densities may indicate the presence of animals such as deer. Squirrels often leave tell-tale piles of pine cone scales called "squirrel middens." Such a location may be excellent for setting a snare.

5. **Beaten Grass.**   In grassy areas, animals as small as mice may beat grass down by their continuous passage. Some animals may also be harvesting grass along their travels and further define the path. These trails are often traveled at a run and make very good snare locations. On some advanced survival courses, it has been possible to drive rabbits down their trails at top speed. In the animals' overconfidence, snares set there were surprisingly effective.

6. **Compacted Soil.**   Heavier animals with hoofs such as deer, elk, or water buffalo may beat a regular "cattle path" into the soil.

TRAP TYPES

Traps and snares may be divided into three categories: those that (1) strangle, (2) mangle, or (3) hold.

Strangle.
As a general rule, the strangle types are most effective and easiest to construct.

Fixed Noose
By far, the easier snare to build is the fixed noose. Single-strand #24 wire is good material to use. Bend the tip over and twist it to form an eye (Figure 8-14). Then, run the rest of the wire through it to form the noose.

For rabbits, the noose should be about fist-sized and suspended two fingers off the ground in the rabbit run. This will probably appear too small at first examination, but will work well (Figure 8-15). It may be secured to vegetation or to a small stake driven into the ground.

No bait is necessary. Success is dependent on the animal carelessly running along a familiar trail.

The fixed noose may be enlarged and made stronger for larger animals. Two feet in diameter, three feet off the ground, and made of aircraft cable will work well with deer. This is especially true if placed in a location where the deer is accustomed to forcing its way through an obstruction. In one instance, a survival training group caught a black bear in such a cable noose.

Figure 8-14   A wire strangle noose. (Celia Drozdiak)

Figure 8-15   A rabbit caught in a wire strangle noose. (Paul H. Risk)

HOW TO PROCURE AND PREPARE MEAT, FOWL, AND FISH

Small game
trail snare
with drag

Figure 8-16   Wire noose with a drag. (Courtesy of United States Air Force)

Drag Noose
The drag noose is the same simple noose but is attached to something heavy or awkward to drag (Figure 8-16).

Twitch-Up
Using the same slip noose, the twitch-up adds a device that triggers a bent-over bush or sapling (Figure 8-17). It is not necessary that the twitch-up be so

Figure 8-17   Twitch-up snare. (Courtesy of United States Air Force)

TRAPS AND SNARES   123 strong that it snatches the animal out of its tracks and slaps it unconscious to the ground. It is only intended to lift it by the neck and cause strangulation.

The stake portion of the trigger should be driven in the ground far enough to prevent the twitch from pulling it out. This trigger can be used as the basis for many different traps.

A modification of this is to use a weight over a tree limb as the means for lifting the animal (Figure 8-18).

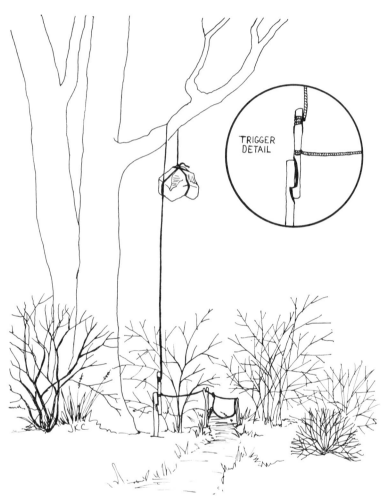

Figure 8-18   Twitch-up snare using a weight over a tree limb. (Jan Kolena Cole)

Figure 8-19   Counterbalance snare. (Celia Drozdiak)

Counterbalance
Again, no bait is necessary. The animal triggers the seesaw by its passage into the noose (Figure 8-19).

Squirrel Pole
Squirrels would much rather go up a slope than climb directly up a tree (Figure 8-20). The squirrel pole is so effective that it never ceases to amaze.

The wire nooses are arranged (see detail in Figure 8-20) so that the wire curves up and around. When a squirrel is caught, it tends to flip it off the pole. In this way the animal falls below the pole and strangles. In one training situation an instructor came back to find three squirrels hanging from the same pole. As one animal was caught, others must have come to investigate, with disastrous results.

The pole is leaned against a tree actively used by squirrels.

Mangle Traps
Deadfall with Figure-4 Trigger
The figure-4 trigger seems almost to be the status symbol of the survival instructor (Figure 8-21). If you don't know how to make one, you probably are not legitimate. However, it requires so much time and energy to make and is

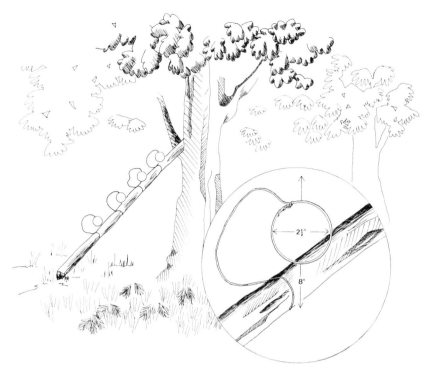

Figure 8-20   Squirrel pole trap. (*Celia Drozdiak*)

so limited in application that there is real doubt about its use. But at least make a miniature to prove you can and then wear it as a tie clasp to impress friends!

Ideally, when the trigger operates, it should fly out from under the deadfall. If this does not happen, it may delay the fall and the animal will escape. Bait is placed on the sharpened end of the horizontal stick and, when the animal attempts to get it, the trap is sprung. Rocks or logs may be used as the weight.

Two-Stick Trigger with Deadfall
This trap, with a trip cord, may be placed across a trail and cause a back-breaking weight to fall on an animal passing beneath (Figure 8-22).

> **Warning:** ANY TRAP CAPABLE OF DROPPING LARGE WEIGHTS ON A DEER IS ALSO CAPABLE OF KILLING OR MAIMING A HUMAN.

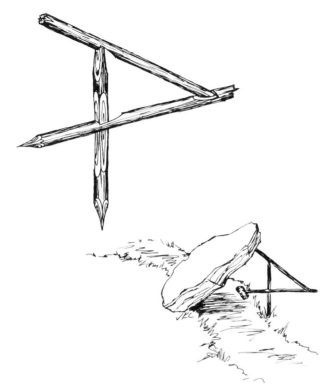

Figure 8-21   A figure-4 trigger. (Jan Kolena Cole)

Three-Pin Trigger with Deadfall
This is merely a modification of the preceding trap using a slightly different trigger (Figure 8-23).

Holding Traps
Ojibwa Bird Snare
This trap grabs the bird's feet when it lands on the perch (Figure 8-24). Although it may be baited with entrails or berries, bits of string or bright foil may attract a nest-building bird. These traps work best in open field or meadow areas.

The weight should not be too heavy or it will cause the noose to cut through the bird's feet and the prey will be lost.

The upright and the perch should both be made of hardwood. The perch and the hole into which it fits are both cut square. The end of the perch that fits into the hole and the hole itself should be firehardened. (This is done by passing

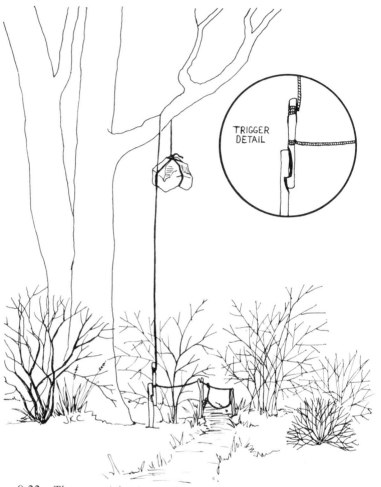

Figure 8-22   The two-stick trigger. This can be the basis for numerous kinds of traps and snares. (Courtesy of United States Air Force)

the object to be hardened back and forth through a flame or over hot coals to harden it. The wood may turn golden in the process but should not be charred.) The purpose of the firehardening is to prevent the cord from cutting into the wood and enable the parts to move quickly and smoothly.

Apache Foot Snare

The hoops are formed from willow or some other easily bent wood (Figure 8-25). The sharp pointed parts may be of the same material. A hole is dug in an area traveled regularly. When the animal's foot goes through the hoop, the

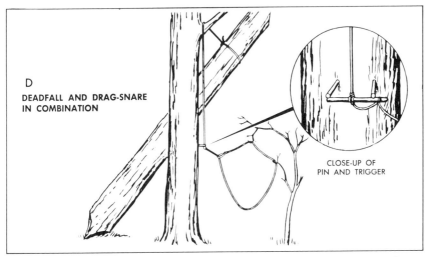

Figure 8-23 A deadfall using the three-pin trigger. This trigger has wide use in a variety of traps. (Courtesy of United States Air Force)

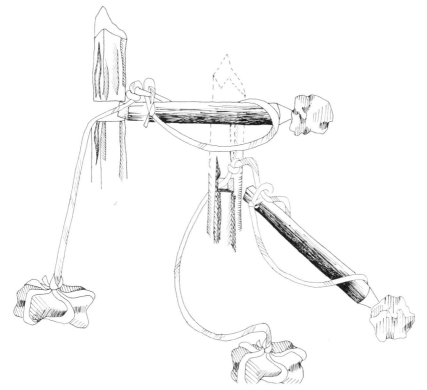

Figure 8-24 Ojibwa bird snare. (Celia Drozdiak)

Figure 8-25   Apache foot snare. (Jan Kolena Cole)

sharp points easily force open. But, picking up the foot, they are unable to spring back and the hoop with the noose is picked up. If wire or cable is used and attached to a stake, the struggle which follows merely tightens the noose.

The trap may also incorporate a trigger to a twitch-up or weight.

V-Trench for Birds

Especially effective for pheasants and quail, the trap appears almost too simple to work (Figure 8-26). The bird, following the bait (grass seed, ration crumbs, etc.), walks down the incline into the narrowed end of the trap. They are then either unable or unwilling to back out.

130   HOW TO PROCURE AND PREPARE MEAT, FOWL, AND FISH

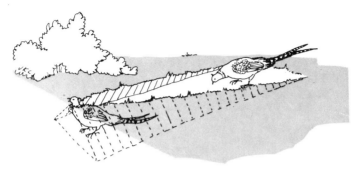

Figure 8-26   V-trench bird trap. (Jan Kolena Cole)

PREPARATION OF GAME

Birds

Birds may be split from the anal opening at the base of the tail up through the breast bone First, cut only the skin and remove. This is the easiest way to get rid of the feathers. Then, open the body cavity and remove the internal organs. As discussed earlier, most of these may be used for food.

Small birds have little meat on their wings, but these may be used in the preparation of soup or stew, as may the feet and head.

Larger birds, especially waterfowl, may be prepared without skinning or plucking. Make a cut through the back and remove the internal organs. Pry the bird open so that the breast bones fracture, and allow the bird to flatten out. (Figure 8-27). It may then be placed on the coals, body cavity down, for a few

Figure 8-27   A bird split open for cooking. (Paul H. Risk)

moments to sear the meat. Then, turn it over and lay it feather-side down directly on the coals. The smell is spectacular since the feathers char, but this does not seem to affect the taste. The fat between the meat and the skin will melt and the charred feathers will form a crust—sort of a form-fitted skillet—with the bird literally cooking in its own juices.

Mammals

Follow the dotted lines in Figure 8-28. Cut through only the skin of the legs and down the belly. Carefully work the skin off. With a large animal like a deer, this will require a shaving action with the knife between the skin and the flesh. Smaller animals such as rabbits, squirrels, and racoons are less attached to their skins and it may simply be pulled loose.

Figure 8-28   Skinning a deer on the ground. (Jan Kolena Cole)

HOW TO PROCURE AND PREPARE MEAT, FOWL, AND FISH

Figure 8-29   The author skinning a rabbit during survival course field experience. (Paul H. Risk)

Small animals may be tied to a branch by their hind legs to skin or secured with a sharpened branch driven through the leg behind the main tendon (Figure 8-29). While it is handy to hang a deer or other large animals while preparing, it is not necessary. The skin may be removed from one side at a time and the animal kept clean by rolling it on the skin as it is finished on one side.

Scent Glands and Bleeding

Some animals such as deer have scent glands located on their rear legs. These are only active during the mating season and even then are not the problem some people claim. They can impart a strong flavor to meat they touch but will not ruin it for use. Removing the lower leg will take care of the problem. If you recognize the exact area where they are located, simply cut them out.

Bleeding an animal is only necessary for aesthetic reasons. If an animal is not bled, the meat may be discolored from the blood in the tissues. But it will be even more nutritious with the blood left in. While it may be stronger in flavor, it is still excellent.

FISHING

In many locations fishing may be a very important source of survival food. While some of the more traditional methods will work, the techniques presented here allow the survivor to go about other chores while the fishing continues automatically.

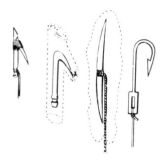

Figure 8-30   Improvised fish hooks. (Courtesy of United States Air Force)

BASICS

In stream areas, fish may be found in quiet pools, near overhangs, and in eddies. In ponds and lakes, areas near aquatic vegetation and off rocky points may be good spots.

It is helpful to find out what the fish are eating if bait fishing is contemplated. When the first fish is caught, open its stomach and examine the contents.

TACKLE

All that is absolutely necessary is a hook of some sort and a line. *Hooks* may be carved in the more traditional shape from the point at which a branchlet leaves a branch (Figure 8-30). Or, a piece of bone may be carved. Perhaps the simplest type of hook is the gorge or skewer hook. It is made from a long thorn, a piece of hardwood, or a bone sharpened on both ends. The line is tied to its center. It is then pushed into the bait so that the line comes out the end. When the fish swallows it, the hook is set with a quick tug, which causes the gorge to orient crossways in the fish's throat. (Figure 8-31).

Line may be twisted from various kinds of plant fiber. Bassfood, elm, cedar, nettle, yucca, and other plants have tough fibers and may be twisted into serviceable line.

The two pieces of fiber required may be easier to manage if soaked for a few minutes before twisting. If the material is safe, place in the mouth. Just don't forget what it is and swallow it.

Holding the two pieces together (or knotting them), begin twisting each fiber clockwise until they are tightly wound. Then wrap them together in a *counter*clockwise direction (Figure 8-32). The two opposing twists work against each other and prevent the cord from unwinding.

To add fiber, just insert a new piece and twist it to the remaining end (Figure 8-33). The line can be made as long as necessary. To form heavier line, twist pairs of this first cord together, and so on, until it is as heavy as desired.

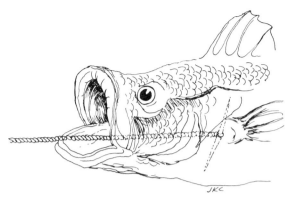

Figure 8-31   Gorge hook in a fish's throat. (Adapted by Jan Kolena Cole from Hafin et al., Surviving Health Emergencies and Disasters)

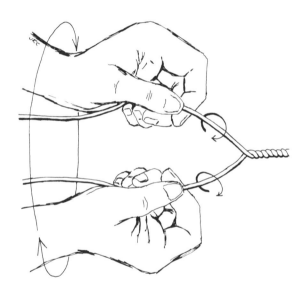

Figure 8-32   Twisting cord from fiber. (Jan Kolena Cole)

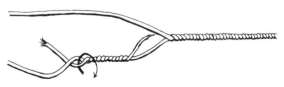

Figure 8-33   Adding fiber. (Jan Kolena Cole)

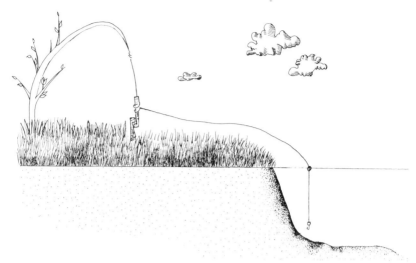

Figure 8-34   The two-pin trigger used as an automatic fishing rod. (Celia Drozdiak)

TWITCH-UP FISHING

The two-peg trigger used in the twitch-up works very well for fishing (Figure 8-34). Attach the line to the movable half of the trigger and throw out the hook. When the fish takes the bait, the trigger (which can be set for desired sensitivity) will release and set the hook. The waving of the sapling will indicate your catch.

A series of these may be set along a stream, river, or around a lake or pond. Then the survivors are free to go about their other chores.

Trot-Lines

A trot line is a multiple hook device (Figure 8-35). The baited hooks may be placed not only at intervals along the main line, but the hooks may also be set at various depths to maximize chances of a catch.

Set-Lines

Generally possessing a single hook, the set line can be arranged to be easily retrievable by making the main line double, as shown in Figure 8-36.

HOW TO PROCURE AND PREPARE MEAT, FOWL, AND FISH

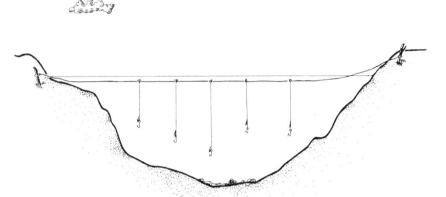

Figure 8-35   A trot line with hooks at several depths. (Celia Drozdiak)

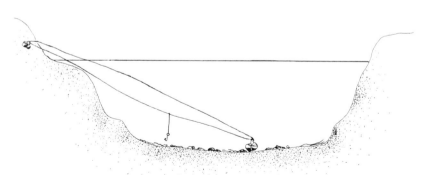

Figure 8-36   A set line attached to a rock in a pond to allow easy retrieval. (Celia Drozdiak)

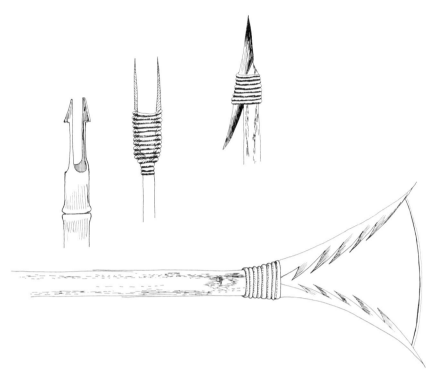

Figure 8-37   Several types of improvised fish spears. (Celia Drozdiak)

Spearing Fish
Spearing fish can be effective in shallow areas and may be enhanced by use of a light (torch or otherwise) to attract them (Figure 8-37).

Fish Traps
In the type of trap illustrated in Figure 8-38, poles are driven into the stream bottom. The fish easily enter the V-shaped front but cannot run the maze to get out again.

The type of fish trap show in Figure 8-39, is really a very open-weave, double-cone-shaped basket. The fish enter the large end and then cannot determine how to get out the small inner funnel. It is made of willow or other easily workable material.

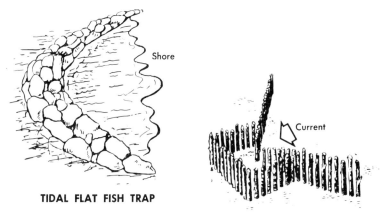

TIDAL FLAT FISH TRAP

Shore

Current

Figure 8-39   Fish traps placed in a steambed. (Courtesy of United States Air Force)

Poisons and Explosives

In tropical areas, there are several plants, such as the Cube, that when crushed yield a substance that will stun fish. Or, rotenone powder from the survival kit may be used.

In North America, the green hulls from black walnuts when crushed will stun fish and they may be picked up from the surface of the water. The toxin has no effect on humans. In the western United States, soapweed will do the same thing.

Rotenone, a chemical used to reduce fish populations, may be carried as a powder in the survival kit. One ounce of 12 percent rotenone powder will stun all the fish in a $\frac{1}{2}$ mile of stream 25 feet wide. It is most effective in water above 60°F. At lower temperatures, its effect is almost negligible. The powder is mixed with water to form a mixture about the consistency of a milkshake before placing in the stream or pond.

Explosives detonated in the water will kill fish. However, those in close proximity to the explosion will probably have their swim bladders ruptured and will sink. Dynamite as well as large, waterproof fireworks and high explosives may be used.

CATCHING FISH BY HAND

Some fish may be caught by hand. Wading in the water, carefully feel under the lip of overhangs along a stream. Especially in trout streams, the fish may actually be touched lightly without them being disturbed. With a smooth, flow-

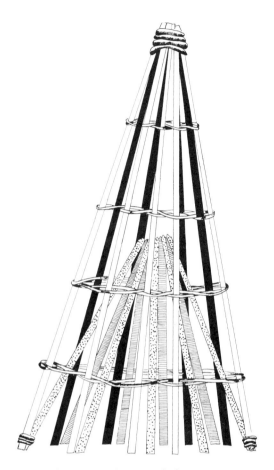

Figure 8-39   Basket fish trap. (Celia Drozdiak.)

ing movement, slide the hand toward the head and at the same time insert the little finger or index finger in a gill. With a sweeping motion, carry the fish out of the water and throw it on the bank.

While this sounds easy, it is not. Nevertheless, an experienced person can catch a number of trout this way.

> **Warning:** It is not recommended that this procedure be carried out in warm waters. Snapping turtles and other undesirable creatures may be encountered.

9

HOW
TO
PROCURE
AND
PREPARE
PLANT
FOOD

Plants, in some environments, can be a substantial contributor to the menu. There are hundreds of thousands of plants and only a small percentage that are poisonous. However, many parts of plants are very low in calories as anyone who has ever been on a weight reduction diet can tell. Since under survival conditions the important consideration is energy, plants and their parts that provide carbohydrates (starches and sugars) and oils should be sought. Yet, even plants low in calorie value may provide an important emotional lift for the survivor. Teas and potherbs may also enable the survivor to acquire needed vitamins and minerals in extended survival situations.

It is not possible in this book to teach everything there is to know about edible and useful plants. That is really the undertaking of a lifetime. But it can be very rewarding. Plant material can also add dietary variety to traditional food sources. Often wild plant food will be better tasting and fresher than that from the market.

At each season of the year, plant familiarization is something that should be practiced. A plant appears markedly different at various stages of its development. Start now to recognize useful ones in all stages. There are numerous books that present information on edible and useful plants. Several excellent ones are mentioned in the recommended reading at the end of this book.

Start with the poisonous ones first. Once you are confident about the ability to recognize these, there is more safety in experimenting with others. But do not become overconfident. Just because this chapter describes a plant as edible and even delicious does not preclude the possibility of an allergic reaction. Also, the particular plant may just be a bit more exotic than your gastrointestinal tract is accustomed to and cause temporary difficulties. Don't gorge on a new plant dish. After determining that it is safe, eat only a normal-sized helping. And remember that there is a difference between edible and palatable. While many plants are pleasant as well as edible, there are a number of edible but quite unpleasant tasting ones.

For survival purposes, roots and other underground fleshy parts as well as fleshy stalks, fruits, and nuts are usually the highest in energy value.

RULES TO DETERMINE WHETHER PLANTS ARE EDIBLE

Rules are only rough indicators or averages. All poisonous plants do not have the same characteristics indicated. And, some edible plants have the characteristics listed as warnings of possible toxicity. The only way to be sure is to learn plant identification.

In general, poisonous plants or parts of plants that are toxic taste bad. Some do not. For example, castor beans are very poisonous yet have a taste that is not unpleasant. A friend, in her teens, ate about 20 mature castor bean seeds. She described them as tasting somewhat nutlike. But within a half hour, she suffered intense nausea and vomited them. She was lucky. Had the dose not nauseated her she might have died.

One definite warning may be given. Do not experiment with fungus plants. Poisonous fungi often taste good and their effects may be so long delayed that they have been thoroughly assimilated by your body and treatment becomes almost impossible.

VISUAL WARNINGS

Sap
If the plant oozes white, milky sap it is likely to be toxic and should be avoided. Also, brightly colored sap should cast doubt on the edibility of a plant.

Fruit
The structure that forms after the flower falls is technically referred to as a fruit. If it is *white,* it is most likely to be poisonous. *Red* is next most likely to be dangerous, followed by *blue* or *black.*

Taste
If when a small quantity of the plant is chewed it is very bitter, very sour, quite acid, or has a nauseating taste, it should be avoided.

Effect

If placing a small amount in the mouth or chewing it produces: pain, burning, numbness of the lips, tongue, or throat, dizziness, blurred vision, cramps, nausea, headache, muscle tremors, or difficulty in breathing, it should not be eaten.

OTHER WARNINGS

Avoid Beans or Peas

Although there are many that are edible and choice, there are many in the world that are very poisonous. Eat them only if you know for sure they are edible or have conducted a taste test.

Avoid Bulbs

Disappointingly enough, many bulbs are also poisonous. This is too bad since they are usually very high in starch and therefore energy. There is one exception—any bulb that smells like onions or garlic is safe.

The *Death Camas* is an example of a bulb-forming plant that is deadly. It is often seen growing in open, somewhat damp meadow or field areas throughout many areas of the United States. There is also an edible Camas (*Camassia* sp.) but its flowers are blue while those of the Death Damas are cream colored.

Avoid plants with umbrella-shaped flower clusters. Although Wild Carrots (*Daucus carota*) are in this group and are edible, the Poison and Water Hemlocks are too but are deadly (Figure 9-1). Poison hemlock may occur side by side with Wild Carrot.

Figure 9-1   Water hemlock, poison hemlock, and wild carrot. (Paul H. Risk)

While most edible plants will be identified by observation and with certainty, there are some about which questions will arise. In these cases, it is possible to run a taste test.

However, this should never be conducted with fungus plants. Symptoms are often too delayed to be of use in the prescribed test and may be very severe. Besides, mushrooms and other fungi are so low in calorie value that one person suggested it would take 100 pounds by dry weight to equal 100 calories. And by the time you ate 100 pounds of dried mushrooms, you wouldn't care whether they were edible or not—especially after they began to rehydrate and swell!

THE TASTE TEST

Never taste test two unknowns at the same time. If difficulties develop, it will then be impossible to determine which caused the symptoms.

Also, the test only determines the safety of the plant in the form it was tested. If a plant is tested when cooked, the results only relate to the cooked plant. If raw, only raw. Often a plant that is toxic raw is safe when cooked.

Step 1.

Place about $\frac{1}{2}$ teaspoon of plant material in the mouth. Carefully and slowly chew it. Hold it in the mouth for 3 to 5 minutes. Do not swallow. Saliva will well up in your mouth and you may have to spit some out from time to time. If at any point the plant is unpleasant tasting in any of the ways listed above or any of the undesirable effects become manifest, spit it out and wash the mouth with water. Proceed no farther. If all seems well, spit out the plant and wait 12 hours for symptoms. If nothing happens, go to Step 2.

Step 2.

Twelve hours after the completion of Step 1, place another $\frac{1}{2}$ teaspoon of the material to be tested in the mouth. Chew it well and swallow. Wait another 12 hours. If symptoms develop, discontinue testing this plant in its present form. If all is well, proceed with Step 3.

Step 3.

Eat about an ice-cream scoop full of the material. Wait another 12 hours. If all is well, the plant is safe to add to the menu in normal servings.

Note: For reasons not entirely understood, someone always asks about the 36 hours necessary for the completion of the test series. They are concerned about such a long time without eating. It is assumed that the survivor is eating other foods of known quality during this time.

PREPARATION OF PLANT FOOD

All traditional cooking methods may be used in the preparation of edible wild plants. Also, some may be eaten raw. However, caution should be used in eating foods raw that may have grown under contaminated conditions, unless they are to be peeled. And, sometimes, the peeling process may not be thorough enough to render the food safe. For example, the author collected some cattails from a contaminated swamp area. Their tender shoots were peeled and eaten. Water from the swamp contaminated the shoots, and it took six weeks to recover. Had the disease organism been more serious, the results might have been more extreme. In some areas of the world, human waste is used to fertilize crops. Both amoebic dysentery and cholera may easily be spread in this way.

Cooking is an important means for rendering foodstuffs safe. The processes of baking, roasting, and frying bring the food to temperatures well above the boiling point of water and effectively kill bacteria and other microorganisms. Boiling also is effective but, because of the lower temperatures required to boil water at high altitude, the food may not be hot enough to kill all organisms unless some means of pressure cooking is available.

If there is any question about the safety of food, cook it.

Repeated Boiling

Food that is toxic or unpleasant raw may sometimes be rendered safe or more palatable through the process of repeated boiling. Books on eating wild plants may only say "cook in two changes of water." This means bringing to a boil for about 3 minutes, pouring off the water, and repeating the process again. Where changes of water are necessary, the toxic substance dissolves in the water and is poured off.

In other plants, the heating process involved in cooking is responsible for the destruction of the poison. Such toxic substances are termed *heat labile*—they are detoxified by heating and although present in the water are no longer dangerous. So, boiling makes plants safe by either of two processes: (1) removal by solution or (2) destruction by heat.

Leaching

Leaching is another solution process. Material to be leached is crushed, pounded, or otherwise ground, placed in a porous container through which water is run.

Always grind the material as finely as possible and start with cool water. Some substances coagulate in contact with hot water and cannot then be removed. Leaching is most easily carried out when a strong-tasting substance is being removed. Acorns are a good example. There are two categories of acorns: white and red. White oak acorns may be eaten raw and will not taste bitter.

Red oak acorns have a very bitter taste. In spite of that, some American Indians have used acorns—both red and white—as a staple in their diets.

The mature acorns were first shelled and placed in an open-bottom, funnel-shaped basket. This was then put on a large flat stone, and the acorns within were carefully pounded until they were very finely ground. The acorn meal was transferred to a hole in the ground that had been lined with grass. Or it was placed in a grass-lined, open-weave basket. In either case, cool water was poured through it until the meal lost its bitter taste. The process was long, but the product very nutritious. After leaching, the meal, mixed with water, was slowly simmered and eaten. A modification of this procedure would be to place the ground meal in a T-shirt funnel and put it in a stream where the water could continually wash through.

If the cool water does not seem to be having the desired effect, then begin increasing the temperature. Use warm water for a time. Slowly, a shift may be made to hot water, until a temperature is found that seems most effective. Once that has been determined, use that temperature each time afterward.

Parching

Nuts and seeds are good candidates for parching. If a metal container is available, it may be used as an improvised frying pan. Place the seeds, nuts, or grain in the container and, while heating over coals, keep stirring until they turn a golden brown. Some seeds will even burst a bit like popcorn. (Large, chestnutlike fruits should first be pierced with the point of a knife. If this is omitted, they may build up steam pressure internally until they explode.)

If any type of oil (not machine oil) or fat is available, put a small amount in the container as you would with popcorn. Lacking a metal container, parching may also be done on a flat rock that is heated in the coals.

Production of Flour

When mature, seed from grasses, pine cones, and other sources may be ground for flour. An old technique for this is the *mano* and *metate* (Figure 9-2). The grain is placed on the metate, and the mano is used to pound and grind the material into flour.

A hollow log with a hardwood pounder or pestle will also serve for this purpose, as will an indentation in a rock surface with a manolike rock used vertically.

Flour obtained in this way may be used as a dough with water to make an unleavened bread, which may be baked in the ashes.

HOW TO PROCURE AND PREPARE PLANT FOOD

Figure 9-2   Mano and metate. (Paul H. Risk)

TOXIC PLANTS TO BE AWARE OF

Water Hemlock (*Cicuta* spp.)

Usually growing in semimarshy areas or wet areas along a stream, the water hemlock is one of the most poisonous plants (Figure 9-3). Its roots, looking like small carrots or parsnips and containing air compartments, do in fact have a parsniplike flavor, and children have been fatally poisoned by them. Convulsions and frothing at the mouth are just two of its effects on humans.

Figure 9-3   Water hemlock. (Paul H. Risk)

Figure 9-4 Poison hemlock. (Paul H. Risk)

Poison Hemlock (*Conium maculatum*)
Poison hemlock is reputed to be the plant from which Socrates' fatal draught was prepared (Figure 9-4). He described its effects as a creeping numbness moving in from the extremeties.

Red Baneberry (*Actaea rubra*)
Often seen in moist areas, it may reach a height of 2 to 3 feet (Figure 9-5). It bears fruit mid to late summer and produces beautiful, shiny red berries. Six of them are sufficient to kill an adult. They are white on the inside and very bitter.

White Baneberry (*Actea alba*)
Found in similar areas to the Red Baneberry, its fruit develops later in the summer and is still around in the fall (Figure 9-6). The white fruits are just as toxic as the red cousin and because of a black central spot are sometimes called Dolls Eyes.

False Hellebore (*Veratrum* spp.)
This plant is found in low areas and damp meadows (Figure 9-7). False Hellebore looks a great deal like a stalk of corn with accordion-pleated leaves.

Figure 9-5   Red baneberry. (Paul H. Risk)

Lupine (*Lupinus* spp.)

Widely distributed in the western United States, its small bean pods are a lure to the hungry survivor (Figure 9-8). Readily excreted through the kidneys, its active toxin is not as dangerous as some. But it should still be avoided. The flowers are blue, pinkish, or even white.

Vetch and Locoweed (*Astragalus* spp.)

Another member of the pea family to look out for is the vetch or locoweed (Figure 9-9). The leaf configuration, flowers, and pea pods are reminiscent of sweet or garden peas.

Figure 9-6   White Baneberry.
(Paul H. Risk)

Figure 9-7   False Hellebore. (Cour
tesy of Carl S. Keener, Ph.D.)

Figure 9-8   Lupine. (Paul H. Risk)

Figure 9-9   Locoweed. (Courtesy of Carl S. Keener Ph.D.)

Figure 9-10   Jimsonweed. (Paul H. Risk)

Jimsonweed (*Datura* spp.)

This plant is found in many locations of North America, from desert to the eastern seaboard (Figure 9-10). Its flowers are often 4 or more inches long, trumpet shaped, and white. As they mature, a spiny capsule containing small black seeds forms. Jimsonweed is very poisonous, containing a hallucinogen. Symptoms include respiratory and cardiac irregularity.

Mayapple (*Podophyllum peltatum*)

Arising like a tiny green torpedo from the forest floor in the eastern part of the United States, its leaves unfurl into two large umbrellas (Figure 9-11). It then produces a cream-colored flower and a green thumb-sized fruit. The entire plant is intensely poisonous until the fruit turns yellow in ripening. This soft, custardy fruit may then be eaten, although some are allergic to it.

Figure 9-11   Mayapples. (Paul H. Risk)

Figure 9-12   Cattail. (Paul H. Risk)

SOME RECOMMENDED PLANT FOOD SOURCES

Cattail (*Typha* spp.)

Perhaps one of the best and most widely distributed edible plants is the common cattail (Figure 9-12). It is edible virtually from its roots to its top.

New shoots developing on the rhizomelike roots (Figure 9-13) are tender, nutlike in flavor, and may be eaten raw or cooked. The roots themselves are very high in starch, although they are laced with tough fibers. They may be boiled, baked, or roasted and have a flavor like chestnuts. They may be chewed to separate the fibers and the starch swallowed. Dried or baked until very dry, they may be pounded to separate the starch material. This may then be used as a crude flour to create various kinds of unleavened breads.

As the cattails put up new shoots in the spring, they are easily harvested by grasping the top and pulling. They pull apart much like a tender young grass stem. The basal part will be crisp, white, and taste like raw cucumber. Some think they have a slight radishlike flavor. With salt, they are absolutely

HOW TO PROCURE AND PREPARE PLANT FOOD

Figure 9-13   Cattail roots. (Paul H. Risk)

delicious. But take care about eating them raw if they come from questionable water. Boiled they are very much like water chestnuts. At home they may be diced and cooked with bouillon to create a fine soup.

The cattail (Figure 9-14) develops in two sections—the male or pollen-bearing top and the female or seed-bearing lower section. In the latter part of May the tops, sometimes called Cossack Asparagus, may be harvested. They can then be boiled and taste a bit like corn on the cob. Or the tiny pollen florets may be scraped off the stem and cooked with other food. The seed-bearing part can be harvested in the fall but requires a lot of preparation. They are fluffed out and ignited. The fuzz burns in a flash and the tiny, dustlike seeds fall to the surface. If enough time is available, seed may be accumulated and makes a usable porridge.

Cattail leaves may be harvested during July, dried, and used to thatch shelters or in making rush-bottoms for chairs, baskets, mats, clothing, and other useful items. Truly, the cattail is among the most versatile of plants.

Common Milkweed (*Asclepias* spp.)
Although there are desert species that are toxic, the common milkweed in spite of its milky sap is a useful edible plant (Figure 9-15).

As the shoots come up in the spring, they may be harvested and cooked in two changes of water. Omitting this results in a very bitter, unpalatable vegetable.

As the flower buds form, they may be picked and boiled briefly. No changes

Figure 9-14 Cattail showing the male pollen-bearing section at the upper end and the female or seed-bearing section below. (Paul H. Risk)

Figure 9-15 Common milkweed with buds. (Paul H. Risk)

Figure 9-16   Fiddleheads of bracken fern.
(Paul H. Risk)

of water are necessary. Having an appearance somewhat like broccoli, they are delicious.

After the buds flower, pods begin to form. These may be eaten raw or cooked. They should be collected when they are about the size of sweet pickles. If too much time elapses, they mature, fill with fuzz, and are a bit like eating a down sleeping bag.

But, when they have matured, the fuzz can be collected for insulation or tinder. During World War II, milkweed down was used to fill flotation vests.

Ferns.

Most ferns, in their young stage, are edible (Figure 9-16). Bracken is a good example. The immature fronds are called fiddleheads because of their configuration. These are easily snapped off. They should be washed to remove fine hairs and may then be steamed or boiled. They require only a short time in the pot and are much like asparagus.

Water Lilies (*Nuphar* spp.)

The roots of water lilies look almost like dragons but may be cooked and eaten (Figures 9-17 and 9-18). However, it is recommended that a small piece be tried first. Some of them are very bitter and this author has had no success in

Figure 9-17   Water lily in flower. (Paul H. Risk)

Figure 9-18   Water lily root. (Paul H. Risk)

doing anything to them to remedy that condition. Those that are palatable are very high in starch and therefore excellent survival food.

The roots are often at some depth and require a substantial energy outlay in order to secure them. This should be weighed against their value. Especially if the water is cold, it may be advisable to choose something else to harvest.

Wild Grapes (*Vitis* spp.)

The long vines may, as discussed in Chapter 6 on water acquisition, supply pure drinking water (Figure 9-19). The leaves may be used as a flavorful food wrapping for anything that is to be baked in the ashes of a fire or in a rock-filled steampit.

HOW TO PROCURE AND PREPARE PLANT FOOD

Figure 9-19   Wild grapes. (Paul H. Risk)

Wild grapes look like any grapes that grow under cultivation. However, they are often somewhat smaller. Usually purple when mature and ready to eat, they may in large quantities cause an impressive case of diarrhea. So, don't gorge on them.

Rose Hips (*Rosa* spp.)

The fruit that forms after the wild rose falls is called a hip (Figure 9-20). The same type of structure develops on roses around the home if not pruned as the flowers mature. This pruning usually is constant enough in the garden that the

Figure 9-20   Rose hips. (Paul H. Risk)

SOME RECOMMENDED PLANT FOOD SOURCES   157

hips do not form. But the gardener could allow some to develop and eat them to experiment.

The hips are very high in vitamin C. In fact, vitamin C derived from rose hips may be purchased in health food stores. In some rose varieties, the hip may be 2 inches or more across.

The fruit should be cut open and the seeds removed; they act as a strong laxative. The rest of the hip may then be eaten raw or cooked. Their flavor is a little applelike.

Although they will supply little in calories, their pleasant taste can be important in lifting sagging spirits.

Pine Seed (*Pinus* spp.)

The seeds of pines are found between the cone scales (Figure 9-21). If the cone is torn apart, the seeds can then be collected. They are usually better roasted or parched. Some are very small and hardly worth the trouble. But others such as the Pinyon Pine will yield large seeds or "nuts" of excellent quality.

Squirrels often stockpile these seeds for winter use. If a location is found where pine cone "cores" and piles of scales are heaped up, it may be productive to search for a hollow in a nearby tree where the seeds have been stored. (For that matter, the squirrel itself can make excellent eating.)

Nuts and Berries

Too numerous to cover in detail, such fruit as walnuts, butternuts, hickory nuts, pecans, and many others are good food sources.

Berries such as blackberries, blueberries, strawberries, raspberries, and cloudberries among others are also available in season. These may all be eaten raw or are also good stewed. Use color as basic criteria and if necessary the taste test.

Figure 9-21   Pinyon pine cone showing the seed between scales. (Paul H. Risk)

HOW TO PROCURE AND PREPARE PLANT FOOD

Figure 9-22   Grass seed ready to harvest. (Paul H. Risk)

Grasses (Gramineae)

Grass seed is edible and nutritious (Figure 9-22). This should come as no surprise once it is remembered that wheat is grass. The difficulty in harvesting grass seed is that, like wheat, it must be done at exactly the right time. A day or two off and it will have all fallen.

Locate a stand of mature grass. Bend the tops into a container and strike sharply with a stick to dislodge the grain. When conditions are right, a considerable quantity can be acquired in a short time.

The container will have a mixture of seed, straw, chaff, and small insects. To be most useful it must be cleaned. Grass also has stiff, sharp structures called awns that can cause some damage if swallowed. Cleaning in a survival setting is done by winnowing.

Simply throw the seed up in the air a short distance (over a ground cloth) and let the wind carry off the undesirable material. Once this has been done, if kept dry, the seed will keep for a considerable time. If it is not in a sealed container, it will likely become infested with weevils or other small vermin. These are edible too and when ground with the seed or cooked into whole-grained porridge will not even be noticed.

> **Warning:** Grasses are subject to a fungus disease called Ergot. The fungus causes the plant to produce, along with normal grass seeds, some black or dark brown structures called sclerotia (Figure 9-23). They develop on the same head with the normal seed but are much larger and easily seen.
> Erogotized grain is very dangerous. The toxin in the sclerotia is neurotoxic, carcinogenic, and cumulative in the system. Bread made from ergotized grain has been responsible for the death of thousands of people.

Figure 9-23   Ergotized wheat. The dark grainlike structures are sclerotia of the ergot fungus. The others are normal seed (Paul H. Risk)

Either the black sclerotia must be painstakingly separated from the normal grain or an undiseased area found to harvest.

Inner Bark

The moist inner bark of most pines and birches may be eaten. In some cases, it can be eaten raw. But it generally is like chewing the sole of a boot. It can be softened somewhat by boiling. Some boil it, dry it, and then pound it to a crude flour.

There are many more plants that may be eaten. The interested outdoor person should take time to study this subject in detail. Not only can it be useful in an emergency, but the familiarity gained of native vegetation will enhance any outdoor experience.

10

COLD
WEATHER
EMERGENCIES

Proper clothing combined with the realization of the danger of cold can permit activity in extreme situations. Generally, extreme cold alerts us, and precautions are taken. However, moderate conditions found during spring and autumn often cause a reduction of our "alert status." We tend to become less cautious, assuming that nothing very serious can happen at temperatures above freezing. Because of this, these conditions, especially when rain and wind are present, are inherently more hazardous than colder situations.

Cold weather and its effects are widely misunderstood. Parents, out of concern for their children, are often heard to say, "Johnnie (or Jane) cannot go out in this weather—he (she) will *catch* cold." It sounds as though they will have to run to get the job accomplished. Or there is a refusal to permit a child to go winter camping in fear that they will fall asleep in the cold and fail to awaken. Neither situation will happen.

The British Institute for the Study of the Common Cold has determined that chilling has nothing to do with the likelihood of "catching cold" and also does not affect the intensity and duration of the cold. Furthermore, nobody whose condition is normal when they fall asleep is ever in danger of slipping into a terminal coma and death without reawakening. Anyone who has ever gotten chilly during the night knows that it is impossible to stay asleep under such miserable conditions. They become uncomfortable and sleep is not possible. Nobody has ever "frozen to death" in the history of the world. Many have died from the affects of cold and *then* frozen.

HYPOTHERMIA

The human body is a mobile system of chemical reactions. These reactions are responsible for our very lives. They account for nerve transmissions both within the brain and along our numerous neural pathways to and from that cerebral computer. Muscle contractions are caused by chemical reactions. When affected by cold these vital reactions slow down. In general, reducing the temperature of a reaction by 10°C will cut the speed in half. Another 10° drop will decrease the remaining speed by half, and so on. Ideally, the body's reactions operate best at temperatures of approximately 99 to 100°F. Above and below this range, problems begin to develop.

Hypothermia is a condition of abnormally low body-core temperature. The body's surface and extremities may drop several degrees in temperature without serious difficulty. But when the temperature of the deep areas of the body begin to be affected, hypothermia occurs. The word comes from two roots—*hypo* meaning below and *thermia* derived from the word for heat.

Hypothermia is a condition that sneaks up on the unwary. Its onset is sometimes so gradual as to be unnoticed by anyone around the victim. And, because of its slowing affect on mental processes, victims themselves are almost assured of failure in noticing symptoms. The frightening thing is that from the time symptoms of moderate to severe hypothermia are noted by an observer the victim may be dead in as short a time as 2 to 4 hours.

HYPOTHERMIA'S SEQUENCE OF SYMPTOMS

As cold removes heat from the body, the peripheral circulation (that near the skin surface) begins to be reduced by blood vessel constriction. So does that in the fingers and toes. In an effort to maintain the body's core temperature at normal levels, blood is held away from the chilled body surface. Often an early symptom of this shift will be a numbness in one or another finger and a feeling of chilliness over the body. Shivering initially begins. This is the body's effort to produce additional heat through exercise and enhanced oxidation of food materials. As chilling progresses, it becomes difficult or impossible to carry out fine muscle movements, such as working with the fingers. The chemical reactions enabling finger flexing simply cease to be effective. Shivering becomes more intense as the body attempts to offset cooling. Progressive chilling finally results in heat loss for which the body cannot compensate. The temperature of deep circulation begins to fall. Fatigue sets in, reducing the heat-producing shivering. The body's core temperature drops still more. As chilling continues and the body cools, the chemical reactions that oxidize food and produce heat slow down. Thus, heat is produced less rapidly and the body cools even *more* quickly. An increasingly rapid interacting heat loss pattern is now initiated. As the body cools, it is even less able to chemically heat itself so it cools even

162

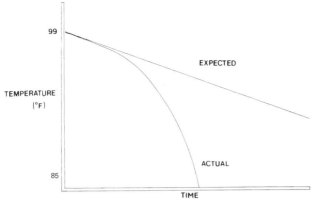

Figure 10-1   Body temperature drop in hypothermia as compared to expected cooling rate in the body. (Celia Drozdiak)

more rapidly. Still less heat is produced by the slowing metabolism, and the body's rate of cooling steepens (Figure 10-1). Thinking becomes sluggish as the blood circulating through the brain chills it. Ability to perform mental tasks is affected. The victim finds it difficult or impossible to recall simple facts such as name or address. Speech becomes slurred and progressively incoherent. Large muscle function is affected, causing a stiff legged stumbling gait. The victim has a glazed expression.

Shivering has, in the meantime, been producing metabolic products. Lactic acid, normally carried away by increased circulation through the muscles, tends to accumulate producing a feeling of intense exhaustion and often inducing pain and cramps. Plodding stoically forward the victim finally is no longer able to remain upright and falls forward. Consciousness wanes and waxes. Losing consciousness completely, the hypothermic person gradually passes into a coma. Heart action and respiration become erratic, with cardiac arrest or fibrillation developing. Fluid fills the lungs, and a froth pink with blood may appear at the nose and mouth from pulmonary edema. Death follows quickly.

Symptoms as Temperature Falls

96–99	Shivering begins; it may be violent
91–95	Shivering continues; thinking is sluggish
86–90	Shivering decreases and stops; begin muscle rigidity; consciousness lapses; thinking more sluggish
81–85	Stuporous; possible hallucinations; pulse slowing
78–80	Unconscious; comotase
Below 80	Cardiac and respiratory control centers fail; pulmonary edema; death

TREATMENT OF HYPOTHERMIA

Prevention is the best treatment. But, failing in this, it is important to quickly treat the ailing person. Victims have died because companions did not take the situation seriously or react quickly enough.

There is a complex set of conditions operating in hypothermia. Treatment is determined by its severity as well as the duration of onset. And, due to the very nature of the disorder, a person may be successfully resuscitated even after respiration or heartbeat has become undetectable for unusually long times.

Hypothermia is easiest to treat in the early stages. Keep a careful eye on members of the party especially if they are wet and in windy conditions. At the first sign of intense shivering, lapses in memory or uncoordinated movement take action.

Stop traveling and establish camp. If heat loss exceeds the body's ability to restore or maintain normal core temperature, death from hypothermia is guaranteed in time. Build a fire and if possible change wet clothes for dry. Provide hot drinks even if only hot water is available. At this point the victim's body is still able to restore normal function. But remember, the difference between discomfort and hypothermia is narrow. And it is far easier to deal with discomfort than the medical emergency of hypothermia.

If lapses in memory, slurred speech, and staggering gait have developed, the situation may have progressed to critical. Dry clothing, shelter, and a warm fire are still mandatory. But the victim's own metabolic processes may no longer be able to restore normal core temperature. If lapses in consciousness have developed, this is definitely the case. Moderate to severe hypothermia is immediately life threatening. Victims, if placed in a dry sleeping bag alone, even with dry clothing, no longer have the capability of restoring normal body temperature. They will continue to drift down the heat loss curve until they pass into a comatose condition and die. Encourage them to walk. Be sure that their clothing is dry. Provide them with hot drinks. But here is where the situation becomes extremely shaky. A severely hypothermic person may be literally killed in short order by inappropriate treatment. Above all, NEVER GIVE A HYPOTHERMIC ALCOHOLIC BEVERAGES! Two things may happen. If the hypothermia has been induced by anything other than cold water immersion, there is usually a fairly prolonged period of shivering. You will recall the earlier comment regarding the buildup of lactic acid in the muscle tissues by this action. So there is a large component of this acid waiting in reserve.

Second, the body has tried to limit heat loss by reducing to an absolute minimum any blood flow near the cold surface of the body. It has done this by peripheral vasoconstriction—the blood vessels near the skin surface have been reduced in diameter. Blood flow is concentrated near the core of the body. Because of this, the outer layers of body tissue are quite cold. Alcohol taken into the body causes almost immediate vasodilation. Those narrowed surface

COLD WEATHER EMERGENCIES

vessels suddenly open wide permitting the warm blood from the body's core to surge into the cold tissue near the surface, where its temperature drops precipitously. As this blood rushes toward the surface, it also picks up large quantities of the lactic acid produced in shivering. This changes it chemically, making the circulating blood more acidic. In effect, what is happening is that suddenly a mass of severely chilled, abnormally acidic blood is now rushing through the circulatory system toward the heart. When it gets there it is very likely to cause the heart to immediately stop beating regularly—to fibrillate. This uncoordinated quivering of the heart muscle does little or nothing to keep blood moving normally. Or, the cold acidic blood that reaches the heart may simply cause heart action to stop completely. In either case, without immediate and heroic treatment, death is only moments away. Remember, if you want to kill a hypothermic person, give them a good stiff shot of whiskey or some other alcoholic beverage!

Why, then, have people for so many years been under the impression that brandy or other alcoholic beverages help to warm a person? The answer lies in the perceived effect of the alcohol on the system. As the alcohol passes down the throat, there is a feeling of burning warmth. This is caused to some extent by the irritating effect of the alcohol. The same feeling occurs in the stomach, caused there both by the irritation and the stimulation of blood flow in the lining of the stomach. As the alcohol is rapidly taken into the general circulation from the vessels of the stomach's lining, peripheral vasodilation occurs. A feeling of spreading warmth suffuses the body.

Of course, what is really happening is that the body's system for reducing heat loss has suddenly and catastrophically gone awry. The only thing that may now be said is that the person will experience a fleeting sense of returning warmth and security—just before they die.

But alcohol is not the only culprit. In a seriously hypothermic person rough handling as clothing is being removed or as they are being transported may cause cardiac arrythmia (irregularity in beat) and sudden death. Massaging or rubbing the skin brings blood to the surface and can do likewise. So, handle the victim with great gentleness.

In general, field treatment involves the following steps.

1. Prevent further heat loss; add insulation. This may involve dry clothing, placing the victim in a sleeping bag, or adding clothing to what they are wearing. The victim may be removed to a cool room, but caution should be exercised here. If the room is above 65°F, cardiac irregularities may develop in severe hypothermia.

2. Force victim to exercise if possible.

   Note: Some victims of hypothermia become combative until their temperature begins to rise.

3. Provide warm fluids by mouth (only if victim is conscious). Sweetened beverages may be of some additional help.
4. Apply CPR (cardiopulmonary resuscitation) as necessary.
5. Apply external heat to the trunk of the body by immersion.

There is some controversy surrounding the immersion procedure. But it is especially recommended in "forever" situations and cases of cold water hypothermia. The victim's body is placed in *circulating*, renewable warm (104 to 110°F) water up to the neck. The arms and legs should *not* be in the water. Cooled water should be constantly drawn off at the bottom of the tub while warm water is added and the water stirred to keep it mixed. Otherwise, the chilled body will rapidly cool the bath, and severe and sudden core-temperature drop may kill the patient. Under hospital conditions heated, humidified oxygen (maximum temperature 115°F) may be used to advantage since the warmed bronchial tree lies in close proximity to the heart. Also under hospital conditions warmed fluids may be surgically introduced into the abdominal cavity. In the field, skin to skin contact may be provided by removing the clothing of the hypothermic person and a healthy person, and placing them both in a sleeping bag.

6. Transport the victim to a hospital as rapidly as possible.

FROSTBITE (FREEZING)

Frostbite is the process of physically freezing the body tissue. In its mildest form it only involves superficial skin layers, but deep freezing may involve muscle tissue down to the bone.

In the slow freezing characterized by exposure to cold outdoor environments, relatively large ice crystals form within the cells of the body and ultimately cause bursting of the tissue. While frostbite and freezing may involve the actual production of ice crystals in the cells of the body, serious damage occurs before actual rupture by crystal formation. Skin, muscle, and other tissues of the body are made up of microscopic cells. Each contains a solution of chemicals that enables the living cells to function. An oversimplified explanation might be that each cell is a small enclosure containing water in which some salt has been dissolved. As freezing commences, the water in this cellular solution begins to freeze, concentrating the remaining salt. As the salt concentration increases, it becomes toxic to the cell. It no longer functions properly and finally cell death occurs. Ice crystals may later reach sizes sufficient to cause cell rupture.

Frostbite often starts with exposure to extreme temperatures coupled with wind. But exposed flesh, especially in thin layers over bone or poorly supplied with blood, may freeze without wind when temperatures reach −30°F. If a

COLD WEATHER EMERGENCIES

wind of 20 mph is blowing, the air temperature may be as high as $+10°F$ and still cause freezing. At $-20°F$ with a 25 mph wind, exposed flesh may freeze in as short a time as 30 seconds!

Nose, ears, chin, and cheek areas are highly susceptible. But feet and hands are also likely candidates, especially if circulation is restricted either because of tight clothing or the effects of smoking. Smoking causes vasoconstriction, reducing blood flow into extremities and increasing chances of freezing.

While exposure to cold air may cause frostbite, the symptoms develop much more easily when skin is brought directly in contact with very cold objects such as metal tools or vehicles.

SYMPTOMS

1. Whitening or Blanching
In a light-skinned individual, the constriction of surface blood vessels first becomes apparent by a clearly demarked white patch. Often a sudden sting may herald the onset of this stage. At this stage, frostbite is easily treated merely by placing a warm hand on the affected area to restore normal temperature. But do not massage or rub. Tissue damage may occur. When an area that has been painfully cold suddenly feels better, be careful. It likely is frostbitten and sensation has been lost.

2. Waxy-white
In this intermediate stage serious freezing is developing. The condition is no longer superficial. Deeper tissue is being affected. However, warming with the hand may still be effective. A frostbitten hand may be placed under the armpit.

3. Gray-white
Deep freezing is present. Ordinarily, the flesh will either feel solid when pressed or will depress and remain indented at this stage. Serious tissue damage is likely. Rapid rewarming by immersion in warm water is the preferred treatment (104 to 110°F).

Some General Notes
A frostbitten foot may be rewarmed by a cooperative friend. Have them unfasten the clothing over their stomach down to the skin. Remove the footgear from the affected foot down to the skin and place the foot on the donated stomach. (This kind of assistance is really a wonderful experience! The pain will likely be intense for both of you.)

Never rub or massage a frozen part of the body. If you aren't sure why not, take a bag of frozen strawberries out of the freezer and while it is thawing vigorously massage it. You will end up with a bag of strawberry jam. And that's about what you will have if you massage a frozen hand or foot.

Also, rubbing with or immersing in snow should not be done. This will only compound the damage. After all, the injury was *caused* by cold and it is not reasonable to assume that application of snow will help.

TREATMENT

The treatment of choice is rapid rewarming. The affected part of the body should be immersed in water warmed to between 104 and 113°F. This is barely lukewarm. However, there are several considerations to keep in mind before proceeding.

1. The treatment is excruciatingly painful. Shock may result both from pain and from sudden reentry into the circulatory system of chemical products of the freezing process.
2. Once thawed, a frozen hand or foot is not functional for a prolonged time. Therefore, the victim usually becomes a stretcher case.
3. Swelling is immediate. It rapidly becomes extreme. A thawed foot cannot be reinserted into a boot.
4. Once frozen, severity of tissue damage is static. Therefore, it may be better to leave the part frozen until evacuation is possible. Thawing may cause much more serious problems.
5. A frozen part of the body is unlikely to be further damaged by use. For example, a frozen foot, although feeling like a piece of deep frozen beef roast, can be walked on without increasing the damage.
6. A thawed part of the body is very fragile. The slightest pressure or abrasion usually will increase tissue damage and predispose the area to serious infection.

Once an area is thawed, it must be carefully protected. A thawed foot must be supported on soft padding with resilient cotton pads placed between the toes to minimize pressure.

Swelling, blistering, and discoloration may follow almost immediately (Figure 10-2). Blisters may contain clear or bloody fluid. Do not open them. This only increases chances for infection. As the days progress, the frozen area may turn many hues of blue, black, purple, yellow, and green from blood released into the tissue. Swelling may be so severe as to make the skin appear shiny, and a foot may be as large as the leg above it. Often this swelling causes

168   COLD WEATHER EMERGENCIES

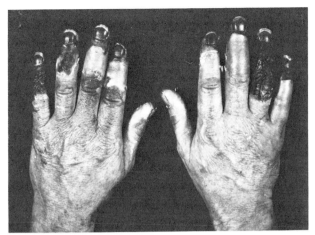

Figure 10-2   Frostbite symptoms. (Courtesy of Gustavo A. Espinoza, M.D.)

pressure that closes blood vessels that enter the affected area. Under hospital conditions incisions may have to be made through the skin to relieve this and permit proper circulation. In any case, the affected area may burst, allowing fluid to be discharged.

A few days after thawing, a clear line of demarcation may develop at the juncture where affected and unaffected tissue meet. A word of caution is needed here. Even medical doctors have been deceived by this.

The line is so clear and unmistakable and the damaged tissue appears so devastated that an erroneous decision may be made to amputate. It would appear that there is no hope for the damaged area to ever be restored to normality. In fact, this is often not the case. Although weeks of rehabilitation and treatment may follow, most of the affected area is likely to heal. Large portions of the frozen tissue may slough away, and supportive antibiotic therapy will be necessary to prevent infection. But, in time, little or none of the frozen area may be lost. It is wise to consult with a physician who has had considerable experience with freezing before irreversible decisions regarding amputation are made. It is far easier to amputate than it is to reattach a limb afterward.

WIND CHILL

Wind chill simply means that wind causes heat to be lost from the body faster than would be the case in still air. When there is no air movement, our bodies are surrounded by a thin blanket of warm air. Heat from the body has warmed it. In effect, the warm air gets in its own way (Figure 10-3). It is difficult for

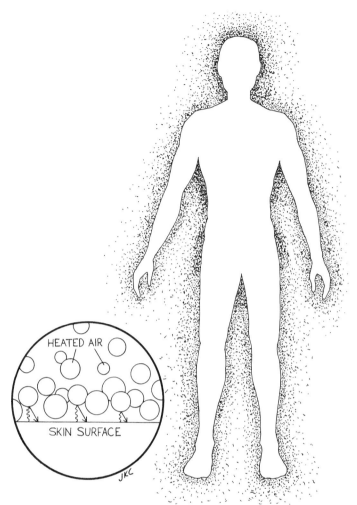

Figure 10-3   Blanket of warmed air over the skin surface. (Jan Kolena Cole)

the body to lose additional heat unless the warm air blanket can be thinned or replaced with cool air. As the wind begins to move it gradually carries away some of the warm air, allowing heat to be lost more rapidly. Up to a maximum of 40 mph, the faster the wind blows the faster heat is lost. So there is really nothing mysterious about wind chill. Figure 10-4 illustrates in chart form how to determine the wind chill factor.

First, read the temperature of the air from a thermometer placed outdoors, out of the sun and preferably away from buildings. Find the temperature by

170   COLD WEATHER EMERGENCIES

COOLING POWER OF WIND EXPRESSED AS "EQUIVALENT CHILL TEMPERATURE"

WIND SPEED			TEMPERATURE (F)																				
KNOTS	CALM	MPH	40	35	30	25	20	15	10	5	0	−5	−10	−15	−20	−25	−30	−35	−40	−45	−50	−55	−60
CALM	CALM		40	35	30	25	20	15	10	5	0	−5	−10	−15	−20	−25	−30	−35	−40	−45	−50	−55	−60
			EQUIVALENT CHILL TEMPERATURE																				
3 - 6		5	35	30	25	20	15	10	5	0	−5	−10	−15	−20	−25	−30	−35	−40	−45	−50	−55	−65	−70
7 - 10		10	30	20	15	10	5	0	−10	−15	−20	−25	−35	−40	−45	−50	−60	−65	−70	−75	−80	−90	−95
11 - 15		15	25	15	10	0	−5	−10	−20	−25	−30	−40	−45	−50	−60	−65	−70	−80	−85	−90	−100	−105	−110
16 - 19		20	20	10	5	0	−10	−15	−25	−30	−35	−45	−50	−60	−65	−75	−80	−85	−95	−100	−110	−115	−120
20 - 23		25	15	10	0	−5	−15	−20	−30	−35	−45	−50	−60	−65	−75	−80	−90	−95	−105	−110	−120	−125	−135
24 - 28		30	10	5	0	−10	−20	−25	−30	−40	−50	−55	−65	−70	−80	−85	−95	−100	−110	−115	−125	−130	−140
29 - 32		35	10	5	−5	−10	−20	−30	−35	−40	−50	−60	−65	−75	−80	−90	−100	−105	−115	−120	−130	−135	−145
33 - 36		40	10	0	−5	−15	−20	−30	−35	−45	−55	−60	−70	−75	−85	−95	−100	−110	−115	−125	−130	−140	−150

WINDS ABOVE 40 HAVE LITTLE ADDITIONAL EFFECT.

LITTLE DANGER

INCREASING DANGER
(Flesh may freeze within 1 minute)

GREAT DANGER
(Flesh may freeze within 30 seconds)

DANGER OF FREEZING EXPOSED FLESH FOR PROPERLY CLOTHED PERSONS

Figure 10-4   The wind chill factor. (Courtesy of the United States Air Force)

reading across the top of the chart. Then find the wind speed. If it is gusting, use a rough average. Locate this wind speed by reading down the left side of the chart. Scan across the equivalent temperatures until you get to the column under the observed air temperature. The number found will correspond to the effective temperature. For example, if the air temperature is 10°F, the equivalent temperature will be found in the column under 10°F. If the wind is blowing at 20 mph, read across the row to the right of the 20-mph point of the estimated wind speed column. This will intersect the equivalent temperature of −25°F. In other words, exposed flesh would be chilled at the same rate as if the air temperature were really 25° below zero.

A common misconception is that somehow the actual temperature would be lower when the wind is blowing. This is not so. To understand the meaning of wind chill, think about this situation. A gun has been repeatedly fired until the barrel is quite warm. It is then leaned against a tree outdoors overnight. Throughout the night the air temperature is 20°F. A wind of 25 mph is blowing. In the morning will the gun barrel be warmer than the air, colder than the air, or the same temperature as the air? The answer is that it will be the *same* temperature as the air. The only thing the wind would have done was cause more *rapid* cooling of the gun barrel. It would have gotten down to 20° at a rate equal to that expected at −25°F. In effect, wind chill is then an indication of cooling *rate*.

COLD WEATHER SHELTERS

While the usual lean-to or other brush-type shelter may be constructed in very cold weather, snow itself is an excellent insulator and the survivor may be most comfortable in a shelter constructed from it.

In Chapter 6, it was mentioned that melted snow reduces in volume by a factor of 10. Or to put it another way, snow is about 90 percent air. In this lies the means for its insulating value. Literally filled with millions of tiny spaces containing trapped air, snow can be used to provide a really cozy home away from home.

THE ESKIMO QUINZHEE

Many times there is not enough snow to enable the survivor to carve a cave. But, even with limited amounts, the quinzhee or snow heap can be made if the air temperature is 20°F or less.

Mark off a circle in the snow between 8 to 10 feet in diameter. Thoroughly stir the snow in this area down to ground level. Then place a stick about 7 feet long upright in the center of the circle (Figure 10-5). Lay another along the snow from the center pole to the edge of the circle and continue to pile

COLD WEATHER EMERGENCIES

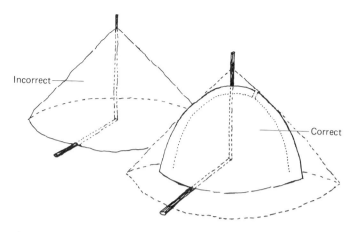

Figure 10-5   Construction of a quinzhe. (*Jan Kolena Cole*)

more snow in until a heap is formed with just the top of the upright pole showing. Let the pile remain undisturbed for at least 2 hours. During this time because of the mixing done while piling, a recrystallization process will be going on. This will result in the snow binding together. Without this process, the quinzhee would not be possible. And, anyone who has ever tried to make a snowball with very dry powder snow may already wonder how this snow could hold together. Test the pile to assure that it is solidifying. When it is firm you are ready to proceed. Note that the pile of snow is somewhat shaped like an inverted cone. Scrape off the apex of the cone so that the remaining heap is more nearly circular (Figure 10-5). If this is not done, the top will be too thick, weigh too much, and likely collapse as you hollow out the interior.

Now, locate the tip of the horizontal stick that is jutting out from the upright pole. This is the point at which to start digging into the center of the heap. Both this stick and the vertical pole are there to serve as road guides to keep you from accidentally digging out through the side of the shelter. The middle of a pile of snow tends to be rather uniformly white. So, it is very hard to know if you are headed in the correct direction.

Continue to dig along the horizontal stick until you reach the vertical pole, and then begin hollowing out the interior of the living space. The thickness of the walls should taper from about 10 inches near the bottom to about 6 inches in the ceiling. A thin stick may be used as a probe to check wall thickness as you progress. Figure 10-6.

Be sure that the shelter rests directly on the ground. Strange as it may seem, the earth in extremely cold environments will actually serve as a source of heat. Under 2 feet of snow cover, the earth will never be less than 18 to 20 degrees above zero even if the air temperature is 50 below.

Figure 10-6   The quinzhe in use. (Jan Kolena Cole)

The entrance should be kept small—no larger than is necessary to permit entry of the largest member of the party crawling on their belly. It may be closed with packs, extra clothing, or fabric from a disabled vehicle. Brush the earth as clear of snow as possible, and lay a thick bough bed if that is all that is available. Otherwise, grass or materials secured from a vehicle may be used. A small (2 inch) hole should be cut near the apex of the shelter to permit ventilation. This is particularly important if anything is burned in the quinzhee. Carbon monoxide is a real danger in any enclosed shelter such as this.

And, that is all there is to it. Such shelters are very warm, with interior temperatures varying from about zero degrees near the floor to as high as 50 near the ceiling. This in itself may pose a problem. The interior walls should be kept carefully curved and ought to be smoothed with a gloved hand. This is called glazing although it has nothing to do with freezing a slick surface on the snow. Its purpose is to allow any melt water forming in the very warm upper part of the shelter to trickle down the walls, be absorbed, and refreeze down below. If this procedure is omitted, melting will produce a continuous shower bath dampening everything and everyone. And, dampness compromises insulation and threatens life.

SNOW HOLE

In deeper snow, dig down to ground level leaving a bench around the entire shelter for sitting or equipment storage. Radiating from the snow hole are sleeping tunnels. Line the floor and the sleeping tunnels with boughs or other

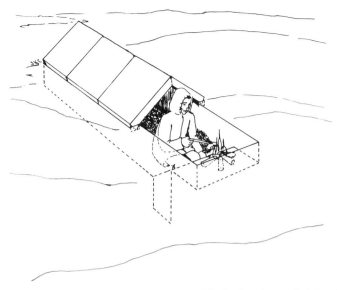

Figure 10-7   Snow trench shelter using snow blocks for the roof. (Jan Kolena Cole)

insulation. The roof is then constructed with poles and boughs covered with snow.

SNOW TRENCH

For one person it may be simpler to dig a trench in the snow. This is sometimes called a fighter trench since it has also been recommended for ski or mountain troops (Figure 10-7). But, for the roof blocks to be effective, the snow must be very firm. Wind-packed snow that has stood for a prolonged period of time is ideal for this. Again, the floor and the sleeping area should be well insulated.

SNOW CAVE

Where snow is very deep, has drifted, or been plowed, a snow cave may be made. Figure 10-8 is self-explanatory. The entrance should be lower than the rest of the shelter to prevent warm air loss. Often a sink-trap—down and back up—entrance may be made. Walls again should be carefully curved to prevent dripping.

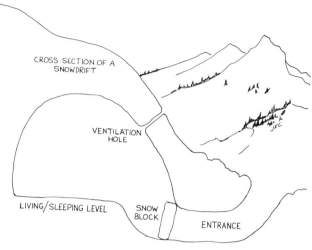

Figure 10-8   Snow cave. (Jan Kolena Cole)

TREE WELL

In heavy snow areas where evergreen trees grow, the area beneath the dense boughs may be relatively snow free. A survivor can crawl into this area, cut out interfering branches, and remove the rest of the snow. The result will be a spacious area nicely protected from snow and wind.

IGLOO

To construct an igloo is no simple task. The author has seen eight people with limited experience work 4 hours to complete one. On the other hand, an experienced Native American working alone can often complete one in 45 minutes to an hour.

The diagrams which follow will greatly simplify igloo construction if followed carefully. It is recommended that the entire process be practiced before the necessity arises. This will assist in working out any rough spots in construction and familiarize the survivor with the sequence.

The two key concepts that must be held firmly in mind are (1) spiral layout of the snow blocks and (2) the three-point contact method of shaping the blocks.

Contrary to popular belief, igloos are constructed, as are all other similar shelters, from snow. They are not made of ice. An igloo made of ice would be fine for a deep freeze, but most survivors would not like to qualify as frozen meat.

Constructed properly, the igloo is warm and surprisingly quiet, since the 6-

176

inch thick walls effectively block sound. A candle or two turns the interior into a crystal palace. Under other than survival situations, the experience of living in an igloo can be a lot of fun.

Igloos have a limited term of usability. As slight melting continues to occur and water is reabsorbed, the air spaces in the snow are blocked and slowly the insulating characteristics are compromised. In the far north, 6 to 8 weeks is probably the outside limit before reconstruction becomes necessary again.

Construction

Ideally, snow for construction should be from wind-packed areas or locations in which the snow has become very firm. Such snow may be so solid that it requires a saw for cutting and shaping. Snow knives or snow saws are manufactured for this purpose. However, one can be constructed from a machete. The design is shown in Figure 10-9. If nothing else is available, boot laces or parachute suspension lines may be used to make an improvised saw. Knotted every 2 inches with a stick tied on the ends, the laces form a flexible saw (Figure 10-10).

Once suitable snow has been located, dig out a clear vertical face (Figure 10-11). Blocks should be about 4 feet long, 20 inches wide, and 6 inches thick. Cut the blocks from the area where the igloo will be constructed. (There is no

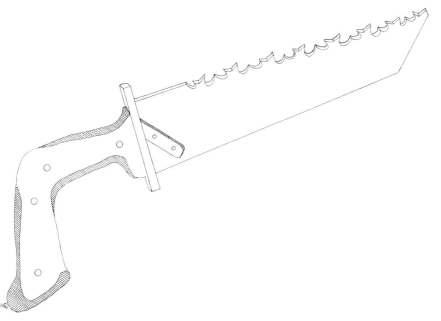

Figure 10-9   Snow saw. (Celia Drozdiak)

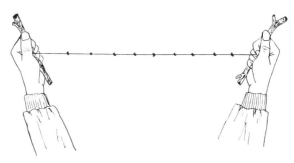

Figure 10-10   Improvised snow saw using knotted boot laces and stick handles. (Rosalie R. Risk)

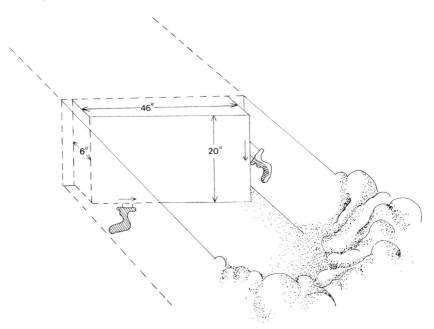

Figure 10-11   Dimensions of snow blocks for igloo construction. (Celia Drozdiak)

sense in double digging.) Blocks this large may seem awkward but they are actually easier to work with than smaller ones and, in the long run, reduce the time needed in construction.

Lay a single row, angling the blocks slightly inward. A smaller block must be placed under the point at which the circle crosses the block cutting trench. Be sure that the end joints are radial with the center of the shelter. Anything else will create stability problems (Figure 10-12).

After the initial circle of blocks is laid, begin the spiral by angling a cut

178   COLD WEATHER EMERGENCIES

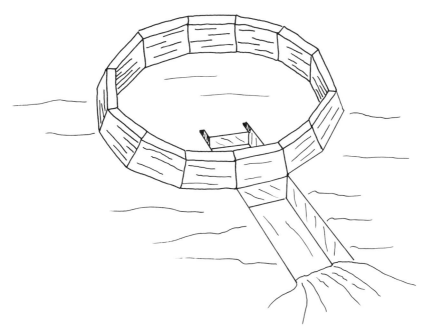

Figure 10-12   The first row of blocks in an igloo. (Adapted by Rosalie R. Risk from Down But Not Out. *By permission of the Canadian Department of Defence)*

from the top of the fourth block down to half the height of the first. Then, starting with a slightly smaller block, commence laying the second tier. The blocks should be staggered so that the vertical joints do not line up. If the first block of the second tier is smaller and all subsequent blocks are again 4 feet long, this will be the case. A spiral going from right to left as viewed from the inside of the igloo is shown in Figures 10-13 and 10-14, but the reverse is also possible. The person doing the building should work from the inside. This enables them to properly support the blocks during the trimming and setting process. Each subsequent tier of blocks should lean more toward the igloo center. This will rapidly appear to be approaching disaster since it will seem impossible for the blocks to lock in place. However, if the pressure or contact points are designed as shown in Figure 10-15, they will not fall in.

Three points of contact are critical. Each block must be cut so that the bottom corners and the upper right corner bear against the blocks beneath and to the right. The easiest way to form the required three bearing points is to place the rough block and then make the finishing cuts. Brace the block with the hand and make a slightly curving cut along the underside. When it is then tapped down on the right end, it will tilt and the a, b, c surfaces will automatically lock into place.

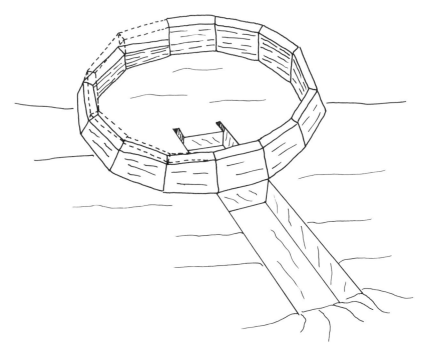

Figure 10-13   Carving the spiral in igloo building. (Adapted by Rosalie R. Risk from Down But Not Out. *By permission of the Canadian Department of Defence)*

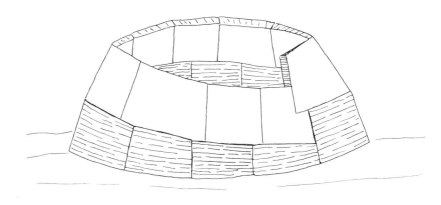

Figure 10-14   The second row of snow blocks in an igloo. (Adapted by Rosalie R. Risk from Down But Not Out. *By permission of the Canadian Department of Defence)*

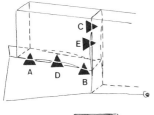

Figure 10-15 The important bearing surfaces of the blocks. (Adapted by Celia Drozdiak from Down But Not Out. *By permission of the Canadian Department of Defence)*

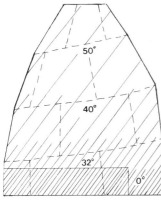

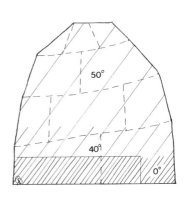

INCORRECT

CORRECT

Figure 10-16 Temperatures in an improperly and properly proportioned igloo. It is important to keep the dome low. (Adapted by Celia Drozdiak from Down But Not Out. *By permission of the Canadian Department of Defence)*

Be sure to continue tilting each subsequent tier of blocks inward. Keep in mind the desired finished shape of the shelter. Usually, beginners tend to make an igloo that is too straight sided near the bottom and then they have trouble completing the dome. At the very least they end up with an igloo that is too high in its base-to-crown interior dimension and most of the warmth is too high up. Ideally, an igloo's interior temperatures should be about zero at the floor of the foot hole, 40° at the level of the sleeping platform, and nearly 50° at the ceiling. A too tall structure will have temperatures at the sleeping platform closer to 32° (Figure 10-16).

The interior layout is shown in Figure 10-17. Pegs may be inserted in the walls to support cooking utensils and keep them out of the way and to act as clothes hangers. Interior cracks are chinked with snow and the entire inner surface carefully smoothed to prevent dripping. Resmoothing and the application of a handful of snow will usually stop any drips that do occur.

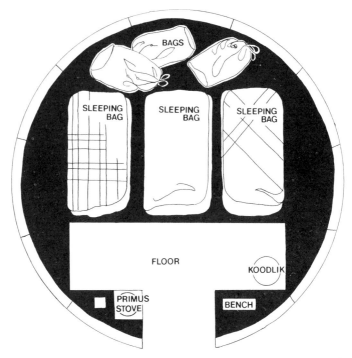

Figure 10-17 One way to place items in the igloo. (Adapted by Celia Droz-dirk from Down But Not Out. *By permission of the Canadian Department of Defence)*

Ultimately there will remain only a relatively small hole in the ceiling. A kingblock should then be cut. Bevel the edges of the hole and the kingblock to about 15 degrees. The kingblock is carefully pushed through from the interior, turned, and manipulated until it can be allowed to settle into place. Careful trimming with the snow knife will permit it to fit snugly (Figure 10-18).

Then descend into the trench entrance and carefully cut out a small entry door. Outside, this may be protected with an A-frame cover or any other modification necessary.

In very cold environments with high wind, blowing snow can erode the lower tier of blocks rapidly. It is almost like a sandblaster. Pile loose snow against these tiers to prevent this (Figure 10-19). As this protective blanket is eroded away, replace it. Also, a windbreak of snowblocks may be used on the windward side. Chink all external cracks and joints with loose snow. Recrystallization will freeze this loose material into place, and the structure will soon become extremely solid.

COLD WEATHER EMERGENCIES

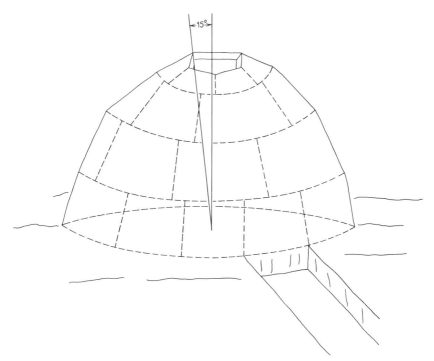

Figure 10-18   Detail of the kingblock placement. (Adapted by Rosalie R. Risk from Down But Not Out. *By permission of the Canadian Department of Defence)*

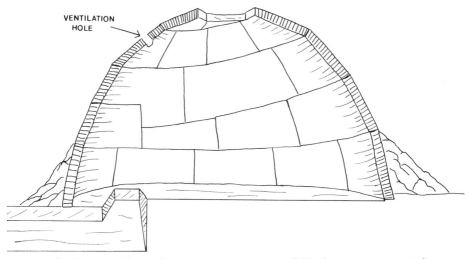

VENTILATION HOLE

Figure 10-19   Snow banked against the first row of blocks to prevent wind erosion. (Adapted by Rosalie R. Risk from Down But Not Out. *By permission of the Canadian Department of Defence)*

HUMAN WASTE DISPOSAL IN SNOW SHELTERS

Nobody enjoys braving the wintry blasts to go to the bathroom. This problem is solved by the Eskimo equivalent of a chamber pot—the kovik. It is merely a snow block into which has been carved a depression. Used during the night, a handful of snow improves the appearance afterward until it can be disposed of in the morning. Be sure that all human waste is placed in a common area known to all. Otherwise, the snow all around the shelter area slowly turns yellow or worse, and it may become virtually impossible to locate clean snow for water. Nothing is as demoralizing as melting snow for drinking water only to find fecal material floating in it!

WATER PROCUREMENT

Even in very cold areas, it may be possible to chip through the ice of a lake and find liquid water. Cover this hole with boughs as insulation. This will slow the formation of ice over your water source.

Both snow and ice may be melted for water. Since snow will produce only about one-tenth as much water as the volume of snow you start with, it is desirable to use ice where possible. Ice melts in a ratio of 1:1. Be careful in melting snow to keep the bottom of the container wet to prevent its burning out. This is not a problem with ice.

But, remember, freezing does *not* kill disease organisms. Ice formed from contaminated water will still be contaminated and produce water unfit to drink. Either boil it thoroughly or use water purification chemicals or microfiltration equipment.

An easy method of melting snow is to place it in a plastic bag between layers of the clothing. As it melts, add more snow. In this way, the heat produced by normal activity may be used to assist in the production of drinking water.

SEA ICE

At extreme temperatures even seawater freezes. Ice formed from salt water tends to have a granular texture, be milky or cloudy, and break in a crumbly manner. Freshwater ice is smooth, fractures like glass with sharp edges, and is clear to bluish.

FIRE CONSTRUCTION

Where it is possible to build fires on the ground, difficulties are minimal. But, sometimes, snow is too deep to permit this. In the winter of 1846, when the Donner expedition was attempting to cross the Sierras, the group had to deal with extreme snow depth. The journal entries indicated that they would build a fire on the snow surface but by morning it would have melted its way down to ground level, leaving them crowded in a snow hole 9 to 12 feet deep with several inches of water sloshing around the bottom, threatening to extinguish the fire.

Fire may be built on the snow surface, but some form of insulation is necessary. Perhaps the simplest way to do this is a layer of 4 to 5 inch green logs. A double layer is even better. A fire can be constructed on this platform and burn for several hours before it penetrates the ground.

Where a disabled vehicle is available, parts of it may be used to improvise a fire platform. For example, an automobile or snowmobile hood supported on logs makes a fine fire support.

In tundra areas fuel for fires may be scarce, and in ice cap areas almost nonexistent. Shrubs and brush as well as dwarf birch may be the largest things around. In some areas peat can be cut and burned, but generally only in the summer.

Gasoline, jet fuel, diesel fuel, and lubricating oil will all burn. So will animal fats. However, gasoline vapor when mixed with air in proper proportions is explosive and very hazardous to burn alone. Experiment with mixtures of gasoline and lubricating oil, or other fuel, until one is found that burns in a controllable way. The mixture will depend on temperature and elevation. Diesel and jet fuels do not pose the vapor problems of gasoline and may be used alone. But, if crankcase oil is to be used, get it out of the engine while still warm. At extreme subzero temperatures, it will thicken and congeal to the consistency of very soft rubber.

Simply run it out directly onto the surface of the snow if the temperature is below about $-25°F$.

> **Note:** Gasoline and other fuels remain liquid far below the freezing point of water. For example, gasoline becomes mushy at about $-45°F$. However, this means that a severe frostbite and freezing hazard may be represented by their presence. An accidental spill can saturate clothing with the supercooled fluid and cause almost instant and severe frostbite.

SIGNALS

Anyone who has ever observed tracks in the snow realizes that they stand out against the white because of their shadows. This is enhanced on sunny days. An overcast sky tends to produce a diffused light which reduces contrast. Driving down a snow-covered road on a sunny day, wheel tracks and ruts are easy to see and to avoid where necessary. But, on overcast days, it is often difficult to see where the road ends and the ditch begins.

Because of the shadow contrast, one of the easiest methods of signaling under snow conditions is tramping down the snow surface. Remember that there is no rush about this and do not overexert. Set a leisurely pace and walk out the signals desired. First, stomp out a large X, with arms at least 20 yards long. Then, if it would feel more secure to also have an SOS, tramp it out.

Contrast may be increased by cutting snow blocks and standing them on edge along the signal pattern. Or, boughs may be cut and the tramped signals filled with them. If it is available, sea dye marker can be used to sprinkle on the snow surface to impart a bright yellow-orange coloration. Lacking this, powdered fruit-flavored beverages will do the same thing. Thin snow may be scraped away to reveal the stark contrast of earth or sod beneath.

Vehicles and shelters built from vegetation are far more visible from the air than are people. So they also form a sort of signal. Keep any vehicles free from snow so that they are easily seen by search aircraft. The same is true of brush shelters.

Unused clothing, tarps, ground cloths, or other material may also be laid out in emergency signal patterns and, especially if bright or reflective, will be excellent signals.

Finally, pieces of a disabled vehicle such as wings, tail sections, or panels removed from engine covers should be considered and utilized where possible.

> **Note:** Snow shelters are *not* visible. Obviously, they are the same color as the surrounding snow. Be sure that your predicament is identified well with signals.

MISCELLANEOUS COLD ENVIRONMENT CONSIDERATIONS

Travel, as in most survival situations, is not advisable. Magnetic compass readings may be greatly in error. In the far north, the magnetic deviation may be as high as 180 degrees! Thus, it would be possible to travel west when the plan called for east.

Travel on sea ice is very hazardous both because of open leads (cracks exposing the sea) and pressure ridges (large blocks of ice thrust up on their edges by the crushing and grinding action of moving ice). Landmarks are virtually nonexistent and may change as the ice moves. The large blocks of ice in the crush zone fall from time to time without warning and may be as large as a railroad boxcar. Especially during spring breakup, the ice masses shift and drift, isolating survivors on floes that may drift miles to sea or may break up and plunge survivors into frigid water where life expectancy is measured in minutes.

Where limited travel is contemplated, improvised snowshoes can be built

186

from willows, metal tubing from a vehicle, electrical wire, or other material. They may mean the difference between being able to move around the area to search for fuel and other necessities and being completely immobilized.

Crude sleds or toboggans may be constructed from aircraft doors, access panels, snowmobile or automobile hoods, and so forth. They make transport of equipment, shelter materials, water, and game much easier.

WHITEOUTS

Whiteout conditions exist when everything up, down, and around appears white. It may involve an overcast sky over snow, such that reflected light from the snow surface matches that from above, and this can be complicated by drifting airborne ice crystals or falling and blowing snow. The result is that it is impossible to see anything. Disorientation is so complete that vertigo (dizziness) may be present.

Fog may compound the situation. In any case, travel could be virtually impossible. The story is told of an Eskimo woman caught in a whiteout and blizzard who calmly removed her mits, placed them under her for additional insulation, drew her arms up into the inside of her parka to conserve warmth, and sat that way for three days. When clearing occurred, she was fine and merely walked the short distance back to camp.

When whiteout conditions prevail, stop and establish improvised camp. Attempting to travel is almost guaranteed to bring disaster. Lines from suspension cords or other rope may be strung around camp in areas where blizzard conditions or whiteouts are frequent. They can easily mean the difference between life and death.

SNOW BLINDNESS

Radiation from the sun, reflecting off snow surfaces, is the cause of snow blindness. Especially in mountain areas, travelers are sometimes afflicted even during overcast or whiteout conditions. Onset is usually sudden, either without warning or heralded only by a brief period during which the vision appears to be suffused with pink coloration. Pain, tearing, and increased sensitivity to light are the prime symptoms. And, once they appear, damage has been done. The difficulties will then get worse before they get better.

A person suffering from snow blindness quickly becomes unable to function. Pain varies from a sensation of grit in the eyes to an intense stabbing pain on exposure to even reduced light levels. The condition lasts from 1 to 5 days. The treatment is simply cold compresses over the eyes and control of the pain with drugs and rest. Headache and depression may accompany the condition.

Figure 10-20   Improvised snow goggles. (Celia Drozdiak)

Once having suffered from the malady, a victim seems predisposed to getting it again and becomes snow blind more easily for a period of years.

Like many other difficulties, prevention is the key. At the least, the eyes should be protected with sunglasses. Ideally, the protection should block rays from the sides as well. Mountaineers often use a goggle similar to that which a welder wears, fit snugly against the face. Those who wear glasses may use a type of goggle with a smoked lens similar to that used by ski racers.

Caught in the open under conditions that can cause snow blindness, an improvised masklike shield should be used. The slit should not be over a sixteenth of an inch wide. It is surprising how much can be seen through a minute slit. This can be demonstrated by squinting through the opening between two fingers. They can almost be touching and clear vision still is available.

Materials for the improvised goggle should not be metal or anything that transmits heat quickly. Otherwise, the cold may damage the skin of the face. Leather (the tongue of a boot), cloth, or heavy cardboard can be used and secured to the face with a cord. Goggles may also be carved from wood or bone, as Eskimos have done for generations (Figure 10-20).

SUMMER CONSIDERATIONS IN NORTHERN AREAS
INSECTS

During summer months northern environments teem with biting insects such as midges, blackflies, and mosquitos. A person who has never experienced arctic insects in summer cannot appreciate how dense they can become. Not only are they individually large but literally clouds of them seem to be present during all daylight hours. And, during the arctic summer, that can be nearly 24 hours! An injured traveler, unable to take protective action, could be bled so seriously as to compromise survival, not to mention the psychological problem of this assault.

To discourage them, smoky fires of punky wood or damp, smoldering vegetation should be maintained. These so-called smudge fires will help to discourage the insects. However, the dense smoke is also irritating to the eyes, nose, throat, and lungs. But, most people seem to feel that they would rather put up with incipient emphysema than the mosquitos and flies. Leaf mold and ferns could be tried for this smudge protection. Where it is available, clay or other mud may be used to cover exposed skin.

Commercial insect repellants are also of great help and those should be selected that have the highest possible percentage of diethyl-meta-toluamide.

11

HOT
WEATHER
EMERGENCIES:
ARID
REGIONS

People unfamiliar with desert conditions often exhibit one of two extreme responses. They are either unrealistically frightened by the desert or show a cavalier disregard for the potential hazards.

While it should be apparent that water is a serious limiting factor, newcomers often are entirely unaware of the quantities necessary to sustain life. General environmental dryness coupled with extreme heat during much of the year combine to place severe stress on the survivor.

Deserts more often are characterized as harsh, demanding, and dangerous by those who are unfamiliar with them. Yet, globally many people live and thrive in desert country. In fact, deserts are beautiful and very habitable but must be treated with informed respect. They are no more and no less dangerous than many other environments. There is no reason why a trained person should not be able to survive limited, unforeseen stays there. But, in all honesty, there are desert areas in the world where a victim will find it almost impossible to sustain life long. There simply are not ways to cope with *all* the extremes possible in the environment.

GENERAL CONSIDERATIONS
WATER

Anytime travel off main roads or flights over desert country are planned, it is advisable to carry plenty of water. Empty bleach bottles make handy containers. Any residual trace of bleach will only assure the purity of the water. Desert water bags made of coarse fabric were once seen hanging on most vehicles traveling the highways. They are designed to not be entirely waterproof; becoming soaked, they continuously evaporate water, which keeps them cool. However, they are also *losing* water for the same reason. Cool water may be more pleasant to drink but is by no means a necessity. Even hot water is drinkable. It has always seemed strange that a treatment for poisoning has been to drink warm or hot water to induce vomiting. After all, coffee, tea, and other such beverages are mostly hot water with only a tiny quantity of flavoring, and they do not nauseate.

Plan to carry at *least* a gallon of water per person on backroad trips.

TRAVEL BY MOTOR VEHICLE

It is a good idea when traveling remote desert areas to have at least two vehicles. If one breaks down, the other may be the only reliable source of rescue. At the very least, spare parts and tools should be carried. Items to take would include a spare distributor cap, points, and rotor. Those who travel the desert a great deal also have an additional spark coil.

Drivers in the desert usually learn quickly that a vehicle can easily become stuck in sand in the same way it would in loose snow. Avoid dry, light-colored, sandy areas. They are often very loose, and the car will immediately sink to its hubs.

If this should occur, there are several ways to get out. Some carry strips 2 feet wide by 12 feet long of either closely woven wire mesh, heavy carpet, or canvas. These can be placed under the drive wheels and used to assist in enhancing traction.

Tire pressure may also be reduced by about one-half the normal amount. This will allow the tires to mush down and spread out, giving additional pulling power. But do not lower the pressure below this. Tire damage is likely to result and it will be impossible to continue to drive after getting out of the sand. Either special compressed gas tire refill cylinders or spark-plug type tire pumps work very well to reinflate a tire, either after a repair or this procedure.

DEHYDRATION

DO NOT RATION DRINKING WATER. In spite of various fictional accounts of travelers severely limiting water intake and thus living through a dangerous experience in desert country, water should not be rationed. Emphasize rationing sweat, not water.

As the surface of the body rises above a certain point in temperature, sensors cause pores to open and sweat glands to produce perspiration. This slightly salty solution flows out on the skin surface and acts as an evaporative coolant.

The more heat stress to which the body is subjected, the faster flows the perspiration. Under extreme conditions sweat may be produced at a rate of 2 quarts an hour. Obviously, this water must come from somewhere. Its source is food and drinking water. The body is literally drying itself out in order to facilitate cooling and to prevent the core temperature from rising too high. But this water is coming from a limited reservoir—the body.

As the body's water content drops 1 percent below normal, the sensation of thirst is manifest. If water loss continues, efficiency drops markedly. Fatigue sets in and a feeling of lethargy occurs. There seems to not be enough energy or desire to accomplish even the simplest tasks. The victim becomes impatient and irritable. A headache is often one of the earliest signs of dehydration. As the dehydration progresses, appetite is lost followed by the onset of nausea.

Urine becomes darker than normal and if the deficit is not met may become almost as dark as tea. Urination may produce a burning sensation. When water balance is down by 5 to 6 percent, nausea becomes a serious problem as it comes and goes in waves. A general feeling of malaise—that rotten achy feeling associated with colds and flu—sets in. Vomiting begins, making it impossible to retain anything by mouth and, in itself, further removes water from the body. When this stage is reached, the victim may be in a no-win situation. Even if water becomes available, it may be impossible to retain it and only intravenous methods will be effective in restoring a balance. As water deficiency approaches 10 percent, thought processes become impaired. No permanent harm will be done by deficits up to 10 percent, providing the water shortage is made up afterward. A loss of 20 percent is usually fatal.

HOW TO RATION SWEAT

1. *Limit all physical activity.*   Confine what is absolutely necessary to night-time hours when temperatures will be cooler. Put simply: "Don't work up a sweat." Physical labor means muscles are required to contract, a process that generates metabolic heat. In an effort to keep the body temperature within normal limits, sweat glands will be activated and an increased flow of perspiration will occur.

2. *Keep your body covered.*   While first impressions might indicate that you will be cooler without clothes, you actually will be better off covered. A relatively cool layer of trapped air between the clothing and the skin will tend to reduce sweating. Clothing will also protect you from sunburn.

THE BODY'S WATER REQUIREMENTS

Another widely told myth is that the human body when given time will develop a certain capacity to withstand periods of dehydration—that it will require less water after it becomes accustomed to the heat. This is just not true. Studies indicate that, although psychological thirst may be reduced, physiological thirst

192

is not affected. Given the same amount of physical activity, a person who has spent an extended period under desert conditions will physiologically require the same amount of drinking water as one who has not.

The four variables that affect water requirements are: (1) air temperature, (2) exercise, (3) food intake, and (4) health. The first two can be graphically understood by reference to Figure 11-1: Expected Survival Time in the Desert. As temperature and exercise rise, so do water requirements. Ingestion of food also causes the body to require additional water as a means for digestion and assimilation. Furthermore, various pathological conditions may increase the body's requirements.

WATER RATIONING

Rationing drinking water is counterproductive. In general, it is safe to say that under desert conditions you should drink when you are thirsty whether or not you have adequate water. When you scrimp on water you soon reduce the body's efficiency and likely reduce survival chances.

Loss of efficiency begins with relatively slight water losses. For example, a $2\frac{1}{2}$ percent body weight loss (about $1\frac{1}{2}$ quarts) will result in a 50 percent loss in efficiency. Although it may be impossible to predict exactly how much a person operating at peak efficiency might accomplish, it is safe to say that a 50 percent drop will not *enhance* accomplishment.

Let's look at an analogy. Using containers of water with identical holes punched in them to represent two people under the same desert conditions, it is possible to clearly understand what happens in water rationing.

The holes release a gallon of water (sweat) a day, a condition possible in very hot deserts. At the end of the first day, both cans are down by a gallon from their ideal levels. There are only two gallons of reserve water available. One gallon is poured into the first can, bringing it's level back to normal. But in an effort to conserve and ration water, only a cup of the remaining gallon is added to the second can. So the second can is still down almost a full gallon; the cup of water did virtually nothing to reduce its water deficit. By the end of the second day the first can will be down only a gallon, while the second is nearly two gallons low, even after another cup is poured in.

In human terms, the first can has had sufficient water during most of the two-day period to allow efficient operation. However, the second can has been extremely low and is operating at greatly reduced efficiency for most of the time. The improved efficiency in the first case could enable a person to develop shelter and be in a better survival condition in the long run.

Efforts to conserve body moisture include avoidance of wind. The drying effect of the wind can be profound. Shelter formed either from brush fastened into a crude windbreak or supplied by existing rocks or vegetation may assist.

No walking at all

MAXIMUM DAILY TEMPERATURE (°F) IN SHADE	AVAILABLE WATER PER MAN, U.S. QUARTS					
	0	1 Qt	2 Qts	4 Qts	10 Qts	20 Qts
	DAYS OF EXPECTED SURVIVAL					
120°	2	2	2	2.5	3	4.5
110	3	3	3.5	4	5	7
100	5	5.5	6	7	9.5	13.5
90	7	8	9	10.5	15	23
80	9	10	11	13	19	29
70	10	11	12	14	20.5	32
60	10	11	12	14	21	32
50	10	11	12	14.5	21	32

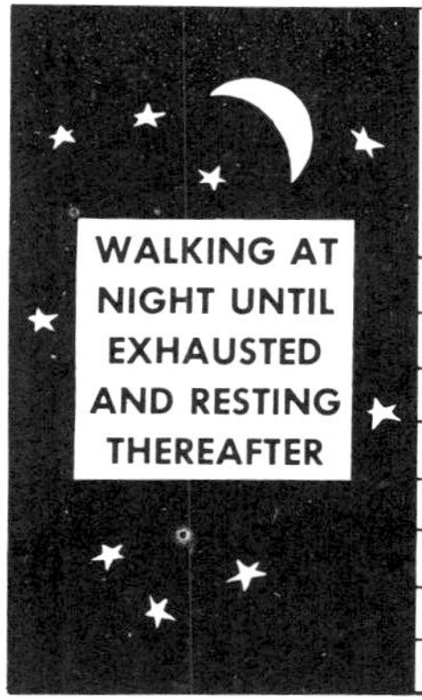

Walking at night until exhausted and resting thereafter

MAXIMUM DAILY TEMPERATURE (°F) IN SHADE	AVAILABLE WATER PER MAN, U.S. QUARTS					
	0	1 Qt	2 Qts	4 Qts	10 Qts	20 Qts
	DAYS OF EXPECTED SURVIVAL					
120°	1	2	2	2.5	3	
110	2	2	2.5	3	3.5	
100	3	3.5	3.5	4.5	5.5	
90	5	5.5	5.5	6.5	8	
80	7	7.5	8	9.5	11.5	
70	7.5	8	9	10.5	13.5	
60	8	8.5	9	11	14	
50	8	8.5	9	11	14	

Figure 11-1 Survival time in the desert. (Courtesy of United States Air Force and by permission of Dr. E. F. Adolph)

Avoid sitting or lying on the ground if it has been in the direct sun. An improvised platform a foot off the ground is ideal, but a 6-inch elevation may reduce the temperature by 30 or more degrees. The surface temperature of dark-colored rocks may reach as high as 160°F!

If you are exhausted and must sit or lie down in a sandy area, first scrape away at least 3 inches of dirt or sand. This will reduce the surface temperature of your seat by up to 30°.

Keep your mouth closed. Breathe only through the nose. Mouth breathing dries the oral cavity and the mucous membranes of the throat quickly and will greatly enhance the sensation of thirst. Because of this, smoking is inadvisable. It tends to promote mouth breathing, and the inhaled smoke is often very warm and will further dehydrate the mouth and throat. Strictly avoid alcohol. As we have seen before, alcohol accelerates dehydration. The process of conversion of alcohol to sugar in the body requires water. In effect, drinking alcohol is like eating. And in a water short situation, no food should be eaten.

WEATHER

Storms in desert country can be extremely violent. Especially during summer months, thunderstorms may develop during the afternoon and evening hours as rising hot air cools and clouds form. This effect is often enhanced over mountains, mesas, and buttes. Thunderstorms should, however, be regarded as a potential hazard rather than a reliable source of water. Winds gusting up to 70 mph may precede or be part of the storm's passage. These are likely to generate a sand or dust storm of spectacular proportions. The daylight gives way to dusk and ultimately to darkness, while visibility may be reduced to almost zero. Dust and grit fill the air and seep into everything including the nose and mouth. A moist or dry handkerchief will help under these circumstances.

Place it over the mouth and nose, and breathe through it to filter out the debris. Hail, sometimes of baseball-sized stones, often falls from these storms. A person caught unprotected can be killed by large hailstones. Some desert thunderstorms may produce only thunder, lightning, and wind. Others give way to intense cloudbursts. One at Grand Canyon National Park's South Rim dropped $2\frac{1}{2}$ inches of rain in 20 minutes. Two hikers ascending the Bright Angel Trail were swept away in the resulting flashflood and killed.

FLASHFLOODS

Never establish camp in a dry wash or for that matter in the lowest areas in the environment. Be suspicious and cautious any time thunderheads build in the afternoon (Figure 11-2). Although no rain may fall in your immediate area, flashflooding may still endanger you. Storms several miles away may be filling

Figure 11-2   Thunderheads building with rain streamers beneath. (Paul H. Risk)

tributaries with turbulent rushing water. Anyone who has witnessed a desert flashflood or its aftermath will certainly take every precaution. Sand, gravel, rocks, and boulders sometimes half the size of a house or larger come careening down a watercourse. Anything caught in the path of the flood is subjected to the same action as that of an ore crusher. Victims of these floods are frequently unrecognizable, having been so severely mauled and beaten by the debris in the water. Besides stony materials, bushes, branches, and entire trees frequently are carried along by the force of the torrent.

Ordinarily, a flashflood caused by rain at some distance from your location will provide no warning. And it need not be deep to be devastating. Many such floods cover the desert with water about 2 to 4 feet deep. But they strike with such force that victims can be swept off their feet. And, once down, there is almost no chance of regaining footing.

Narrow canyons are especially dangerous since there may be no way to climb out as the water rushes through. Some years ago a group of Boy Scouts and their leaders were caught in a portion of Zion National Park called The Narrows as a huge wall of water descended upon them. The water struck with virtually no warning and five were killed.

On August 10, 1981, while this chapter was being written, the author witnessed a massive thunderhead building west of the Moapa Valley near Las Vegas, Nevada. Within minutes a violent windstorm developed, followed by torrential rains. The storm passed, but a short time later water began coursing down several of the dry washes in the area. Where moments before only dry sand had been, a wall of water, at times 30 feet deep, surged into Logandale and Overton. Diversion dikes gave way and, with a sound like a freight train, water covered large areas of the valley. Cellar doors burst, and in one case a woman was swept down the steps as her basement filled with water. She was just able to swim to a window and climb out. Large double-wide house trailers were picked up and flung about like toys. The railroad right-of-ways were washed out in several locations, and there were many twisted tracks. Hundreds of people occupied emergency shelters during the night as secondary floods poured down the tributary streams of the area. Luckily, the office in which the manuscript for this book was housed was spared.

Following the passage of such storms, depressions in rocky surfaces are often filled with rainwater and can provide for the needs of a large party. This water, providing it has not flowed in from a contaminated location, will be pure. It should be allowed to settle and may then be used as needed.

Although these water-filled depressions—called *tanks* in the western United States—may hold water only for several days after storms, they almost miraculously become spawning grounds for aquatic and amphibious creatures that have lain dormant in caked mud at their bottoms. The water may swarm with them. Simply strain them out through a shirt and utilize the water. To be on the safe side, use water purification chemicals or boil the water when it has reached this stage.

WATER SOURCES AND INDICATORS

In Chapter 6, *Water Procurement and Treatment*, we looked at some desert sources where one can find water. Here are some others.

SOURCES

Plants are among the best sources of water in an arid region. Ripe cactus fruit is largely water and is also pleasant to eat. But the fruit of the prickly pear cactus (Figure 11-3) received that name for a reason. The white spots or slightly fuzzy appearing areas on the surface are made up of almost microscopic, pointed hairs. When the fruit is handled, they stick in the skin and feel like small fibers of spun glass or steel splinters. Hence the name. So pick them with care using

Figure 11-3 Prickly pear cactus with mature fruit ready for harvesting. (Paul H. Risk)

gloves or a layer of cloth to protect the hands. It is a good idea to pare the skin before any further use is made of them. The inner pulp is juicy, sweet, and filled with seeds of about the right size to get stuck between your teeth. In a nonsurvival setting, they make excellent jelly.

The fleshy pads of the prickly pear cactus, handled with care to avoid the sharp spines, may be skinned or the spines burned off. The pulp, although not sweet, is moist and can alleviate thirst.

> **Note:** There are plants that look like cacti in certain parts of the world that are actually of the family Euphorbiaceae. They have a milky sap and are very poisonous. Any cactuslike plant that oozes milky sap should not be used either for food or water.

Yucca (see Figure 11-4) is a plant that occurs in deserts of various parts of the world. Its fruit, when ripe, is also moist and may help to slake thirst.

The agave or century plant (see Figure 11-5) is another supplier of moisture. Both the stalk and the fruit can be used for this purpose.

Both yucca and agave fruit are also good sources of food since they are high in sugar content.

Other sources of water, most discussed in Chapter 6, include dew, dry washes and streambeds, cliffs, seeps, perched water tables, and stills.

INDICATORS

Animal Movement
All animals require water to some extent, though some like the kangaroo rat may manufacture it solely from food. Nonetheless, most animals must have some source of liquid water. Be alert to birds especially in the early morning or at late afternoon and evening. Quail, pigeons, doves, parrots, as well as other birds, often fly toward water at these times and their flight patterns may help locate drinking water. Sometimes birds may be seen circling a water source or their chirping and singing may give away its location. Game trails made by deer, antelope, cattle, or other animals often lead to water. An aerial view may show these trails clearly.

Plant indicators of moisture include cottonwoods, willows, tamarisk, cattail, sedges, and arrow weed. However, water in these locations may be at some depth and require much energy to obtain.

SHELTER AND TRAVEL
Emphasis has already been placed on the importance of keeping clothed. Where possible, the clothing should be light in color to reflect as much sunlight as possible and also porous to permit good vapor passage. Long sleeves and long

pants are recommended, not only to reduce evaporative loss of water but to protect against brush, briars, and snake bite. (Loose pant legs will certainly not stop a snake's fangs but will provide an indefinite, unsubstantial target. The result is likely to be a hit on the loose pants material rather than a solid strike into a bare leg or ankle.)

Headgear is advisable but not for the reasons often given. There appears to be no correlation between wearing a hat and protection from heatstroke or heat exhaustion. The human body is able to adapt to a variety of circumstances, and the brains will *not* bake without a hat in the desert. However, the hat does help to shade the eyes and protect the face, ears, and neck from what might be serious sunburn. But, if the crown of the hat is not well ventilated, the temperature on the top of the head can be far higher than it would without the hat. It is then like wearing a hotbox on the head.

Another method of protecting the neck is to hang loose material down the back of the head and over the shoulders. If they are available, leaves from palms or other vegetation may be used to make an improvised hat/sunshade.

If impure water is available it may be used to dampen clothing to increase evaporative cooling and reduce the body's need for water.

Travel, as in most areas, is not recommended. Not only will travel likely take the survivor out of the area being searched, but the heat of the desert makes it dangerous. As the temperature advances above 100°F, travel becomes increasingly hazardous. By referring to Figure 11-1, it can be seen that traveling only at night compared with no travel at all decreases survival expectancy by about 50 percent. But, if travel is deemed necessary, it should be done during the coolest portion of the day. This is certainly the hours of darkness. A person traveling then may be able to move up to 20 miles on a gallon of water, while daytime travel at temperatures above 105 may only allow movement for 10 miles or less.

Leave a note at the original campsite. Build trail markers along the path of travel. Then stop and set up camp. Shade is of great importance. If the ground surface has been heated by the sun, scrape off the top 3 inches of sand. Arrange whatever is available such as sticks, brush, or other vegetation to form an improvised shade. This may take the form of the typical lean-to, A-frame or other shelter. If tarps or ground cloths are available, use them folded over double in order to have an insulating air space between. Aluminized blankets should be arranged with the reflective surface toward the sun. This will not only protect the survivor but also form a bright signal easily visible to passing aircraft. Stones may be used for the basic support part of any shelter. And, in some areas, there may be stone outcrops that will be usable as part of the shelter.

Sometimes, caves or erosional features will be present. But, be careful. The twilight zone at the entrance of caves may be a home to creatures such as scorpions, spiders, and snakes. They do not make cooperative roommates.

SIGNALS

Visibility on the desert is often great because of the low humidity. This can be both a curse and a blessing. Mountains and other natural features appear to be much closer than they are. There may be a great temptation to hike to a land feature that is actually miles away. On the other hand, signals are visible for long distances. Signaling may be done to advantage during the night. A fire in a strange location may excite the curiosity of a local inhabitant. Three certainly will. Pyrotechnic devices such as railroad or highway flares may also be used at night to attract attention.

As in any other area, arrange extra clothing or vehicle parts into an X on the ground or use vegetation for the same purpose.

Desert vegetation such as creosote bush even though green, contains an oily substance that burns intensely and produces dense black smoke. Try several kinds of plant material until you find one that will do the job.

Because of the many days of sunny weather, mirrors, shiny metal sheets, pieces of plastic or glass from aircraft, or automobile windows will work well to flash reflective signals. They may also be placed on the ground so that they will function without tending.

USEFUL PLANTS
YUCCA

The Yucca (Figure 11-4) is truly a general purpose plant. Its root, pounded in water, will yield a frothy soapy substance that is ideal for washing. In fact, it has been suggested as the best detergent for cleaning Navajo rugs.

The leaves are tough and fibrous and have for generations been carefully split and shaped and their ends used to apply paint to Hopi pottery. Either dried or allowed to rot in water, the fibers may be easily separated from the leaf and can then be twisted into a tough cord. If done carefully, the sharp spine on the end of each long leaf can be removed with fibers still attached and used as an already threaded needle. Hopis use the leaf fiber for making baskets, bleaching some in the sun, and allowing some to dry in darkness to retain a darker, greenish coloration.

When flowering time comes, a stalk arises from the center of the leaves. It attains a height of 2 to 4 or more feet depending on the species. Cream-colored blossoms then develop from the buds. Both the buds and the flowers are edible and delicious. They may be eaten raw or cooked by roasting, boiling, or baking. By mid or late summer the Yucca fruit has formed and is ripening. In some species it is as large as a banana. In fact, Banana Yucca is its common name. Containing thin black seeds, this fruit is edible raw or cooked. It is very sweet and in fact has been used to make candy. The Hopi Indians collected the

Figure 11-4 Yucca with mature fruit. (Paul H. Risk)

fruit when ripe, chewed it in a communal get-together, spat it into a large container, and carefully boiled it down. As it thickened to the required point, the mass of sugary material was poured out on a flat rock and allowed to congeal. It often spent a couple of days on the rock, outdoors. Since it was sweet, most every insect that could crawl or fly headed for it and became attached to its sticky surface. This seemed to bother no one since the large pancake was rolled up (enclosing the insects like raisins in a cinnamon roll) and sliced. The slices were then placed on the roofs of the dwellings to dry in the sun for about 10 days. By this time, they were nearly bulletproof but made an excellent candy or sweetener.

Of course, the insects encased in the candy were merely bits of protein. Any microorganisms would have been rendered harmless by the very high osmotic pressure of the sugar—the same reason fruit and other things are canned in sugar syrup.

AGAVE (CENTURY PLANT)

Although the plant does not take a hundred years to bloom, they often wait 15 to 20 years (Figure 11-5). Perhaps the first botanist to wait for this flower to bloom coined the common name out of pure frustration.

The base of the plant can be roasted. In fact, it was cooked this way in huge stone-lined pits in the western United States by Native Americans. Its flower

Figure 11-5 Century Plant with flower/seed stalk. This plant has completed its cycle and is now dead. (Paul H. Risk)

stalk is usually much taller than the Yucca. It may reach 15 or more feet, sometimes growing at a rate of 6 inches in a single day. High in moisture and sugar, this plant can represent an important part of a survivor's checklist. The stalk can be cut into segments and the center eaten raw or cooked. The young buds and flowers, as in the case of the Yucca, are also edible as are the fruits.

Agave leaves are also fibrous and can supply any needed cordage or fiber. As well as having a sharp spine at the end of each leaf, there are also recurved teeth along the leaf margin. Since these teeth are turned toward the heart of the plant, it is easy to push the hand down into the leaves but very uncomfortable to remove it—especially with any speed.

MESQUITE

Both the Screw Bean Mesquite and its straight-pod relative (Figures 11-6 and 11-7) produce beans that are excellent food sources. This is one of the bean producers whose fruit is not toxic. But it is well to realize that many beans found in nature are poisonous.

202   HOT WEATHER EMERGENCIES: ARID REGIONS

Figure 11-6   Mesquite with mature beans. (Paul H. Risk)

Figure 11-7   Screw bean mesquite with fruit. (Paul H. Risk)

The most important source of nutrition from the Mesquite is the pod itself. The seeds contained therein are like little ball bearings and to attempt to bite one is to invite dental disaster. Their seed coat is so hard that if eaten whole they will pass through the alimentary canal unscathed. The result is that many large, mature clumps of Mesquite now occur around Native American waste areas dating back to the ancient past.

The pods have a distinct though mild, sweet, floury flavor and may be eaten raw or cooked. When they are mature, they are ordinarily heavily infested with the larvae of a small weevil. But, if they are not visually examined, this will never be revealed since the larvae are not the least bit apparent to the taste.

Mesquite wood is very hard. It resists rot and can be used to manufacture eating utensils and bowls or as a source of pegs, posts, and poles. However, it is very hard to cut without proper tools.

JUNIPER

Juniper (Figure 11-8) is usually referred to as Cedar in most of the West and Southwest. Technically, there are no native Cedars in the United States. Real Cedars are found natively only in North Africa and Asia. Nevertheless, the wood of the Juniper is reddish at its heart and aromatic in the same way as Cedar. Its berries when ripe are edible, although the author has not found them to be particularly pleasant. They have a resinous, strong flavor. It has been said people who enjoy gin will find these berries just fine. (Gin is flavored with Juniper berries.)

Juniper bark is very fibrous and peels easily from the tree. Generations of Native Americans diapered their babies and started their fires with this bark.

Figure 11-8   Juniper with fruit. (Paul H. Risk)

204

Pounded on a rock, the fibers fuzz out and become very soft. In this way they make a very absorbent, clothlike material. The same technique produces an excellent tinder.

PINE NUTS

The seeds of many pines are large enough to serve as a high-protein, high-energy food. Most notable in high desert areas are the Pinyon Pines. Their seeds, which usually ripen in October, may be as large as a peanut and delicious raw or roasted. The procedure for gathering is the same no matter what pine is involved. The seeds are found between the cone scales (Figures 11-9 and 11-10). Pinyon cones are usually very pitchy so the process is messy. But the seeds, usually referred to as pine nuts by locals, are well worth the mess. Anyone who has ever tried to purchase them knows that they sell like gold. Pine seeds are usually better tasting if they are lightly roasted before eating.

Since the cones of many of the pines are so pitchy, they are excellent for starting fires, burning even when wet. Knots from the Pinyon are also very good fuel.

Figure 11-9   Pinyon pine tree. (Paul H. Risk)

Figure 11-10   Pinyon cone with nuts (seed). (Paul H. Risk)

USEFUL ANIMALS

Since essentially all animals of the desert are edible, there is no need to discuss most of them. A few that are representative of this environment will be mentioned.

JACKRABBITS AND COTTONTAIL RABBITS

These may be shot or snared. At certain times of the year grubs (fly larvae) may be found in fluid-filled pockets under their skin. Although the appearance is somewhat repulsive, they in no way render the animal unfit for food.

However, if the animal appears unusually lethargic or the liver is speckled with small cream or yellowish spots, it may have tularemia. The disease is transmittable to humans. On the other hand, it is most often spread through open wounds in the process of skinning or handling. Since by this time you may have already contracted the disease, don't waste the meat. Cooking renders it harmless. Wash hands well if possible. A member of the party without scratches on their hands should be delegated to the duty of preparing any other rabbits. Tularemia is easily treated with antibiotics.

PORCUPINE

Easily killed with a blow to the head, these animals may be picked up afterward by grasping their underside where there are no quills. They do not have the capability of throwing quills. They simply are *not* walking missile launchers. But, when threatened, they put their nose between their forelegs and circle to keep their tail toward an enemy. If the aggressor gets too close, they suddenly swat with the tail. This vigorous movement may occasionally dislodge a quill. But they are not purposely thrown.

Porcupines are generally found in the high desert where their diet is often bark from conifers. As a result, their flavor is much like the pine trees on which they have been dining. They should be carefully skinned and cooked.

RATS AND MICE

The desert seems to abound in small rodents. They may be snared during the night with small slip nooses and may then be skinned, gutted, and prepared.

GRASSHOPPERS AND CRICKETS

In some desert areas these may be abundant. They can be caught by hand, but an improvised net made from a T-shirt or undershirt will increase success. Skewered on a thin, green stick, they may then be roasted over the coals. Or, a hot rock will serve the same purpose. The taste is not bad, with grasshoppers generally more pleasant eating than crickets.

GRUBS

Grubs are the larvae of various insects. These are usually found under the bark of dead trees and are delicious roasted.

DESERT SNAILS

These, in some areas, can be a very important food source. They should be well cooked before eating.

OTHER FOOD SOURCES

There are many other animal foods available, including deer, sheep, quail, birds, skunks, racoons, bobcats, coyotes, ground and tree squirrels, lizards, snakes, and wild pigs. Many of them will require a gun in order to add them to the menu. Others are simply too rare or sparsely distributed to worry about.

MEDICAL CONSIDERATIONS
HYPERTHERMIA

This is the opposite of hypothermia. Instead of a fatal cooling of the body's core, a dangerous or terminal overheating of the body takes place.

Heat Stroke

Caused by the improper functioning of the body's heat control center—the hypothalamus—this condition is the most dangerous of the problems encountered in hot temperatures.

The core temperature may exceed 106°F and, unless quickly lowered, death is imminent. There is danger of permanent brain damage, even if life continues, from temperatures this high.

Weakness, nausea, and headache sometimes coupled with heat cramps are symptoms of approaching heat stroke. Just before collapse sweat stops as the hypothalamus malfunctions. Blood pressure and pulse rate rise. The skin feels dry and hot to the touch, and the victim quickly loses consciousness. The face is often red.

They must be removed from the sun and placed in the shade. Cooling must take place rapidly. If there is any way to do it, immerse them in cool or cold water. Otherwise, pour water over their body. Fanning will help to increase evaporative cooling. Elevate the head and give no stimulants. If possible, the victim should be evacuated to a hospital.

Heat Exhaustion

Another heat problem is heat exhaustion. It is characterized by a cold, clammy skin; weak, rapid pulse; and low blood pressure. The victim may be nauseated and vomit but is generally conscious. The symptoms are very similar to shock and the treatment basically the same. They should be in a supine position with the head either level with the feet or at a slightly lower position. They may feel cold and a light blanket may be placed over them. However, the problem is too much heat and exertion, so don't overload with blankets. They may be given fluids by mouth with some salt added.

SALT REQUIREMENTS

Salts—especially sodium and potassium—are deeply involved in the chemical balance of the body. Muscle contraction and nerve transmission as well as a number of critical regulatory functions are closely related to the body's need for these substances. Perhaps because of their vital nature, they are lost from the body only under extremely stressful conditions.

Over the years it has been popularly assumed that salt must be taken orally whenever the body sweated a great deal. However, recently this has largely been shown to be inaccurate. In fact, it is very possible and easy to take an overdose of salt. Under all but the most arduous conditions, it is simply not necessary to take salt tablets. A steel foundry worker laboring under intense heat and great physical exertion may need to supplement salt intake. But the average hiker, climber, or hunter does not. In fact, they are more likely to induce nausea and vomiting by the use of salt tablets.

208

Furthermore, any time it *is* deemed necessary to take salt, adequate water should be available to balance it out. In desert survival conditions it is almost never possible to get enough water to do this.

Also, salt or salt tablets that dissolve directly in the stomach are likely to cause distress. There are wax-treated tablets and tablets covered with an enteric coating that allow them to pass into the intestinal tract before dissolving. They are highly recommended.

As a general rule, don't worry about salt intake.

INSECTS AND ARACHNIDS

Scorpions

Varying in size from an inch or less to well over 7 inches, scorpions have a stinger located on the last joint of their flexible tail (Figure 11-11). Although these eight-legged creatures—and therefore arachnids, not insects—have well-defined pincers, they do not sting with them. The pincers are for holding food.

With the exception of the small Bark Scorpion, there are none in the United States that have the potential of inflicting a life-threatening sting. The Bark Scorpion, although more dangerous than most scorpions, is likely to cause death only in a very small child, an elderly individual, or a hypersensitive person. The Bark Scorpion's sting causes pain at the site, numbness, restlessness, and possible respiratory impairment. There may also be fever and a fast pulse. Although a fast pulse may merely be an indication of fear.

Figure 11-11   Scorpions. (Paul H. Risk)

The sting of other scorpions may be intensely painful, but there are generally none of the neurological symptoms such as numbness and difficulty in breathing. Some have said their sting hurts far more than a wasp's.

Scorpions are usually found under rocks, in crevices, and beneath bark. They may also be found in the tangles of grass and in other material lodged along with the watermark of washes.

Cooling the sting site may help to alleviate pain. If dangerous symptoms are manifest, the victim should be transported to a hospital.

Velvet Ants or Cowkillers

These wingless female wasps are the fuzzy or velvety insects sometimes seen running along the desert floor (Figure 11-12). They will generally avoid contact if given a chance. Although their sting is painful, they are not particularly dangerous to humans. And they certainly do not kill cows.

Tarantulas

Often covered with hair and very large, these spiders are far more feared than necessary (Figure 11-13). Over the past ten years, they have begun to appear in pet shops. Those who have kept them say they are docile and they handle them with little concern. Handling them is, however, not to be recommended. Their bite is about as painful as a bee sting. And while they are not particularly

Figure 11-12   Velvet ants. These are female wingless wasps. (Paul H. Risk)

210 HOT WEATHER EMERGENCIES: ARID REGIONS

Figure 11-13   Tarantula. (Paul H. Risk)

dangerous, secondary infection may create more severe problems. At certain times, the desert seems to come alive as hundreds of tarantulas migrate.

It is good practice to shake out boots in the morning and hang clothing where spiders and scorpions will not crawl in. Bedding should also be hung off the ground when not in use. And if possible, the bed should be off the ground to minimize sharing it with an undesirable companion.

Black Widow Spider

The Black Widow, although carrying a neurotoxic venom, is not as fearsome as popular stories would have us believe (Figure 11-14). They frequent dark holes and crevices, and a favorite location is under the seat in old-fashioned outhouses. As a result, a significant number of bites occur on portions of the anatomy exposed during the utilization of the old "one holers." Otherwise, a bite would only be likely if a person reached into a dark area inhabited by a Widow.

Black Widows do not always have a clearly defined hour glass marking on the underside of the abdomen. Variations are considerable, and the patterns may change as the spider grows and molts the old exoskeleton. Some of the variations along with the oft-seen hour glass are shown in Figure 11-15.

Figure 11-14   Black widow spider exhibiting the typical marking on the abdomen. (Courtesy of Thomas Smyth, Jr. Ph.D.)

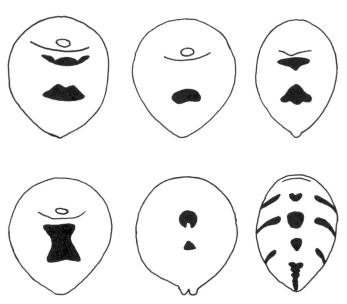

*Figure 11-15 Marking variations that may be found on black widow spiders.
(Rosalie R. Risk)*

The author has had the dubious privilege of having been bitten twice by
Black Widows. During the first episode, the classic symptoms of general malaise,
nausea, abdominal rigidity, and extreme abdominal pain and muscle spasms
were manifest. These symptoms are much like that of appendicitis or peritoni-
tis. As a result, I was rushed to the hospital with that in mind. It was not until
a white cell count disclosed no startling elevation and the spider was found
dead in my bed that a careful examination located the bite. Symptoms subsided
of their own accord, as is usually the case. The second bite occurred several
years later and did not elicit any symptoms.

Although the bite can be dangerous to all ages, it is seldom fatal. Chill the
bite area with cool, moist cloths and evacuate the victim.

Desert Centipede
A bite from this animal is very painful but not particularly dangerous except in
cases of anaphylactic shock (Figure 11-16). Cool, moist compresses will reduce
pain. The symptoms merely have to run their course.

Figure 11-16   Desert centipede. (Hal H. Harrison/Photo Researchers)

SNAKES AND LIZARDS

Rattlesnakes

These snakes have retractable fangs, and with a solid strike, they can penetrate a boot (Figure 11-17). Called pit vipers, they have heat-sensitive organs on each side of their head. However, like most snakes, they are shy and, when given the opportunity, will avoid contact with humans. Do not reach into places you cannot see. Shake bedding and anything else left lying on the ground to minimize your chances of accidental encounters. They do not stalk humans and will bite only if startled, stepped on, or grasped. The bite is rapid, but they can only reach forward about one-third of their body length. Easily killed with a stick, they are edible. Cut off the head to avoid accidental contact with the fangs, and clean and cook the body.

Their venom is hemolytic and proteolytic—attacking red blood cells and

Figure 11-17   Rattlesnake. (Paul H. Risk)

YELLOW OR WHITE
BAND SEPARATES
BLACK AND RED

BLACK NOSE

Figure 11-18   Coral snake. (Courtesy of United States Air Force)

muscle tissue. Permanent muscle damage may result from their bite, which can require weeks or months to treat.

Coral Snakes

Usually very retiring, these brightly banded snakes are very small and do not have retractable fangs (Figure 11-18). To inject venom, they must grasp and chew. Instead of the more triangular head of pit vipers, they have blunt heads and a tapering tail. Their mouths are so small that they would be successful only in biting a finger. To have that happen, the victim would have to pick one up.

They possess wide red and black bands, separated by narrower yellow ones. The Mountain King Snake, which is not venomous, has red and black bands that are not separated by yellow. Hence, the saying, "Red on black, venom lack. Red on yellow, kill a fellow."

The Coral Snake has neurotoxic venom. The bite is not painful, with only a slight numbness at the site. Subsequent symptoms involve the heart and respiratory centers and may cause difficulty in breathing and heart failure.

Gila Monster

To be bitten by a Gila monster requires either extreme youth or gross lack of caution (Figure 11-19). Looking like a beaded bag with legs, these interesting animals do not have retractable fangs. They generally are slow moving but, when threatened, can muster a surprising amount of speed. An animal, human, or other unwelcome guest, approaching too close and attempting to pick one up, will find immediately that they can move their head with lightning speed

Figure 11-19   Gila monster. (Allan D. Cruickshank/Photo Researchers)

and that they clamp down like a bulldog. In fact, when approached from the rear they can, in an instant, jerk around and snap at an assailant.

The venom is neurotoxic and flows along grooves in the teeth of the lower jaw. Because of the low efficiency of the venom-transport mechanism, it is unlikely that a significant amount of the venom would enter the body. If bitten, simply grasp the animal behind the head and yank it off or cut the jaws apart.

Treatment would include a ligature above the bite site, application of cool, moist cloths, and medical treatment. Since the venom is neurotoxic, difficulty in breathing and cardiac irregularity would be included in the symptoms.

Tales about them include *myths* that (1) once bitten, the jaws cannot be opened until sundown; (2) their breath is poisonous; (3) they are poisonous to touch. If one is seen, consider yourself lucky. Most desert travelers will never see one in their lives. It is an interesting animal and one that need not excite much anxiety.

12

HOT WEATHER EMERGENCIES: TROPICS

Whenever people talk about survival, invariably tropical areas come up in the conversation. The general consensus seems to be that they are exclusively steaming jungles that are filled with howling wildlife bent on taking human life. Actually, tropical areas are easier to survive in than many less exotic environments.

Animals of the tropics are seldom dangerous to humans. Snakes may never be seen, although there are many varieties. Travel is often very difficult when moving cross country, but waterways are frequently numerous and civilization is usually found along them.

The greatest dangers in tropical areas are infection and disease. Especially in hot, humid areas, slight scratches heal very slowly and tend to become infected or develop fungus disease. Insects carrying disease such as mosquitos, biting flies, and kissing bugs can transmit serious illness.

However, contaminated water is one of the prime sources of disease. And in relation to *any* disease considerations, keep in mind that native populations may be immune to a disease that can completely debilitate a stranger. Just because you observe others doing something such as drinking directly from a stream or eating food that may be unsafe does not mean you can get away with it.

Tropical environments vary widely around the world. Mangrove swamps and tropical rain forests probably come the closest to matching what people expect when they contemplate survival in the tropics. But there are also tropical scrub and thorn forests that are fire climax regions as well as open grasslands or savannas. Some tropical areas are semiarid.

Since most of the drier areas require action identical to that discussed in desert survival (Chapter 11), this chapter deals largely with more moist tropical areas. Suggestions given here apply well to areas of the south and southeast United States where conditions can almost exactly duplicate those of Central and South America.

HEALTH AND HYGIENE

HEAT

Although the temperature in tropical areas may be lower than in deserts, the humidity is usually much higher. Because of this, the body is less able to cool itself through the evaporation of perspiration. The result is a more extreme heat load on the body. This can be a serious problem. Heat-caused illness often occurs at relatively low temperatures in moist tropical areas. Care must be exercised whenever exertion is necessary in such locations. Clothing, in order to increase cooling, should be light colored and loose fitting. What might have been only uncomfortable in drier conditions may bring about serious illness or death in humid, hot areas.

WOUNDS

Even very minor wounds may become infected in the moist tropics. Not only do they not heal rapidly, but they tend to become prime sites for the invasion of fungus spores and subsequent disease. The author abraded his hand very slightly on a machete scabbard during a jungle survival exercise. The wound was cleaned and an antiseptic swabbed on it. It almost immediately appeared to be drying and improving. But, by afternoon, it was again moist and oozing serum. Again, it was cleaned and disinfected. Once more it appeared to be healing. But within a few hours it was again moist, inflamed, and oozing. During a period of a week in the rain forest, virtually no healing took place. But once back in the low humidity and cooler temperatures of the Officers' Quarters at the base, it had almost disappeared within 36 hours.

So, try to keep wounds as dry as possible. This may mean dressing them twice a day. Antiseptics such as Merthiolate, Mercurochrome, or even isopropyl (rubbing) alcohol are counterproductive and probably should not be used. Iodine should be avoided like the plague. Most of these compounds are tinctures (the active component is dissolved in alcohol), and their alcohol content causes tissue damage. In addition, the active ingredients, especially in the case of iodine, cause rather spectacular tissue damage, destroying some of the cells in the wound. Because of this the dead cells become ideal candidates for decomposition and sites for the start of infection. This recommendation applies to all environments. A few years ago most first aid books recommended the use of these antiseptic compounds. But more recent information has cast serious doubt on their use.

Simply wash the wound with mild soap and pure water. If it is superficial, it may be best to avoid placing a dressing on it. Free air movement and drying are very beneficial. If a sterile dressing is necessary, it should be porous enough to not retain the moisture produced from serum and blood soaking into it. Don't be tempted to swab the wound with alcohol. Save it for washing hands or cooling hyperthermia victims. (It is interesting to note that swabbing the skin with alcohol prior to giving an injection is of value only in preventing lawsuits from people who still think it is necessary. In order to kill bacteria on the skin surface, the site would have to be immersed in isopropyl alcohol for 30 minutes! The swabbing merely moves the bacteria around a bit.)

If the wound is serious or infection has begun, an antibiotic ointment or powder may be applied.

INSECT DISEASE VECTORS

Mosquitos, flies, and to some extent, a Hemipteran, or kissing bug, are responsible for the spread of numerous diseases. A complete list of tropical diseases carried by them would be staggering and so discouraging that few people would voluntarily enter the jungle areas of the globe. In fact, most of the more exotic diseases are confined to certain microhabitats such as tree-canopy areas. Others are found only in close contact with native people. But some are essentially impossible to treat, becoming chronic. There are a few untreatable diseases, such as one form of sleeping sickness which is spread by a kissing bug, and these have a fatality rate near 99 percent. But worrying about this unrealistically will not help. Deal with those that can be avoided, prevented, or treated and just go on about your business. In other environments we seldom see people worrying themselves to death over similar killers—for example, heart disease and cancer.

Use insect repellent when available to discourage biting flies and mosquitos. Malaria and yellow fever are both transmitted by mosquitos. Oral medication is available as a preventative for malaria but must be started at least 10 days prior to entering the areas where the disease is found. It must then be taken regularly (daily or weekly depending on the drug used), during the stay, and for about 10 days after your return. Yellow fever innoculations are available through local health departments in larger cities. However, health officials will want strong reasons before they give them. Most large cities in the tropics are essentially free of malaria and yellow fever, and health authorities tend to be geared toward vacationers who may not need the protection. If your plans are more exotic and travel will take you into remote areas, it is a good idea to be immunized for whatever may be found in the outback. This may include cholera, tetanus, typhoid, and other diseases as well as those already mentioned. In some locations gamma globulin injections for protection against hepatitis are recommended. However, gamma globulin's protection is not 100 percent and some medical authorities question the validity of using it.

Head nets and mosquito netting will also be of great assistance in thwarting these disease carriers.

Human Ectoparasites
Especially in areas of human habitation, fleas, ticks, and lice may be sources of disease. If the survival situation necessitates living with native populations, try to establish a shelter for yourself. This may be impossible. If it is, be especially careful about personal hygiene, examining the body and in particular hairy areas for insects.

Fleas and lice may be physically removed by careful combing. Ticks, after inserting their mouthparts, become firmly attached and care must be exercised in their removal. Do not squeeze them. All this does is to squirt part of their liquid interior into your body and greatly increases the chances of disease and infection.

Contrary to some of the wild stories told, ticks do not have threaded heads! One old timer swore that they screwed themselves into the skin and that this process always proceeded in a counterclockwise direction. Because of this, he said, removal involved carefully twisting them clockwise (the opposite way a screw would normally be removed) until they came off!

Avoid trying to remove them with a lighted cigarette. Some have advocated the application of a lighted one to the posterior in the belief that the ticks would then quickly depart. In fact, it only fries the little critters and they die in place. Similarly, avoid pouring alcohol or iodine on them. These substances will also likely kill them before they have a chance to release themselves.

A far better procedure is to smear something oily or greasy on them. Better yet, cover them with grease. It may be lubricating grease, oil, or vaseline. This clogs their breathing apparatus and they will soon release and fall off.

FOOD

Hepatitis, cholera, and amoebic dysentery are three diseases that may be contracted through food. Occasionally, typhoid is also transmitted from a carrier via food when hands are not washed after defecation. The only prevention against amoebic dysentery is avoidance of the organism which causes it.

Uncooked or incompletely cooked meat may contain trichina cysts. Unfortunately, this disease is not that uncommon in the United States—a fact that many Europeans find appalling. Here it is usually spread through raw or poorly cooked pork. The tiny encysted organisms revitalize when taken into the human body and migrate into various muscles where they again form hard cysts.

Weakness, fever, and malaise characterize the disorder. There is no treatment for it. Where possible, avoid eating any raw or incompletely cooked meat.

Raw fruit or vegetables unless they can be peeled should also be avoided. Both amoebic dysentery and cholera are transmitted on their surface. In a survival situation involving native peoples, it may be very difficult, even impossible, to help them understand that you cannot eat certain foods or that your meat must be cooked thoroughly. This complication may breed hard feelings and be construed as insulting to your hosts.

Raw shellfish are especially good candidates as carriers of hepatitis and should definitely be avoided. Thorough cooking removes this hazard.

Raw freshwater fish may harbor parasites such as liver flukes that can be fatal. Cook all fish well. Marine fish are far less likely to have harmful parasites.

Keep shoes or boots on. Walking barefoot in the tropics is dangerous for several reasons. Thorns, sharp rocks, and sticks may damage the feet. The danger of insect or snake bites is also increased. Parasites that live in the soil may enter through the bottoms of the feet and take up residence in the body.

Even when traveling in waterways, the footgear should be worn to protect against cuts and bruises from slippery rocks or logs and to minimize the chances of stepping on harmful aquatic life.

At the end of each day, the footgear and clothing should be dried. This will reduce problems with funguses and other disease organisms that otherwise might thrive in the damp confines of the boots or clothes.

Boots may be placed upside down on stakes placed near the fire and clothing arranged on improvised racks.

Allow the feet to dry and gently massage them for a few moments. The ability to move about and obtain the basics of survival are largely determined by the condition of the feet. Treat them with care. Constantly wet feet become wrinkled, blistered, and open wounds develop if they are not cared for properly in the tropics.

WATER

One of the most important sources of disease in tropical areas is contaminated water. Assume all water to be unsafe and treat it. It is virtually a guarantee that drinking untreated water will introduce you to hepatitis, amoebic dysentery, or typhoid.

The source of contamination is human waste. Defecation and urination may be done directly into waterways, and contamination is especially heavy near settlements and villages.

The amoeba (*Endamoeba hystolytica*) that causes amoebic dysentery is very unsatisfactorily treated with chemicals. Iodine compounds are more effective but even these will not always kill the encysted form of the organism. (When hard times come upon the amoeba, it forms a spherical shape and develops an impervious wall around itself until conditions improve. In this way it can survive periods of dryness.)

The only assured methods of dealing with this amoeba are thorough boiling or filtration through an approved filter. Sand, ordinary filter paper, and activated charcoal filters are inadequate for this.

Do not underestimate the difficulties of amoebic dysentery. The organism causes a dissolving of intestinal tissue and abcesses of the liver. It can be fatal if untreated. Even with modern medical treatment, it is possible to have recurring bouts with the disease. And, its almost a certainty that a serious encounter will hospitalize the victim for up to three months during which time they may lose several feet of intestine surgically in an effort to stem the infestation.

So remember that water *may* be obtained from streams, rivers, and ponds but *must* be boiled or filtered to be safe.

WATER SOURCES
PLANTS

Palm or banana trees (Figure 12-1) may be cut off and the interior hollowed out to form a cup-shaped depression. Root pressure will continue to force water up through the trunk. This water will be clear and pure since it passed through the cell walls of the plant tissues to get to the collecting basin hollowed out. Such a cut-off tree may continue to produce good, drinkable water for 3 to 4 days. Make a leaf cover to put over it to discourage bugs from falling in. But, if they do, just strain them out. They will not hurt the water.

Coconuts
Especially in areas near the coast, the tropics may provide one of the best food and water sources—coconuts (Figure 12-2). Be advised to depend on the green nuts rather than those that are completely ripe. Ripe coconut milk makes a potent laxative in large quantities. While a severe case of diarrhea may be something to cause a good laugh under other circumstances, it is not funny in survival settings. It produces weakness and rapidly dehydrates the victim.

Green coconuts are easily opened. Cut through the pointed end of both husk and nut until you get to the fluid interior. In an immature nut the meat will not be solid and white. Instead, it will be semitransparent and rather soft. This is normal and is discussed more fully under *food sources*. The milk may be drunk directly from the fruit and is completely free from contamination.

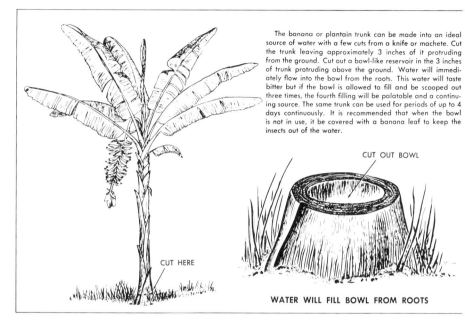

The banana or plantain trunk can be made into an ideal source of water with a few cuts from a knife or machete. Cut the trunk leaving approximately 3 inches of it protruding from the ground. Cut out a bowl-like reservoir in the 3 inches of trunk protruding above the ground. Water will immediately flow into the bowl from the roots. This water will taste bitter but if the bowl is allowed to fill and be scooped out three times, the fourth filling will be palatable and a continuing source. The same trunk can be used for periods of up to 4 days continuously. It is recommended that when the bowl is not in use, it be covered with a banana leaf to keep the insects out of the water.

CUT OUT BOWL

CUT HERE

WATER WILL FILL BOWL FROM ROOTS

Figure 12-1   Cut off banana tree showing a method for obtaining drinking water. (Courtesy of United States Air Force)

Bamboo

Hollow sections of bamboo may contain trapped rainwater and it can be located by shaking. Gurgling will identify the filled ones. Cut a notch to release the water. It too is pure.

Vines

Jungle vines or lianas can also be an important pure water source. In tropical rain forests their leafy sections may be widely separated or may only be near the top of the tree crowns. This can be 200 or more feet up. So identification by leaf or flower is not easy. Simply reach over head and cut through the vine. Then cut lower down so that a 3 to 4 foot section is removed. Tipped horizontally it will not lose water so quickly. If the fluid is clear and runs like water, taste it. If it is not sour, bitter, burning, or sticky it is safe to drink. But, if it is milky or sticky or brightly colored, it should be avoided since it is likely to be poisonous.

Jungle vines often look very much alike, so try a number of them even if they appear to be the same. When a suitable type is located, it is often possible to fill a 1-quart container from a single 4-foot section.

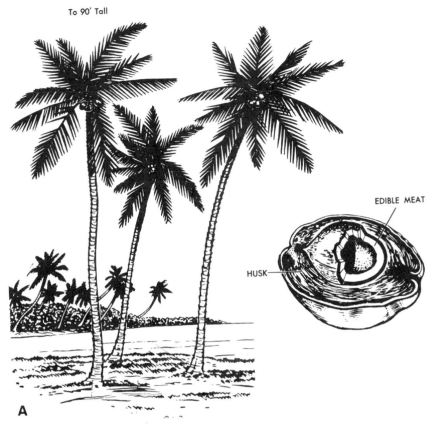

To 90' Tall

EDIBLE MEAT

HUSK

A

Figure 12-2   Coconut palm. (Courtesy of United States Air Force)

Air Plants and Other Epiphytes

If you have ever seen the top of a fresh pineapple you know what to look for. Pineapples are members of the Bromeliad family, and many have the same kind of cylindrically arranged leaves (Figure 12-3). They are usually found perched on branches or in the crotch where a limb connects to the trunk. Rainwater is usually found in the center of their leaf arrangement.

However, a whole community may also exist there, merrily swimming about. Do not be discouraged. Just strain out the various leaf bits, dirt, and insect larvae. The water is pure. (Remember, human contamination is the problem you are concerned with!) Even if there are mosquito larvae bobbing around in your Bromeliad, they cannot transmit disease in this way. They have to bite you and this they cannot do so early in their lives.

Figure 12-3   Bromeliad. (Paul H. Risk)

Hollow Trees and Other Depressions
Any place that rain may collect is fair game for drinking water. As long as there is no inlet from a potentially contaminated source, the water will be fine. In rain forests precipitation annually is from 200 to 300 inches per year, so there are many places rainwater is trapped.

Fruits
If edible, all fruits can assist in providing pure water.

RAIN

In many areas, especially during the rainy season, it will rain every day. Sometimes it never seems to stop raining! This water may be collected from a slanting ground cloth, tarp, raincoat, or shirt as discussed in Chapter 6. Or a hole can be dug, lined with a waterproof ground cloth, and used to collect water.

CAMPSITE SELECTION AND SHELTER
1. Establish your camp on the high ground above the high watermark. Mosquitos will be fewer there and chances for sleep will be better.
2. Avoid caves. Their mouths frequently harbor biting or stinging insects as well as snakes and other unfriendly roommates.

224

3. Game trails should be avoided. They may be heavily used during the night by large animals.

4. Don't seek shelter in tree tops. They may be dead and break off. Also, they often are the home of large numbers of wasps.

5. Don't sleep on the ground. Build a raised sleeping platform to lessen the opportunities for spiders, scorpions, and snakes joining you. The ground is often damp and uncomfortable.

6. Be sure only sound trees are used for hammock supports. A tree weakened by termites was selected by a trainee in jungle school. Several inches in diameter, the tree appeared sound and the student fastened one end of a hammock to the tree. During the night the tree snapped off and the upper end fell across him, causing fatal internal injuries.

7. Clear away grass and underbrush around the campsite. This makes movement easier and also makes it easier to see snakes.

8. Have a place for each item in your possession. The jungle is no place to lose items of importance to you. Each time an item is used it should be carefully replaced. Small objects seem to have a habit of falling into grass or disappearing mysteriously.

SHELTER

Lean-To

The same basic frame used in temperate forests is used in the tropics. However, the thatching material can more often be palm leaves. Banana leaves will also do a good job, as will any other broadleaf. Figures 12-4 and 12-5 show a method for splitting a palm leaf and laying it on for thatching. Note that each leaflet on the frond is concave. The split fronds should be placed on the shelter so that the concave sides are down. Banana and other broad leaves are put on like shingles, so that they overlap and shed water. Several variations are shown in Figures 12-6 and 12-7, including methods for constructing a raised sleeping platform as part of the shelter.

In savanna areas, grass huts are also a possibility but require much more energy in the collection and utilization of materials.

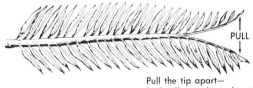

PULL

Pull the tip apart—
leaf will tear down the middle.

Figure 12-4   How to split a palm frond. (Courtesy of United States Air Force)

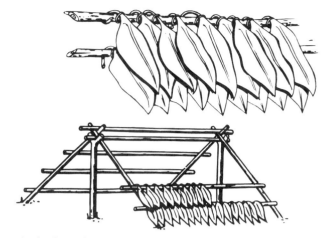

Lay the thatch shingle-fashion, with the tips of leaves pointing downward, starting from the bottom and working up, to shed the rain.

Dig a small drainage ditch just inside the eaves of your shelter and leading downhill—it will help keep the floor dry.

Figure 12-5   Thatching a hut. (Courtesy of United States Air Force)

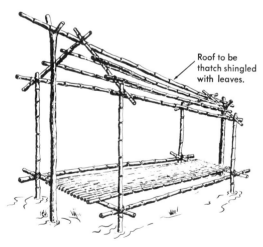

Roof to be thatch shingled with leaves.

Figure 12-6   Jungle hut frame work. (Courtesy of United States Air Force)

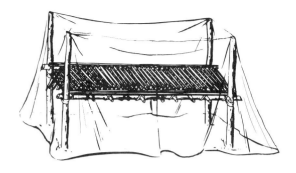

Figure 12-7   Sleeping platform. (Courtesy of United States Air Force)

TRAVEL

The tropics are areas where the rule of never traveling may need to be broken. Native populations are generally not found randomly distributed throughout the forested areas. They tend to be localized along waterways. So unless the plan is to homestead, it may be necessary to travel to a river or stream and then follow it to a village. Part of the determination to travel will depend on whether you will be missed.

Travel only during the day. At night there is too much chance of stepping on a snake or being injured by thorns or through falling. Some jungle trees have trunks covered with sharp, brittle thorns several inches long. An encounter with these can be serious. They enter the flesh and break off.

Even during the day, care is in order. Often the ground is very high in clay content and, when wet, is like walking on grease. When this surface is combined with steep terrain, a majority of the time can be spent just getting up after falling. If a fall or stumble does take place, be careful what you grab. Often a traveler grasping by reflex will take hold of a Black Palm or other very thorny plant. Look before you grab.

Scouting may help locate a trail. Follow trails wherever possible. They may be game trails or trails used by the locals in hunting, or both. But they will ordinarily lead to water sooner or later or to a village. But be careful along trails. Sometimes natives have set traps for large animals. If the ground is disturbed, covered by a grass mat, or the trail is obstructed with a cord or braided grass rope, avoid it. You may be headed for a pitfall or into an area off limits to strangers. Either could prove fatal.

Twilight is very short in the tropics. It is wise to set up camp or cease activities for the day well before it starts to get dark. Otherwise, the sudden loss of light (and it seems to rise right up out of the ground and swallow you) may endanger you.

Another misconception is that all travel in the tropics requires hacking through miles of tangled vegetation. There are actually many tropical areas through which relatively unobstructed cross-country travel is possible. But where this is not so it is usually possible to push aside the vegetation. Do this with care because some grasses have sharp, sawlike edges and can inflict deep cuts.

If cutting becomes necessary, a 14-inch machete is a great help. Make upward cuts instead of swinging the blade down as you would normally. In this way any plant juice that sprays out is deflected toward the ground rather than in the eyes. There are some plants that have very dangerous sap. Splashed in the eyes it causes blindness.

WATERWAY TRAVEL

Following waterways may be necessary in order to locate help. Floats may be improvised from any type of lightweight wood. In some forest areas balsa is available. A piece of this, 5 inches thick and 2 feet long, under each arm will make a good underarm float. The two pieces should be fastened body width apart with cord or vines.

Float with the current and keep the feet forward to ward off driftwood and rocks. But keep alert. If the current seems to be increasing or a roaring sound can be heard ahead, you may well be approaching a rapids or falls. Move to the bank and investigate on foot.

Also, floating indiscriminately down the Amazon or its tributaries may be hazardous to your health. Piranhas inhabit these waters! In such areas it may be possible to float the river on an improvised raft but capsizing can be an exciting experience!

FLOODING

Intense rains upstream may cause sudden rises in the water level of streams. Sometimes this is indicated by bits of drifting vegetation or a sudden increase in muddiness. If any of these indications occur, get out of the water and seek shelter above the high watermarks along the stream. This zone is usually indicated by grass, leaves and other debris lodged above the normal water level.

In all river or stream travel it is wise to float near the bank.

Shallow streams can be waded and may be far easier than bushwhacking. Keep shoes or boots on. A slip on rocks may bring you to a halt because of a foot injury. Carry a stick to help probe the stream bottom. This will be an aid in locating concealed potholes. Water in jungle streams is often murky, making

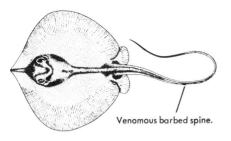

Venomous barbed spine.

Figure 12-8 Stringray showing the characteristic barb on the tail. (Courtesy of United States Air Force)

it impossible to see the bottom. The stick can also be used to turn over rocks. Turtle or lizard eggs may be found in this way.

Especially when wading in brackish (partly salty) water near the point at which freshwater streams meet the ocean, stingrays may lie along the bottom. They will get out of the way if you travel with a shuffling movement. But, if they are stepped on, the barb at the end of the tail can inflict a very painful and serious wound (Figure 12-8).

If you are wearing a pack or any kind of improvised sack, it should be equipped with quick-release capability. The slipknot will allow the pack to be quickly dropped in the event of sudden flood, falls, or other emergency. This is very important. A trainee in the U.S. Air Force Jungle School in Panama failed to take this advice. A flashflood developed and he was knocked to a sitting position with his back against a rock. The average water depth was probably not over 2 feet, but his pack filled with water and held him down. Also, water striking his chest and cascading over his head made rising doubly difficult. He drowned.

FIRE

There is generally plenty of fuel in the tropics. Some plants which are green have oils that permit them to burn. The difficulty is finding *dry* fire-building materials. The rule is the same here as in other environments. Be alert for tinder, kindling, and fuel. Gather it whenever possible. Keep the tinder in a dry location.

The frequent high humidity does not help in this process. Even material that is dead and fuzzy may be too damp to burn. Anything lying on the ground is almost assured to be too wet.

Dead palm leaves make very good fire-starting material. But be careful in gathering them. The "beards" of dead leaves that are often seen hanging under the living palm top are favorite habitats for wasps and scorpions. Palms cut down for shelter-building materials sometimes hum as they fall because of the wasp nests in them. Before grasping the dead leaves to cut them loose, knock them around with a stout stick to dislodge any concealed scorpions or snakes.

Bamboo is another plentiful fuel in some areas. But watch for snakes in the thickets. Also, green bamboo releases toxic fumes when burned.

SIGNALS

Especially in the rain forests, visibility from the air is almost nonexistent. Try to locate campsites near a clearing when possible so that search aircraft can see the location.

Signal fires and smoke signals (pyrotechnics) operate at a definite disadvantage in tropical areas. The high humidity tends to hold down the smoke. It drifts to a height of 15 to 20 feet and then spreads in a horizontal layer (Figure 12-9). Smoke flares may be lashed to a long pole and held over the rapidly rising heat of a large hot fire. This will force the signal smoke to rise above the tree canopy.

Radio signals tend to be less effective in the tropical rainforest areas unless the antenna is above the trees.

FOOD

Food in tropical areas is easily available. Its sources are so broad in scope that it is not possible here to discuss them completely. Therefore, only selected sources will be covered. While there are a number of toxic plants and animals unfit for eating, many are delicious.

MAMMALS

Many animals may be shot or snared along game trails. Deer, wild pigs, rodents, monkeys, bats, and squirrels are only a few. Various snakes and lizards are also available and will make excellent additions to the menu. It is only necessary to overcome food prejudices so that partaking of the rather exotic fare will be less difficult.

Most game animals are not repulsive or shocking, and survivors would have no difficulty eating them. Monkeys, however, are a different matter. Some find them particularly hard to deal with. When shot, they often die rather theatrically, screaming and clutching at themselves as they fall. Skinned, a monkey looks a great deal like a human child and it is not unusual for strong men to balk at eating them. If this is likely to be a problem for you, have someone else do the chores. Once the meat is cooked, it loses its identity and is delicious.

230

Figure 12-9   A smoke signal is held down by high humidity in the jungle. (*Jan Kolena Cole*)

Large animals should generally be left alone. This is especially true in the absence of a heavy caliber weapon. Wounding a large animal is so dangerous that it far outweighs the possible benefits of a great quantity of meat. In addition, preservation or utilization would be very difficult under survival conditions.

FISH AND SHELLFISH (FRESHWATER)

Most fresh bodies of water are potential sources of fish. They may be caught by traditional methods or speared. Construct spears using hardwood for the points. Several designs will work well (see Figure 8-37). Success may be enhanced by wading shallow areas after dark with a torch. Fish attracted by the light are easier to spear. Interestingly, piranhas are excellent eating.

Some tropical vegetation when crushed produces a fish poison that can be used to stun fish in warm water. The fish are still safe for human consumption. Plants producing fish poisons include: crushed, ripe seeds of *Barringtonia* that have stood overnight in a container and the crushed husks of green Black Walnuts.

Freshwater clams and mussels are often found in sandy areas along streams and when cooked may be important food sources.

FISH AND SHELLFISH (MARINE)

While most marine fish are edible, it is well to be aware that especially in the South Pacific and Caribbean near coral atolls there are fish that are extremely dangerous to eat.

TOXIC FISH

Any fish that does not look traditional should be suspect. Some of the warning signs include:

1. Skin rather than scales.
2. Beaklike mouth.
3. Prominent spines.
4. Fish with boxlike bodies or with armored plates.
5. Ugly, deep-set eyes.
6. Flesh retains indentation when pressed with the finger.
7. Exudes a foul smell.

Such fish are almost never found in deep water. Their toxin sources are stinging spines and neurotoxic flesh. The sting of some may be very serious.

There is no way to detoxify the flesh of a poisonous fish. And it takes very little to kill an adult. The poison is water soluble and is not deactivated by heat. It cannot be deactivated by drying, leaching, or any other process. Its toxicity is extreme.

The following material is adapted from Information Bulletin #13, *Edible and Hazardous Marine Life*, Air Training Command, Environmental Information Division, Maxwell Air Force Base, Alabama (Revised September 1978).

Fish that should never be eaten include Puffers (an ounce of flesh can kill),

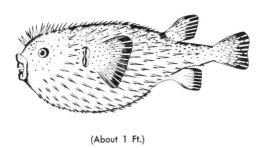

(About 1 Ft.)

Figure 12-10   Porcupine fish. Flesh is toxic. (Courtesy of United States Air Force)

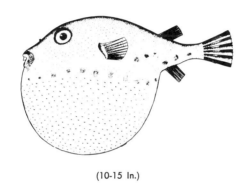

(10-15 In.)

Figure 12-11   Puffer fish. Flesh is toxic. (Courtesy of United States Air Force)

Porcupine fish, and Molas (sunfish). Porcupines and Puffers inflate with water when disturbed and Molas look like they are all head (Figures 12-10 and 12-11).

Some fish secrete a poisonous foam or slime from their skin. The material is toxic if ingested or allowed to contact the eyes or sensitive skin areas. These fish include Soapfish, Toadfish, Hagfish, Moray Eel, and Boxfish (Cowfish). However, these may be used for food if they are carefully skinned (Figures 12-12 and 12-13).

In addition, it is wise to avoid eating the brain, sex organs, liver, and other internal organs of fish since they may be toxic when the rest of the animal is not.

In some areas another problem with marine life is called ciguatera poisoning.

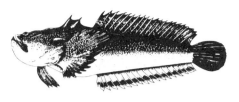

(About 1 Ft.)

Figure 12-12   Toadfish. This fish secretes a toxic slime on its body surface. (Courtesy of United States Air Force)

(6-12 In.)

Figure 12-13   Cowfish. This fish secretes a toxic slime on its body surface. (Courtesy of United States Air Force)

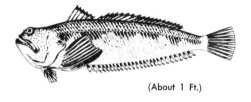

(About 1 Ft.)

Figure 12-14   Weeverfish; its spines are venomous. (Courtesy of United States Air Force)

(10-30 In.)

Figure 12-15   Zebra fish; its spines are venomous. (Courtesy of United States Air Force)

It is thought to be caused by the fish eating a particular type of algae. However, it is usually confined to fish whose teeth form a parrotlike beak.

Fish that sting include stingrays, catfish, Weeverfish, Toadfish and Stargazers, Surgeonfish, Stonefish, Zebra fish, and Scorpion fish (Figures 12-14 and 12-15).

Although fish with venomous spines could be eaten if the spines and poison glands were removed, the process is so involved and hazardous that their value as food is outweighed by it. The spines and venom apparatus remain dangerous even in dead fish.

SYMPTOMS AND TREATMENT

Toxic flesh if eaten will cause abdominal pain, vomiting, diarrhea, tingling and numbness of the lips, dizziness, and weakness. Vomiting should be induced to empty the stomach. Symptoms may progress to include respiratory and cardiac difficulty and death. The procedure is essentially to treat the symptoms.

For stings, cleanse and flush the affected area immediately. The affected part should be placed in hot water (120°F or hotter). Or apply hot compresses for 30 to 60 minutes. The toxins are heat labile (destroyed by heat).

USE OF MARINE FISH AS FOOD

There should be plenty of fish that are unquestionably edible without resorting to those that might be toxic. However, if it is deemed necessary, it is possible to test fish by one of three methods to determine their safety.

1. Apply an edibility test. Taste a small amount (a piece less than the size of a marble). If stinging, numbness, or tingling in the mouth results or if the fish tastes unpleasant, do not eat more.

If it passes this portion of the test, swallow the piece and wait four hours. If nothing happens (nausea, vomiting, stomach or abdominal pain, dizziness, double vision, muscle tremors), it is probably safe. A small serving may be eaten.

If no symptoms occur within the next 12 hours, the first sample can be considered edible.

> **Note:** If ciguatera poisoning is suspected, each fish must be individually tested since their diets may vary. DO *NOT* RUN THIS EDIBILITY TEST ON FISH SUSPECTED OF SPOILAGE.

2. Feed a portion to an animal that can be observed for some time such as a pig, rat, or dog. Cats are less sensitive than the other three animals.
3. Ask locals about the edibility of the fish. (Of course, the presence of local inhabitants likely means that you are no longer in a survival situation.)

Figure 12-16   Toxic Cone snails. They have a venomous spine. (Paul H. Risk)

Be very careful to use fish immediately. Dead fish spoil rapidly at tropical temperatures. If the fish smells differently than it did when caught, it may be spoiled. Slimy texture or nonresilient flesh may also indicate questionable quality. If any fish, but especially one with dark flesh, has a sharp, peppery taste it should not be eaten.

MOLLUSKS

All snails are edible. However, the Cone and Terebra snails have a hypodermic-like spine with which they stab aggressors. It is deployed through the small end of the shell and the result may be fatal (Figure 12-16). Although the animal would be edible with the venom apparatus removed, it is not worth the risk.

SHELLFISH POISONING

During certain times of the year shellfish may feed on toxic microscopic plankton. They then store the toxin in their tissue and become intensely poisonous themselves.

Shellfish poisoning is not limited to the tropics but is also found along coastal areas of North America. The ingested organism is often a dinoflagellate that in massive quantities is responsible for red tides. It is not necessary, however, for a red tide to be present for the shellfish to be toxic. As few as six affected shellfish may prove fatal to an adult. The most likely time for the shellfish to be toxic is during the summer months. It may be helpful to remember that months with an "r" in them in the northern hemisphere are least likely to be dangerous.

There is not necessarily any indication that the toxicity exists since the ingestion of the dinoflagellate does not usually affect the shellfish themselves. However, if there is a question, an edibility test as described for potentially dangerous fish may be run. Bulletin #13 of the Air Training Command Environmental Information Division (Maxwell Air Force Base, Alabama) states that if no symptoms show up within an hour the shellfish may be assumed to be safe in the form tested. In other words, if they were tested cooked, they may be assumed to be safe cooked. But, if they are to be eaten raw, they must be tested for edibility in that form.

PLANTS (EDIBLE)

The tropics abound in edible plants. There are hundreds that could be utilized. There are also some that are intensely toxic, and rules for these are found in Chapter 9, in the discussion on edible and poisonous plants. A few that are representative are all that will be covered here. With the exception of funguses, use the edibility test as outlined in Chapter 9 to determine safety of questionable plants.

Coconut Palm
Immature Stage
Perhaps one of the most delicious forms of the coconut (see Figure 12-2) is when the seed (nut) germinates and begins to produce a shoot (Figure 12-17).

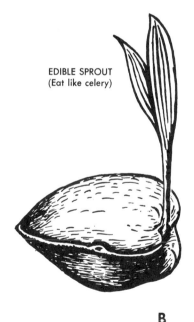

EDIBLE SPROUT
(Eat like celery)

B

Figure 12-17   Germinating coconut. (Courtesy of United States Air Force)

The meat and milk (endosperm) form a moist, breadlike tissue with the shoot coming out of the end. The taste of the breadlike tissue is mild and pleasant, and the shoot itself may be eaten raw or cooked.

As the shoot matures, the nut and its contents shrink but the shoot may, for some time, be split open and the heart eaten. Crisp and cool, it is excellent.

Mature Stage

A mature coconut palm can be a complete general store, providing delectable food and drink as well as building and roofing materials and utensils.

Green immature coconuts have several benefits. First, the fluid (milk) within may be safely drunk as a water source. The meat will be soft and somewhat translucent. It reminds one of firm milky-looking gelatin. As much as 2 pints of fluid may be secured from a single nut. The gelatinous flesh may also be eaten.

The second benefit of using immature nuts is that they are far easier to open than mature ones. A knife or machete can be used to carefully cut through both the green husk and the nut.

Mature coconuts may still be used. However, they are hard to separate from the husk. A husking stake will be of great assistance (Figure 12-18). The husk is brought down smartly against the chisel point of the stake and with a prying, twisting motion the fibers are separated. An experienced islander can complete the husking operation in only a few well-placed blows. However, most inexperienced people find it to be a real chore!

Once the nut is separated, it may be opened by striking blows between the "eyes" with a pointed rock or the blunt side of a machete. This, it might be added, is also less than simple for someone who has never done it before.

However, the milk of a mature coconut, although pleasant tasting, is very purgative. If much over a cup or two is drunk at one time, its laxative effects will be impressive.

The meat or flesh of the nut can be scraped out or the shell broken up and the white meat pried out with a knife. It may be eaten raw or shredded as an addition to other foods.

Coconut oil is extracted from the fruit by pounding the meat or heating it. It can be used as cooking oil or as an excellent sunburn treatment.

Plantains and Bananas (*Musa* spp.)

Plantains are sometimes referred to as "cooking bananas" (Figure 12-19). Their flavor is not good unless they are fried or cooked some other way and in some cases they may cause digestive distress.

And, of course, bananas are well known. When eaten tree-ripened, they are far better tasting than any from the market. Use caution. Spiders and insects

Figure 12-18   Husking a coconut by using a husking stake. (Jan Kolena Cole)

sometimes make their residence in the large bunches of fruit. Although bananas are usually eaten raw, they too may be cooked.

Bamboo
The young shoots of bamboo often grow at the staggering rate of 10 inches or more in a day (Figure 12-20). To be eaten, they should be boiled. They are then tender and good tasting. They may be eaten alone or make a taste-provoking addition to other foods.

Rootstalks and Tubers
Manioc (Manihot utillissima)
This plant (also known as cassava or tapioca) is one of the staples of many jungle people (Figure 12-21). Its starchy rootstalk must be pounded to a paste and leached with water to remove cyanide-based chemicals before use. The paste is then made into a dough and ash cakes prepared from it.

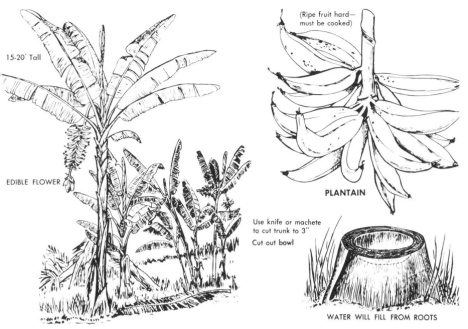

15-20' Tall

EDIBLE FLOWER

(Ripe fruit hard— must be cooked)

PLANTAIN

Use knife or machete to cut trunk to 3"

Cut out **bowl**

WATER WILL FILL FROM ROOTS

Figure 12-19   Banana tree. (Courtesy of United States Air Force)

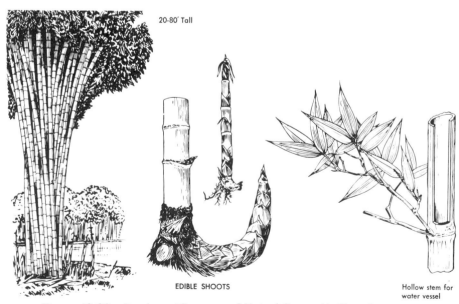

20-80' Tall

EDIBLE SHOOTS

Hollow stem for water vessel

Figure 12-20   Bamboo. (Courtesy of United States Air Force)

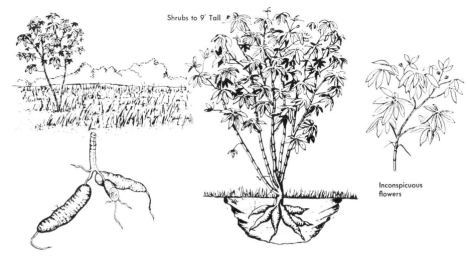

Shrubs to 9' Tall

Inconspicuous flowers

Figure 12-21   Manioc. (Courtesy of United States Air Force)

Tropical Yams (Dioscorea **spp.)**

These are generally soaked in water a few days and then baked (Figure 12-22). This process removes an irritant contained in them. They are also good boiled.

Taro (Colocasia esculenta)

These tubers should not be eaten raw since they too contain chemical irritants (Figure 12-23). Baked, steamed, or boiled they may be eaten like potatoes.

SPECIAL NOTES

Piranha

These oft-maligned fish are found only in the Amazon River and its tributaries (Figure 12-24). Ranging from tiny to 10 to 12 inches in length they have minute razor-sharp teeth. A bite is typically small (about the size of a dime), painless, and bleeds profusely.

Their reputation stems from the fact that they are often found in large schools and attack en masse. Although a single bite may be insignificant, a massive attack can be fatal as the group of fish enter a feeding frenzy.

Nevertheless, native people often swim, wade, and wash in streams where the piranhas live. They often bear the scars of single attacks on their legs as well. Use caution in waters where they may be found. Do not needlessly expose your body.

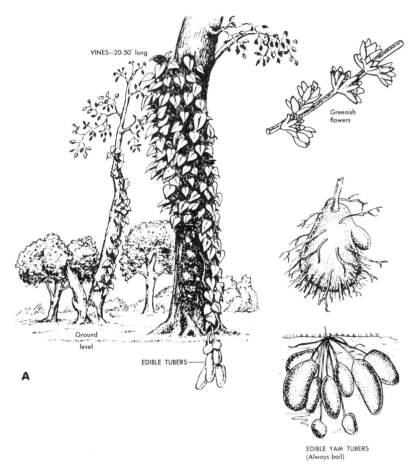

Figure 12-22 *Tropical yams.* (*Courtesy of United States Air Force*)

Parasites in Streams

In some tropical streams there are parasites that are attracted to urine. Do not urinate while floating down waterways. These organisms swim rapidly toward the urine and enter the urethra. They can cause extreme problems.

HOT WEATHER EMERGENCIES: TROPICS

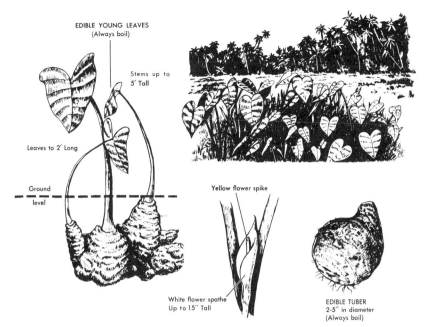

EDIBLE YOUNG LEAVES
(Always boil)

Stems up to
5′ Tall

Leaves to 2′ Long

Ground
level

Yellow flower spike

White flower spathe
Up to 15″ Tall

EDIBLE TUBER
2-5″ in diameter
(Always boil)

Figure 12-23   Taro. (Courtesy of United States Air Force)

Figure 12-24   Piranha. (Toni Angermayer/Photo Researchers)

13

WATER
SURVIVAL

Survival on water is similar whether it's salt or fresh. On large bodies of water many of the same environmental factors found on land are present. It is essential that the body be protected from temperature extremes. So shelter in the form of clothing and other protection is critical. Signals also enhance the chances of rescue and shorten the duration of the experience. In marine environments water is an important limiting factor. Generally, food is not a particularly important consideration in freshwater survival. But the extreme duration of some sea survival experiences can bring food back into the picture.

COLD WATER IMMERSION

Heat loss from the body immersed in cold water is 48 times that in dry air. Because of this, a person immersed in water becomes hypothermic much more rapidly than in dry air. The list below (U.S. Coast Guard data) gives some idea of life expectancy at various water temperatures.

Temperature	Life Expectancy
28 degrees (saltwater)	15 minutes or less
32 degrees	15 to 30 minutes
40 degrees	30 minutes to $1\frac{1}{2}$ hours
50 degrees	1 to 4 hours
60 degrees	2 to 24 hours
70 degrees	3 to 40 hours
80 degrees	Indefinite

Actual situations impose wide variations in survival time, depending on physical condition, age, and thickness of adipose tissue insulation. These figures are for people in nonwaterproof clothing.

Dr. Martin Collis of the University of Victoria, British Columbia, Canada, has done research in heat loss from the human body and survival during water immersion. His work answers some of the common questions outdoors people often ask. This list gives predicted survival time in hours according to different behavior in water at 50°F.

No Flotation	Survival Times (hours)
Drownproofing	1.5
Treading water	2.0
With Flotation	
Swimming	2.0
Holding still	2.7
HELP*	4.0
Huddle	4.0

* HELP = Heat Escape Lessening Posture.

First, it is important to get as much of the body out of the water as possible. The major heat loss areas are (1) the head, (2) the sides of the neck, (3) the sides of the chest, and (4) the groin. The more of these areas that are out of the water, the longer a person can survive. Most small boats when capsized or even damaged will float to some degree. The victim is far better off perched on top of whatever floats than immersed in the water.

WITHOUT FLOTATION DEVICES

Boaters without flotation devices deserve only limited sympathy if that situation was under their control. A cardinal rule for boating is that each person should have a personal flotation device (PFT).

At any rate, the alternatives are not happy ones. Any movement accomplishes two things. (1) It brings blood to the surface of the body where it is cooled faster, and (2) it brings the skin into contact with fresh supplies of cold water by replacing that warmed from contact with the body. Drownproofing tends to cause the greatest heat loss because it immerses the head and face. At 50°F, a person treading water can expect to live approximately 30 minutes longer than one executing drownproofing. Put another way, a person practicing drownproofing cools about 82 percent faster than one floating still with the head out of the water.

WITH FLOTATION DEVICES

Flotation devices of the jacket type protect the sides of the chest from heat loss. Loose fitting ones do not extend survival time. The best types as determined by the University of Victoria study are full survival immersion suits that, according to their data, produced a 400 percent increase in predicted survival time. A convertible jacket modified to allow water to become trapped within insulating foam was also highly recommended. Foam vests adjustable for close fit and garment-type flotation jackets increased thermal protection by 50 to 75 percent.

When flotation devices are used, the victim still should not swim. There is a tendency on the part of good swimmers to assume that they can swim to shore after a boating accident. Drowning records do not support this idea. The average person can swim less than a mile in water at 50°F. As water temperature falls, this distance is greatly reduced. Because of the rapid onset of hypothermia at temperatures below 40, swimming is virtually impossible because of the loss of control of the voluntary muscles.

THE HELP PROCEDURE

HELP stands for Heat Escape Lessening Posture (Figure 13-1). A modified fetal position, it involves drawing the arms down against the sides of the chest with the forearms crossed. The knees are drawn up to protect the groin area, and the head is out of the water. Of course, this is only possible when wearing a flotation device. The HELP procedure can increase survival time approximately 50 percent. A group of people huddling together can accomplish the same percentage increase.

Figure 13-1   A survivor floating in the HELP position (Heat Escape Lessening Posture). (Jan Kolena Cole)

246

However, these figures can vary considerably. Also, women whose body dimensions are less than that of men studied tend to cool more rapidly. Children, because of their smaller size and generally reduced amount of fat as compared to adults, are particularly endangered by immersion in cold water.

PREVENTION

Throughout this book the importance of *prevention* has been a theme. Nowhere is that more true than with regard to cold water immersion. Those planning boating activities should first be sure that there are sufficient flotation devices for each passenger *and* that they are immediately accessible. In small boats, canoes, and kayaks, the devices should be worn all the time.

If water travel is planned in cold water areas, immersion suits (Figure 13-2) should be considered. The complete coverage suit leaves only the face exposed and is quite expensive. But the alternatives are not very desirable.

One of the author's students aboard a fishing boat off Alaska was, with the skipper, forced into the frigid water after the boat filled and sank. The skipper gave her the only complete coverage suit just prior to entering the water. A small dinghy was available but because of high winds it could not be kept righted. In what she estimated at less than 10 minutes, the skipper was no longer able to grasp the edge of the dinghy. His conversation became incoherent and in approximately 15 to 20 minutes he lost consciousness and disappeared under the water. His body was not recovered.

She floated in water estimated at 38°F for about 9 hours before she was able to get ashore and then, still wearing the immersion suit, spent another 11 days along an uninhabited coast before searchers found her. Although tired and hungry, she was virtually unscathed by the ordeal. Without the immersion suit, her life expectancy would have been nearly identical or slightly less than the man whose life was lost.

TREATMENT FOR IMMERSION HYPOTHERMIA

The treatment of this condition is the same as that for hypothermia induced by exposure to cold air. See Chapter 10 for a discussion of hypothermia.

COLD WATER DROWNINGS

An interesting sidelight on cold water immersion deals with drownings. An 18-year-old college student lost control of an automobile and plunged into an ice-covered pond. The car turned over, causing the loss of all trapped air. After 38 minutes rescuers recovered him from the pond. He was pronounced dead at the scene—no pulse, no respiration, pupils dilated, with no response to light.

Figure 13-2   Survival immersion suit. (Paul H. Risk)

As he was being loaded into an ambulance he made a sound. CPR was started immediately and he was rushed to the University of Michigan Hospital where after 15 hours of resuscitation he regained consciousness and recognized his mother. He apparently sustained no brain damage from the ordeal.

Since then, much more attention has been focused on such drownings in cold water, and with increasing frequency victims have been successfully revived.

Such seemingly impossible events involve what has been called the *mam-*

malian diving reflex. It is triggered by sudden contact of the face with cold water (less than 70°F). Water colder than 50° is desirable. Best developed in the very young, it causes severe limitation of blood flow to all but the vital areas of heart, lungs, and brain. The colder the water and younger the victim, the better are chances for survival without injury. The outcome is dependent on the following points.

1. Duration of immersion.
2. Temperature of the water.
3. Age of the victim.
4. Effective and continuous resuscitation.

Treatment for Cold Water Drowning

Do *not* rewarm the victim. Any further heat loss should be prevented with insulation above and below the victim's body. But, as with accidental hypothermia in air, rough handling or improper rewarming can kill your patient. CPR must be commenced immediately and continued until the victim is in the hands of medical personnel. Transport the victim to a hospital.

Do not be discouraged by lack of vital signs. Respiration and heartbeat will usually be undetectable; the skin is often cold to the touch and blue in color (cyanotic). The pupils may be fixed and dilated. In spite of all these indications, treatment should be continued.

IMMERSION THROUGH ICE

Ice is deceptive. It often seems thick enough to support the weight of a person when it is really too thin. The result is that early in winter people fall through. If travel across ice of questionable thickness is necessary, snowshoes will distribute the weight better and may allow travel when boots would break through. However, if a complete breakthrough does occur with snowshoes, it is far more difficult to get out. Even in shallow water the problems are compounded. A trainee in one of the author's survival courses (an Army major) broke through into water up to his knees. The water was so cold that he was having great trouble unfastening the snowshoe bindings. Yet, the awkward footgear made it almost impossible for him to lift his feet around the ice. The snowshoes kept catching. He stood for some time (within a short distance of camp) unable to bring himself to call for help until he was finally able to unbuckle the snowshoes and get out.

Total body immersion through ice usually means a water temperature close to 32°F. At that temperature, life expectance is *very* short. Within a few minutes the ability to close the hands is lost and voluntary control of large muscle groups compromised. Rapid escape is vital.

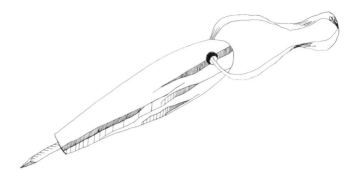

Figure 13-3   Self-rescue ice pick. Two should be carried. (Celia Drozdiak)

Anyone involved in activities on ice such as snowmobiling or ice fishing would be advised to carry a pair of special ice picks, which have wrist loops and are specially designed to assist in self-extrication from just such a predicament (Figure 13-3). Lacking these, place the arms out on the ice and kick with the legs in a swimming motion to lift the body up on the lip of the ice. Continue to kick with the feet and maneuver the body up on the ice. A rolling motion may assist in the final thrust out of the water.

In all honesty, getting out of the water under these circumstances is a very difficult task without assistance.

If help is at hand, rescuers should be very cautious about approaching. It is no easier for a group to get out of the water than it is a single person. A long plank or ladder pushed out to the victim can be used to spread weight distribution. Sometimes a canoe can be slid along the surface to reach the person. If the ice is too thin to support the ladder, plank, or canoe, the canoe may be used to break a path in the ice to the victim.

Ice is not safe for an individual until it is at least 2 inches thick. An individual after a plunge through ice into water may, if the snow is dry, roll in it to blot up excess water. Then brush off as much clinging snow as possible and get to warm surroundings. If unable to get indoors, build a fire. Traveling in wet clothes during winter causes heat loss at far too rapid a rate to be compensated by the body's metabolic heat production.

SEA SURVIVAL

Much of the information contained in this section would also apply to large fresh bodies of water such as the Great Lakes.

DRINKING WATER

The oceans of the world are, in one respect, like the great deserts. Drinking water is hard to find. Also, the constant presence of waves and water imposes a psychological need for water unequaled. Because of this, survivors have convinced themselves that it was safe to drink seawater. This is a very dangerous practice and will ultimately result in kidney failure often preceded by mental disorientation, hallucinations, and convulsions. Death will follow prolonged intake of seawater.

Reducing the need for water must be accomplished. This may be done in several ways.

1. Eating nothing or only sugary foods. Life raft rations are sometimes primarily gumdrops. They require minimal amounts of water to assimilate.
2. Reduce sweat as in desert survival. Stay in the shade. Improvise a sail or shade from cloth, tarps, or extra clothing draped over paddles.
3. Minimize exertion.
4. Use seawater to wet clothing and skin to increase evaporative cooling. After some time, the process of seawater evaporation will cause a buildup of salt in the clothing. This can be very irritating to the skin. Rinse clothing in the sea from time to time to reduce the salt load.
5. Avoid all dehydrated food.

WATER SOURCES AT SEA

Rain Squalls and Storms

In some areas squalls and storms may be major sources of freshwater. Be ready for them, both to facilitate water collection and to prevent capsizing. Frequently the winds accompanying such precipitation will come up suddenly and with destructive force.

A tarp, sail, or clothing may be arranged to intercept the falling rain and run it off into containers. If the cloth has developed an accumulation or encrustation of salt, rinse it in the sea before attempting to catch rainwater.

When inflatable, Mae West-type flotation devices are in use, extra water for storage may be transferred to one half by mouth.

Fill all available containers. Empty ration cans, plastic bags, waterproof clothing may all be used. When all containers are full, everyone on the raft should drink their fill while the storm lasts.

Dew

Sun shades, sails, and rain covers may accumulate considerable quantities of dew during the night. Mop it up and wring it into containers.

Stills and Desalinating Devices

Previously mentioned in Chapter 6 stills should be placed in immediate operation (see Figure 6-6). However, since the desalinating devices have limited capacity, they ought to be used only when other sources of freshwater have failed.

SHELTER

Large rafts carried aboard commercial airliners have sunshades or sun roofs. These can offer considerable protection from rain, wind, cold, and sun.

Protection from *sunburn* is of great importance aboard rafts. Not only is the direct exposure great, but reflected solar radiation may burn a person under the chin, inside the nose, beneath the ears, and under the bony ridges of the eyes. Areas such as the bridge of the nose, receding hairline areas, a bald head, and the tops of the ears should receive special attention. If a sun barrier cream such as zinc oxide is available, it should be applied liberally to these locations.

Keep clothing on to control sweating and to protect from the effects of the sun. Long sleeves and pants should be worn. Shorts or swimming suits without a shirt predispose the tops of the legs, arms, and shoulders and the back of the neck to serious sunburn. A wide-brimmed hat will help protect face and neck. Sunglasses should be worn if available to prevent sunblindness.

Sunburn over large areas of the body can be incapacitating at least and dangerous at worst. In serious sunburn pain is not limited to the superficial layers of the skin. Muscles ache and stiffen. A general feeling of achiness develops and may be accompanied by nausea, vomiting, dizziness, and chills.

Even in large rafts, lack of physical movement can be a problem. It is even more serious in rafts designed for one person. One survivor after weeks at sea in a one-passenger raft said he lost all feeling from the waist down and became unable to move his legs. Interference with circulation as well as pressure on nerves can cause these symptoms. Isometric exercises and massaging the limbs will help to prevent this.

The Raft

Wear and Damage

Be especially careful of sharp or rough objects. If they are not needed for warmth, shoes and boots should be removed in the raft and secured so that capsizing will not cause their loss.

Belt buckles, metal buttons, and fasteners (including large metal zippers) may, because of the motion of the raft, slowly chafe their way through and cause a leak.

Equipment containers, radio equipment, ration cans, and signals may likewise cause holes. They should be stowed so that they do not move around and cannot be lost if the raft overturns.

Most rafts come with a patch kit. Before it is needed, become familiar with its use. Be sure everyone aboard is aware of where it is kept.

Stability

The smaller the raft, the less stable it is. In rough seas a one-man raft is very liable to turn over. This tendency can be reduced by lowering the inflation pressure so that the raft rides a little lower in the water and is more flexible. Water in the raft will provide ballast and also increase stability. (This will make you feel a little better when you become aware that it is virtually impossible to keep the water out of a tiny raft!)

Capsizing might be fun in a swimming pool but it saps energy in emergencies. Climbing back into the raft may be too much for exhausted or injured individuals. Also, the raft could be blown away from you after you fall out. The wind can blow a raft across the surface far faster than a person can swim. For this reason, it is wise to fasten yourself to it by a long tether. Then when you capsize, the raft can be brought back to you and not the reverse.

Try to distribute weight evenly in the raft. A heavy spot can cause the lighter side to lift in the wind and this may flip the raft over.

Righting an Overturned Raft

Very small rafts are not too difficult to right but a 6-passenger raft or larger are a real chore. If the raft has a carbon dioxide inflation tank on one side, attach a line to the side opposite, bring it across the raft and using the feet as a fulcrum, pull the raft back right side up (Figure 13-4). Be sure not to reverse the procedure. If the raft is lifted up with the carbon dioxide tank on the side away from you, it can strike you on the head and fracture your skull.

The very large, donut-shaped rafts have no right side up. They are the same on both sides.

Large rafts often have a boarding position that deflates, allowing survivors to enter at nearly the same level as the water. This is a great help. But smaller

BOTTLE SIDE OF RAFT

Figure 13-4 Righting a life raft. (Courtesy of United States Air Force)

SEA SURVIVAL

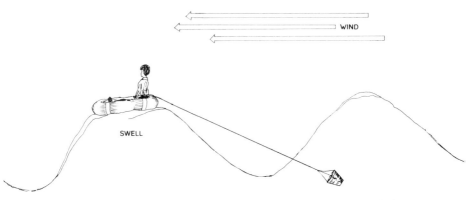

Figure 13-5 Proper placement of the sea anchor. (Celia Drozdiak)

rafts do not have this and to clamber over the side of a 6- or 8-passenger raft may be impossible without help. A one-passenger raft is boarded by orienting its long axis away from you and pulling the raft under you. It sounds easy, but doing it is something else again, especially while wearing soaking clothes.

Fasten everything in the raft. Anything like a radio or signal mirror which is in use frequently should be attached with a long cord which permits use but also makes retrieval possible after a spill. Even if the raft does not flip over, items which are not secured will, sooner or later, be dropped.

Rough Weather

When the wind comes up, so do the waves. A sea anchor can be invaluable. Most larger and some smaller rafts come with them. They look like a canvas bucket, with or without a bottom depending on the style. Trailed from a raft in heavy seas, they will keep it faced into the wind and reduce chances of swamping. The anchor line should be paid out until it is in the wave trough at the same time the raft is in an adjacent one. Or, it should be under the crest of a wave at the same time the raft is at the crest of another (Figure 13-5).

Any improvised shades or sails should be furled if the wind is high, since they may tend to overbalance the raft and promote capsizing.

HEALTH AND HYGIENE

Seasickness

Seasickness is a form of motion sickness. At some point most people suffer from it while at sea. It is easier to treat at onset and during the early stages than it is later. If Dramamine, Bonine, Marezine, or other nausea-control medication is available in tablet form, it should be taken before symptoms are so severe as to preclude oral medication. Some of the seasickness drugs are also available in suppository form. These are invaluable when nausea and vomiting make it impossible to retain anything taken by mouth. But, under survival conditions, seasickness tablets can also be given rectally. Using the index or middle finger, simply insert them through the anus being sure they are placed well up in the rectum. Absorption will then be through the vessels of the rectal walls. A new medication called Transderm is available by prescription. Applied as an adhesive patch behind the ear, it is absorbed through the skin. Its effects last for about 3 days.

Possibly nothing saps the will to live as much as severe nausea. Survivors have reported hearing aircraft while seriously seasick and not caring enough to even raise their head. Not only does it affect a person psychologically, but vomiting can seriously deplete the body's water content and physically weaken a survivor.

For some, it is helpful to keep the eyes focused on the horizon. For others, it is better to watch the raft. Motion sickness stems from a complex interaction between the middle ear's semicircular canals (the body's balancing sensors) and visual cues. Changing the orientation of the head, lying on the back or the stomach, and sitting up may all be tried. Before vomiting starts, eating may stabilize the stomach and make the victim feel better.

There are no absolutely certain methods for controlling this miserable condition. And, the pitching and yawing of a raft is sufficiently different from what may have been experienced in other boats that even experienced sailors are likely to become sick.

Saltwater Sores

The constant buffeting of the raft together with the irritation of salt and pressure on the body sometimes cause large, raw, oozing sores. Saltwater sores usually occur on areas of the body in contact with the raft, such as hips, buttocks, and legs. They are much like bed sores. While they can be very large and painful—covering an area 3 to 4 inches across—they are not as serious as they appear. If possible, the affected area should be kept dry and an antibiotic ointment applied. Once the pressure and abrasion are alleviated, they heal spontaneously, although secondary infection can be a danger.

Disposal of Human Waste

The raft environment precludes most privacy. But human waste disposal is often of minimal concern. Reduced food and water intake will result in less frequent urination and may halt defecation entirely. This should not be a cause for concern. It is normal under the circumstances.

Where defecation or urination is necessary, it can be done in an empty ration container reserved for this purpose and the material thrown as far from the raft as possible to avoid, in warm oceans, attracting sharks. Survivors have indicated that before long taking care of these natural processes is ignored by others in the raft, although in the early stages of sea survival these considerations may be cause for some embarrassment. If this is the case, it may be possible to rig a screen or have someone hold one up. Whatever the case, human waste should not be allowed to accumulate in the raft since it can pose both aesthetic and health problems. Vomitus should also be collected in a container and disposed of as far from the raft as possible for the same reasons.

SIGNALS

The signal mirror should be used continuously during sunny periods. Since it is visible for up to 15 miles, its flash can be seen by an aircraft that cannot be seen from the raft. The task of signaling also keeps a person occupied with something other than worrying about the situation.

Sea dye markers (fluorescein powder) in sealed containers are found in most larger rafts. Dissolved in the water, they will turn the area around the raft a fluorescent greenish-yellow that is very visible from the air. They should not be used until or unless an aircraft is spotted.

An electronic strobe light could be part of the signaling equipment aboard (Figure 13-6). This is an automatic device that, when activated, emits a bril-

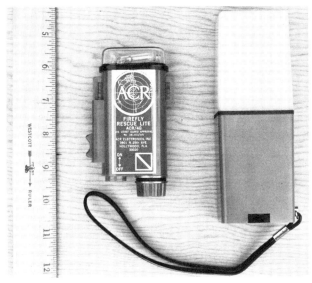

Figure 13-6   Electronic strobe light emergency flashers. (Paul H. Risk)

256

liant white flash at about 1-second intervals. It is visible at night for great distances.

Radio equipment will have operating instructions with it. Today's radios are usually very simple to operate, requiring little more than switching them on and pushing the mike button when talking. They can be very effective over water.

FOOD

Although many larger rafts come with emergency rations, they should be saved until nothing else is available. Certainly, with the exception of the very young, elderly, injured, or ill, it is not essential that food be available during the first few days. Attempt to obtain food from the sea.

Most ocean fish are edible including sharks. Fishing should form an important activity both as a food source and a means of occupying time. Use what fishing equipment is provided and improvise more. But it is not wise to attach heavy fishing line to the raft. A large fish taking the bait may actually take the raft for a ride or tear out the part is is tied to. Improvised fishing equipment is discussed in Chapter 8, which deals with food acquisition.

Small fish may accompany the raft, hovering in small schools in its shadow. These may be netted with an undershirt or other thin fabric on an improvised frame.

During the hours of darkness fish may be attracted to the raft by a flashlight and may be clubbed or speared. Try snagging them with hooks attached to the handle of an oar.

In tropical waters flying fish may leap into the raft and may then be easily caught. But don't get in a rush or do irrational things. One survivor in his zeal to immobilize a fish that had jumped into the raft, slashed at it with a sheath knife. The major leak his rip caused was predictable.

Any fish caught should be cleaned immediately. They will spoil rapidly. Since it is somewhat challenging to build a campfire in a canvas raft, it is good to know that marine fish may be safely eaten raw. Extra fish can be cut into thin strips and dried in the sun by hanging line across the raft. Organs, eggs, and other entrails should not be eaten but can make excellent bait. And, remember, fishing can be a means of alleviating boredom and depression. Have a fishing pool. The winner gets an all expense paid trip to Timbuktu. Set the prizes any way you want.

Sometimes seaweed will drift by. Haul it aboard and carefully pick through it. Small minnows, crabs, shrimp, and other animals are often found this way. They also may be eaten raw.

Turtles sometimes surface near a raft and if an improvised spear has been made they may be caught. However, it is very difficult to kill a large sea turtle, and they are strong. The ride you get before you can either slow it down or cut it loose may be too much under the circumstances.

MARINE HAZARDS

Sharks

To say that the great majority of sharks have never been associated with attacks on humans is little consolation if you are attacked by one of that small minority that are dangerous. Nevertheless, few sharks are hazardous. Even those that *have* attacked cannot be *depended* on to do so. The mere presence of a shark is not a guarantee that an attack will follow. So, the only thing that may certainly be said is that sharks are unpredictable given the current state of our knowledge. And recent popular motion pictures have done little to increase our confidence about them (Figure 13-7).

It is known that sharks, with little or no change, have been around for over 350 million years. So they are well adapted to their environment. They are equipped to sense astounding amounts of certain chemicals. Blood is detectable from a quarter mile away, which represents a 1 part blood to 50 million parts of water. It appears that sharks make use of their finely tuned chemical receptors in stalking and attacking prey. They are also capable of sensing sound waves and minute electrical currents. To a more limited extent, they also respond to visual stimuli.

Sharks may circle the raft or lie quietly in the shadow beneath it. Occasionally they may nudge its bottom. Do not dangle hands, feet, or small, shiny objects over the edge of the raft. You may not get everything back that you dangled.

Sharks tend to move about continuosly and if they find nothing that attracts them often move away. If a survivor is caught in the water without a raft, it is advisable to move as little as possible. Several survivors should huddle together in a group (Figure 13-8). Panicky, jerky motions and splashing in an uncoordinated way may bring about an attack. If movement is necessary, do so smoothly.

If a survivor is attacked and in the water, apply a pressure bandage made of anything handy. The bleeding must be quickly stopped. Sharks in the presence of quantities of blood go into a feeding frenzy in which they will take almost anything including large chunks of metal. Place the injured person in the center of a huddle of others.

A shark slowly circling a person in the water is likely sizing up the prey and may attack momentarily. Keep moving in order to face the animal. Some sharks have stopped an attack because the intended victim seemed to be preparing to repel them.

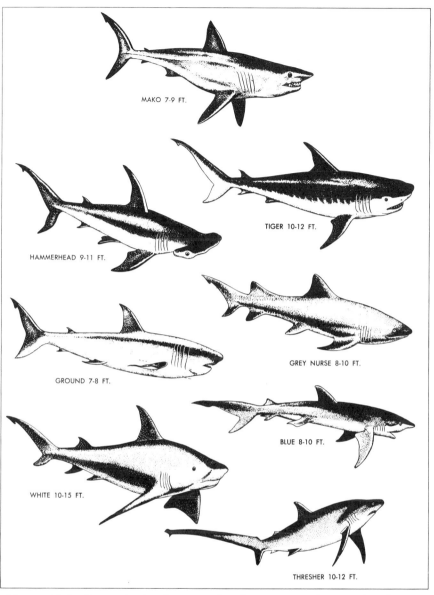

Figure 13-7 Some sharks that may be dangerous under certain circumstances. (Courtesy of United States Air Force)

Figure 13-8 Three survivors in the shark defense position. (Jan Kolena Cole)

If alone, an attack may be cut short by a sudden noise such as slapping the water, yelling underwater, or firing a gun over the water.

If attack is under way, striking with a blunt object at the sensitive areas of the eyes, nose, or gills may discourage the shark. A shark's skin is very rough and bare-skinned contact with it will produce bad abrasions and release serum into the water. Also, it may not be wise to cut or stab the shark since release of blood into the water may attract other sharks.

So-called shark chaser and shark repellent are practically ineffective. Shark chaser was issued by the U.S. Navy during World War II. It came in a water-tight container as a block of copper acetate and nigrosine dye. Although it smelled bad and created a dense black cloud of dye around the survivor in the water, it did little else to discourage attack and is no longer recommended. So far, there is nothing of a chemical nature that shows real promise.

Divers sometimes use a device called a Bang Stick which is a short spear

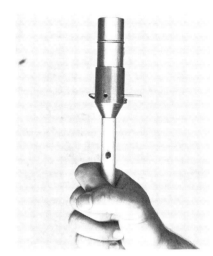

Figure 13-9   Bang Stick. (Paul H. Risk)

tipped with either a 12-gauge shotgun shell or a 30-06 rifle cartridge (Figure 13-9). Thrust into the shark, it is then fired. Another device called the Shark Dart is a sharp-pointed spear with a carbon dioxide cartridge at the end of a shaft (Figure 13-10). It is stabbed into the shark and fired. The contents of the carbon dioxide cartridge blasts into the animal and, inflated, the shark rises to the surface.

Probably the most effective device is the "shark bag" or "shark screen"

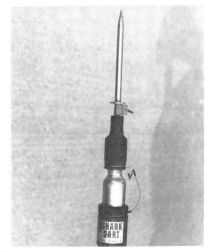

Figure 13-10   Shark Dart (Paul H. Risk)

Figure 13-11   Shark bag. (Jan Kolena Cole)

(Figure 13-11). It was developed by C. Scott Johnson and consists of a poly-vinyl bag 5 feet in length and 3 feet in diameter with inflatable tubes around the top. To use, the survivor climbs inside, allows it to fill with water, and inflates the collar. The shark can then only see an indistinct blob, and all odors whether from blood or otherwise are contained within.

Jellyfish and Portuguese Man-of-War

Trailing delicate tentacles covered with stinging cells, jellyfish can produce a very painful sting. The Portuguese Man-of-War sometimes has tentacles reach-ing 20 to 30 feet (Figure 13-12). Their stings may cause an allergic reaction and death. A somewhat rare jellyfish called the Sea Wasp is found off Austra-lia, the Philippines, and in the Indian Ocean (Figure 13-13). It is extremely toxic and death may occur within seconds or minutes.

Treatment of jellyfish stings includes immersing the affected area in water at 120°F or as hot as can be tolerated. The tenacles on the skin should not be rubbed with sand since this may cause additional stings. Meat tenderizer or papaya juice both work well in detoxifying the active substances. Carefully

262

Figure 13-12   Portuguese man-of-war. (Courtesy of United States Air Force)

Figure 13-13   Sea wasp. (Ron and Valerie Taylor/Bruce Coleman)

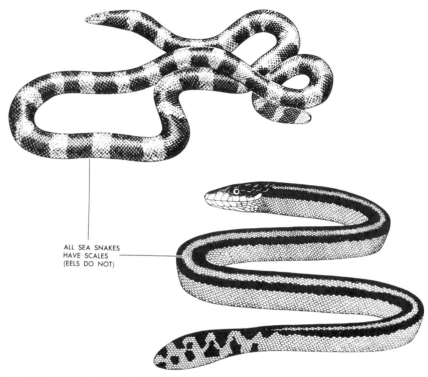

ALL SEA SNAKES
HAVE SCALES
(EELS DO NOT)

Figure 13-14   Sea snakes. (Courtesy of United States Air Force)

scraping a knife blade across the skin will help in removing the tentacles. Flour, soda paste, or dry sand may be sprinkled on the area and then carefully scraped off with a knife blade taking the tentacles with it.

Sea Snakes

These are found in the Indian and Pacific oceans (Figure 13-14). They are about 10 times more deadly than any other snakes. However, they are relatively nonaggressive and their dental structure makes gripping and chewing necessary for venom to be injected.

The venom is neurotoxic and rapidly absorbed. Sea snake bites normally produce little or no pain at the site. Paralysis then develops and death (which occurs in less than 17 percent of the recorded cases) may follow up to a week later. There is a specific antivenin available.

14

SPECIAL CONSIDERATIONS

MOUNTAIN AREAS

Mountain areas have a great deal in common with other environments. But they also have some significant differences. A hiker or climber entering the mountains with the same expectations as the camper in flat country is in for some surprises.

Because of the height differences from their bases to their summits, mountains represent virtually the same mix of climates that one would find if traveling from south to north. Summits may be like the arctic, and areas further down may have weather, wildlife, and vegetation similar to the Canadian forests from Hudson's Bay down to the Great Lakes, with conifers beginning at first as small and stunted and then reaching full stature. The lower elevations may be warmer and have more deciduous trees.

Weather is also influenced by mountains. Towering into the atmosphere, they intercept air masses moving across the land and manufacture their own weather. Rising above the warmer layers of air in the valleys, the temperatures in mountain areas are cooler. For every thousand feet of elevation gained, air temperatures drop 3 to 5°F (Figure 14-1).

The sudden uplift caused by moving air forced sharply upward against the mountains forms clouds and storms that are localized entirely on the mountain. Surrounding lands may be warm and free of clouds. Storms often develop with a frightening suddenness and intensity. Before entering mountain country, it is a good idea to gain some understanding of the extremes that might be found there.

Altitude in itself creates specialized problems. The higher a person climbs,

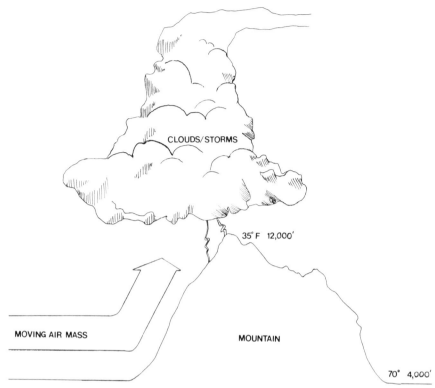

Figure 14-1   Diagram demonstrating the termperature drop with increasing altitude in the mountains. Storms form because of the air masses being forced upward. (Celia Drozdiak)

the lower the partial pressure of oxygen, the drier the air, and the higher the intensity of solar radiation.

MOUNTAIN SICKNESS, PULMONARY EDEMA, AND CEREBRAL EDEMA

Those gaining altitude in mountain areas often develop symptoms of mountain sickness. For years a differentiation between mountain sickness (altitude sickness) and edema involving the brain or respiratory organs was made. More recently, medical authorities have indicated a tendency to consider the development of edema as a continuation of, or part of, mountain sickness.

Mountain sickness may occur because of the lower amounts of oxygen availability at different altitudes, combined with hyperventilation and fatigue. De-

266   SPECIAL CONSIDERATIONS

hydration could also be a factor. The first symptoms of mountain sickness may be noticed between 5000 and 8000 feet elevation, with most people not noticing it until 8000 feet. Pulmonary edema is not ordinarily seen until at least 9000 feet and more commonly at 12,000 feet or higher.

Almost everyone who has climbed or visited a relatively high elevation has experienced the early symptoms of mountain sickness. These include shortness of breath, headache, weakness, slight dizziness, loss of appetite, and nausea. They may also be accompanied by slowed mental processes—a difficulty in the performance of normal, routine chores. As the illness progresses, the much more serious conditions of pulmonary and cerebral edema may follow in about 6 hours.

It is interesting that people under 21 years of age seem to be much more prone to mountain sickness than those 21 and older. Also, people in inadequate physical condition and those who are not acclimatized are more at risk.

Gradually increasing elevation—becoming acclimatized—reduces the chances of mountain sickness. Rather than rushing right to 12,000 feet on a hike, hunt, or climb, it is advisable to take at least 2, preferably 4, days to reach high altitudes. In this way, the body can modify various physiological processes to meet the changing demands imposed by the new environment. The practice of being flown directly to a high camp to commence a climb or hunt may be especially dangerous since the sudden stress on the body is not tolerated as well.

THE ROLE OF DEHYDRATION

Furthermore, it is recommended that adequate water be drunk during high-altitude activities. Due to the dryness of the atmosphere, water may be lost at twice the rate encountered at lower altitudes. Hikers and climbers should plan their meals to provide plenty of fluids (not including alcohol, which not only dehydrates but may impair judgment). Powdered juices, hot gelatin drink, hot chocolate, and soups, all can assist in meeting this need.

While moving during the day, collect snow in a plastic container and melt it by placing it between layers of clothing. However, some medical people feel that snow often contains minute bits of vegetation, dust, and other foreign material that may give the drinker a sore throat. More fluids should be drunk at noon and during the evening meal. Cooler temperatures in mountain areas often fool the hiker into feeling little or no thirst. Thirst itself is not an adequate indicator of physiological need.

The milder symptoms of mountain sickness, if not increasing in severity, may be controlled by remaining in camp a day or so to allow acclimatization. However, if it is apparent that they are not improving or are increasing in severity, the person should go to lower elevation.

Pulmonary and cerebral edema are caused by a breakdown of vessels in the lungs and brain, respectively. Fluid accumulates in the lung or causes swelling of the brain. They are both very serious conditions and are cause for immediate evacuation of the victim to lower elevation. If this is not possible, bed rest with the administration of oxygen is necessary. But it must be emphasized that *the patient who cannot be brought down is in grave danger.*

The victim of pulmonary edema will develop a cough, difficulty in breathing, and an ear or stethoscope pressed against the back will enable one to hear the gurgling sound of air bubbling through fluid. Respiratory distress can become rapidly severe. Mouth to mouth resuscitation is not likely to help since the lungs' ability to absorb air is compromised. A pink froth of blood may form at the nose or mouth of the victim as death approaches.

The prime symptom of cerebral edema is headache. The brain is encased in the rigid structure of the skull. Since it cannot expand, swelling of the brain forces its tissues against the unmoving bony wall of the skull. Pain may be intense, with disorientation, mental incompetence, unconsciousness, and finally death.

Diamox, a carbonic anhydrase inhibitor and mild diuretic, has been recommended by some authorities as a means of preventing mountain sickness. It changes the blood chemistry to slightly more acidic than normal, reduces secretion of cerebrospinal fluid, and slightly increases urine production. However, it is best to rely on acclimatization rather than a synthetic cure.

Some research carried out by Mountain Safety Research indicates that large doses of antacids may also help to prevent mountain sickness.

To summarize, a person contemplating activities at high altitude in the mountains should be in good physical condition, attain altitude in stages—resting at camp in between, keep well hydrated, and minimize exertion until acclimatized.

MOUNTAIN WEATHER

Air masses moving toward the mountain, especially from moist locations, may result in sudden severe weather. Backpackers must be able to cope with these changes. Even during summer months, storms may be violent and drop temperatures several degrees in just a few minutes. Sudden temperature changes can produce dense fogs, making travel impossible. For the inexperienced person, it is difficult to comprehend a fog so dense that visibility is reduced to 5 to 10 feet. It is possible to be unable to see the edge of the trail well enough to continue to move safely. As a result, the mountain traveler should be able to bivouac even under awkward conditions.

When dense fog moves in, the humidity also rises steeply, causing clothing and equipment to become soaked. Coupled with wind, it is very difficult to stay dry. The damp chill penetrates easily and, at the least, the hiker or climber is made very uncomfortable. At worst, the situation becomes dangerous as the threat of hypothermia increases.

Air flow patterns are affected greatly by the terrain, both by the funneling effect of ridges and canyons and the turbulence caused as the wind moves over the tops of ridges. Barometric pressure differences often cause very localized winds as the pressure equalizes by forcing its way along and through valleys and gaps.

In some regions a particular type of wind, known generally as a foehn, may develop. In California it is referred to as a Santa Ana wind and in Alaska as a chinook. Caused by high pressure on one side of a mountain range and lower pressure on the other, it is typically a warm or even hot, dry wind with high velocities (Figure 14-2). As the high pressure spills over the top of the ridges, it surges down the other side into the lower pressure sink, causing rapid compression of the air in the lower elevation. Just as a tire gets warm as air is compressed into it, the descending wind does likewise. Such conditions are associated with sudden thaws during otherwise wintery weather and with severe fire threats in warmer, drier areas such as Southern California.

Velocities are determined by the pressure gradient, with higher winds found with extreme high pressure on one side and very low pressure on the other side

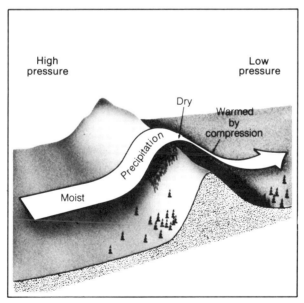

Figure 14-2 Development of chinook winds. (From The Avalanche Handbook)

of the mountain area. In the Southern California area, such conditions occur when high pressure builds over the Mojave desert with low pressure over the Los Angeles Basin. On a positive note, the winds, blowing forcefully toward the sea, clear the air of pollution as the stagnant air is driven out over the ocean. However, the period during which a Santa Ana will blow is generally when Southern California makes national headlines as brush fires and forest fires, driven by the high winds, burn thousands of acres of vegetation.

During the daytime, air movement is usually "up-canyon." A hiker or camper on the floor of a canyon or valley will notice that air, warmed by the earth and sun, moves toward the higher elevations (Figure 14-3). But, during the late afternoon and early evening, this pattern is reversed. The low areas become rivers of cooler descending air.

This more dense air continues to move from the higher elevations toward the valley floors, creating a cooler environment in the low areas. Under very hot conditions, this may be a benefit. But, when conditions are already comfort-

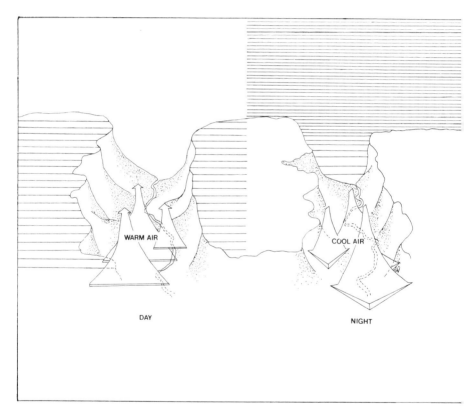

WARM AIR

COOL AIR

DAY

NIGHT

Figure 14-3   Upward and downward moving canyon winds. (Celia Drozdiak)

270   SPECIAL CONSIDERATIONS

able, the air drainage effect may mean that canyon and other low areas are too cool for camping in comfort. This is especially true during winter conditions when low areas often have some of the coldest temperatures.

SNOW AND SNOW-RELATED CONDITIONS

Because of the uplift of air masses caused by the mountains, precipitation may be very heavy. In the Cascade Mountains, Mt. Rainier in one year received over 90 feet of snow. Several feet may fall from a single storm. Although snow is, in small quantities, lightweight, large amounts can impose an amazing stress on tents and other shelters. One group, after retiring for the night in snow caves on the slopes of a mountain near Rainier, awoke the next morning with the roofs of the shelters pressed down almost to their noses by the weight of the single night's accumulation of snow. Needless to say, anyone traveling under such conditions would be in serious trouble.

AVALANCHES

Examination of vegetation on steep slopes in mountain areas will often disclose twisted trunks on large stands of young trees. This is characteristic of the effect of the slow creep of a heavy mass of snow bending the trees down. As thawing occurs in the spring, the trees attempt to grow straight again, and the result is a permanent bend in the lower portion of the trunk.

In other areas observation will show areas devoid of vegetation (Figure 14-4). This should warn the hiker, climber, or skier of avalanche danger.

As the slope approaches 20 to 35 degrees, large avalanche paths are often formed. According to the U.S. Forest Service's *Avalanche Handbook,* avalanches may move at great speed (5 to 30 meters per second) with tremendous impact. Impact pressures may exceed 100 tons per square meter. A chart from that publication may serve to demonstrate potential (Figure 14-5).

Correlation between impact pressure and potential damage

Impact (tons per square meter)	Potential Damage
0.1	Break windows
0.5	Push in doors
3.0	Destroy wood-frame structures
10.0	Uproot mature Spruce
100.0	Move reinforced concrete structures

Figure 14-4 Avalanche chutes on mountain slopes. (From The Avalanche Handbook)

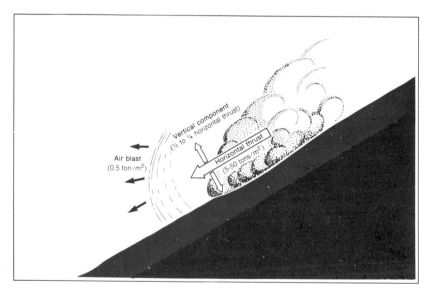

Figure 14-5 Avalanche forces. (From The Avalanche Handbook)

SPECIAL CONSIDERATIONS

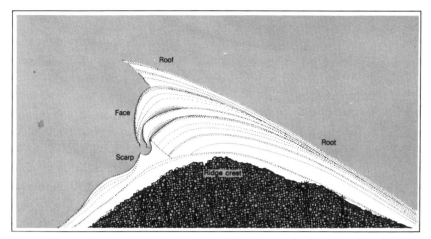

Figure 14-6   Cornice formation. (From The Avalanche Handbook)

Obviously, camp should not be established in areas that are prone to avalanches. With pressures such as those above, no shelter known could survive.

Avalanche information is complex and it is not possible here to provide detail sufficient to cover the subject. But it is recommended that anyone who plans to travel either on snowshoes or skis in the mountains research the subject by doing additional reading and talking to rangers in such areas.

A few guidelines may be of help.

1. Make camp well back from the avalanche runout area. And remember that distances may be deceptive.
2. Stay clear of slopes exceeding 30 degrees.
3. Try to travel on the windward side of slopes. The lee of a slope, because of turbulence, is an area of deeper, less well consolidated snow.
4. If travel across a potential avalanche area is necessary, move quickly across the runout area rather than the startup zone.
5. Be cautious near ridges and summits because of cornices. A cornice is an overhanging lip of snow formed by wind (Figure 14-6). It is usually very unstable and unsuspecting climbers have walked out on them only to have a collapse occur. Cornices are also a severe threat to a campsite. A collapsing cornice can drop a great deal of snow toward the valley and precipitate a secondary avalanche as well.

PRECAUTIONS IN AVALANCHE AREAS

Current information gleaned from accidents shows that only one in five completely buried avalanche victims will survive. But there are some things that can be done to improve those chances.

1. Rope Up

When crossing dangerous areas, use a mountaineering belay line and cross one at a time. But be aware that the forces sustained in an avalanche are higher and more sustained than those in climbing. The belay should not be handheld but should be fastened to a fixed anchor such as a tree, rock, or piton.

2. Carry Probes and Shovels

Avalanche probes are available from some mountain supply houses. These, combined with the ability to dig quickly, can cut search and rescue time greatly.

3. Plan an Escape Route

Carefully examine the situation and plan how to most quickly get to the flank of the avalanche should one develop.

4. Use Avalanche Cord

A brightly colored nylon cord is available that can be trailed along behind a skier or climber. This lightweight cord may ride toward the top of the snow mass and make it easier to locate a victim. However, the *Avalanche Handbook* emphasizes that a completely buried victim can expect that in only 40 percent of the cases will the cord be visible.

5. Remove Ski Wrist Straps

Having the hands free is important, and when ski poles are flailing around, held by their straps, it minimizes the use of the hands.

6. Swim

If a person is caught in an avalanche, a swimming motion may assist in staying toward the upper layer of snow.

7. Raise a Hand

As the moving snow comes to a halt, thrust a hand toward the top. The other hand should be used between the face and chest to help form a breathing space. Some victims have been saved because they have pushed their hands above the surface before the snow set. (Especially in moist snow avalanches, but in others as well, the snow tends to set by recrystallization after the avalanche, making movement impossible.)

CREVASSES

On glaciers, large cracks form as the ice conforms to the surface over which it flows. These cracks, called crevasses, may be more than 100 feet deep and are often concealed by snow bridging (Figure 14-7). The unsuspecting survivor can

274

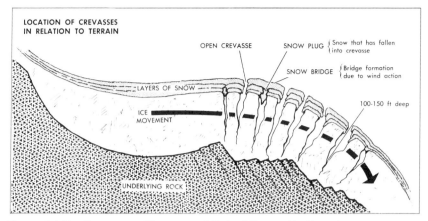

Figure 14-7   Crevasses. (Courtesy of United States Air Force)

easily fall through. Death may come from injuries sustained in the fall or as a result of hypothermia.

Where possible, rope up when crossing such areas. Consult one of the references on climbing and get competent training in snow and ice climbing before undertaking activities in possibly crevassed areas.

If travel is necessary in such locations, use anything available to carefully probe the snow to detect snow bridges before crossing spots that seem to be depressed. Especially a depression which appears to be long and narrow and at right angles to the slope should be suspect. Once located, stay well back from the edge since an overhang may be present that is not visible from the surface.

STREAMS IN WINTER

Because of rapid flow, mountain streams may continue to flow all winter. In some cases they are also snow bridged, and a fall through the snow will plunge the traveler into icy, rapid water. If the stream is of any size, this could assure death since the victim will be washed downstream under the surface of the snow and, even if able to get out, it will likely be impossible to regain the snow surface.

Such streams may or may not betray their presence by the sound of rushing waters. But they will always be in the lowest part of the terrain. So carefully observe the lay of the land, examine topographic maps, and listen for the sound of running water.

Figure 14-8   Lightning. (Paul H. Risk)

LIGHTNING

Lightning is the visible result of an electrical discharge within a cloud or between the cloud and earth (Figure 14-8). An average lightning bolt may release up to 150,000,000 volts at 150,000 amperes. (To determine how many watts of energy this is, multiply the two figures together.) Needless to say, if an outdoor traveler becomes a part of such a high-energy discharge path, it can have a strong influence on the individual's life!

The thunder heard after a lightning bolt is the atmospheric compression wave caused by passage of the bolt through the air.

Generally, lightning, in order to pose a threat to the hiker, climber, or other outdoor traveler, must be in close proximity. It is possible to determine how far away it is by knowing a little about sound and light. Light travels at the staggering speed of 186,000 miles per second. Sound moves at a mere 1100 *feet* per second at sea level, slightly slower at higher altitudes. As a result, when lightning strikes, the light from the bolt arrives at an observer's location instantly. But the sound from the thunder arrives later. So to determine how far away the storm is, merely count the seconds between the flash and the boom. For example, if lightning flash is followed 5 seconds later by the boom, the storm is about 5500 feet (slightly over a mile) away. Or another way is to count the number of seconds and divide by five (a mile is 5280 feet) if the distances are over a mile. But, when the gap between the flash and boom is diminishing, it is time to think about finding shelter. This is especially true when there is *no* gap between flash and boom.

As conditions conducive to lightning develop, a charge difference builds between the earth and a cloud (Figure 14-9). The base of the cloud develops a

Figure 14-9   Electrical charge distribution between a cloud and the earth in thunderstorms. (Celia Drozdiak)

surplus of electrons (becomes negatively charged), and the earth tends to be positive by comparison. As this difference increases, a feeler develops that lasts only for a fraction of a second but that establishes an ionized path along which flows the main charge as the visible lightning bolt.

Sometimes various phenomena occur preceding the strike. One of these is St. Elmo's Fire. It is a visible corona discharge typically seen around pointed objects such as tree tops, summit rocks, and even on ice axes and climbers' heads! Often appearing as a bluish glow, it may crackle or hum. For years mountaineers have talked of the "humming of the bees" to describe the sound of this phenomenon.

While St. Elmo's Fire may not appear, other conditions are likely to give some warning of danger. At Grand Canyon National Park during the approach of a thunderstorm over the South Rim, a small girl's fluffy, fine hair began to stand straight out from her head. Static electricity was building on the observation point on which we stood. The area was cleared of visitors. After the storm moved away we cautiously moved back, using her as an electroscope. When her hair no longer moved and crackled, the charge had dissipated.

Especially when static electricity or St. Elmo's Fire exist, or thunderheads

Figure 14-10   Thunderheads developing. (Paul H. Risk)

form, precautions should be taken. The typical thunderstorm cloud, called a towering cumulus by pilots and cumulonimbus by weather specialists, is a common sight during summer months in the plains states and over mountain areas (Figure 14-10).

Don't be the highest thing in the area. Lightning tends to strike the highest objects. A hiker traversing a large open meadow is at great risk. A climber at the summit is also. A boater on a lake and a golfer on the course are other examples of those who are in the wrong place at the wrong time.

LIGHTNING PRECAUTIONS

1. If on a mountain, descend. Get off the summit. But do not take shelter in overhangs or caves close to the top. The flow of current through these may be deadly. Get as far down as is practical. If that is impossible, crouch on hands and knees. It is unwise to lie down, since the charge differential between head and feet may be too severe in that position if lightning strikes nearby.

2. In the open, take shelter in the forest. However, do not select the only tree in the area. It is liable to become a lightning rod.

278

3. If static electricity is present, leave the area *immediately* or drop to the ground.
4. Don't worry about metal objects in your possession. Lightning is as likely to strike you as it is your metal objects. However, you should not be carrying an ice axe in your pack with the shaft sticking above your head!
5. An automobile is probably the safest place to be. But *not* because of the insulation of the tires. Remember, the lightning to get to you has just jumped an air gap perhaps thousands of feet. It will not have any trouble jumping from the wheel rims to the ground. The safety afforded you is the result of the Faraday Cage effect. The current flows through the car body, but not through you.
6. Do not stand near metal fences. Current induced from strikes miles away has killed bystanders.
7. Do not use telephones or anything plugged into household wiring. Surges may also be induced here that are potentially very dangerous.

BEARS

Over the past 10 to 15 years, bears have come increasingly into the spotlight. In the large majority of cases, bears will avoid contact with humans. But isolated cases of attacks do occur. Many of the wilderness areas of North America have either grizzly or black bears. In fact, this is part of the reason they can qualify under the definition of wilderness. It may be said that most bear attacks involve grizzly bears. But black bears have and do attack humans. Therefore, it's safe to that say that bears are unpredictable. While there is some knowledge about their behavior, much of the information is educated speculation.

Attack by any kind of bear is extremely rare. But, when it does take place, the person on the receiving end is no longer interested in its rarity. Bears are large and their very presence can be intimidating. Black bears—although they may be black, brown, cinnamon, or blond—may stand 5 to 6 feet tall (Figure 14-11). Grizzlies can weigh 1200 pounds and stand 9 feet tall (Figure 14-12). The grizzly has large, exposed claws on the front feet that may be 6 inches in length and make its tracks distinctive (Figure 14-13). The bear may be almost black, brown, or cream. In some rare instances, they are nearly white. But they generally have guard hairs that are tipped with lighter hair and give the animal a grizzled appearance. Hence, the name.

Bears are omnivores, feeding on almost anything. They may pursue a ground squirrel, literally tearing up the landscape, or rip the bark off dead trees in a search for grubs. In season, they devour large quantities of berries.

Although a great many generalities may be said about them, we can most assuredly say that they are unpredictable. However, there are some precautions that will increase your safety if travel in bear country is planned.

Figure 14-11 Black bear. (Courtesy of Joe Van Wormer)

Figure 14-12 Grizzly bear. (Paul H. Risk)

PRECAUTIONS IN BEAR COUNTRY

1. LEAVE THE DOG HOME! Dogs and bears don't mix. For reasons not entirely known, bears sometimes become enraged in the presence of a dog. The dog, running for its life, will then probably come to you. Guess what happens next?

SPECIAL CONSIDERATIONS

Figure 14-13   Grizzly bear track casting.
(Paul H. Risk)

2. Let the bears know you are there. Bear country is not the place to practice stalking. Be a bit noisy. Some backpackers tie small bells to their packs, which they lightheartedly refer to as ''b'ar bells.'' The sound of the bells will give advanced notice to any bears in the area. They will usually avoid you if given the chance. Many attacks have taken place when a hiker surprised a bear.
3. Avoid bears with cubs. Bears with cubs become intensely protective and may go well out of their way to attack. This is especially true if you are between the cub and the mother.
4. Plan an escape route. Bears, especially grizzlies, can outrun a horse; so don't plan to outdistance them in a chase. Keep an eye out for handy trees to climb. Adult grizzlies generally do not climb trees. It has been said the way to tell the difference between grizzlies and black bears is that the black bear will merely climb the tree after you and the grizzly will tear it out of the ground. (Not quite true, but impressive to consider.)
5. Don't hike alone. There appears to be safety in numbers in bear country. This may be because a larger group probably travels less quietly.
6. Reduce odors around the campsite. (a) Store food well away from the camping area in plastic bags suspended out of reach in a tree. (b) Don't cook near the sleeping area. (c) Don't sleep in the clothes you cooked in. (d) Don't have food in your sleeping bag. (e) Don't use perfumes, deodorants, or other sweet-smelling substances. (f) Keep as clean as possible. (g) Cook with stoves rather than on campfires; avoid campfires. (h) Don't prepare especially aromatic foods. (i) Don't enter bear country during your menstrual period. (j) Avoid sexual activity; it may attract bears.

7. If a bear seems to be staying around the area, it would be wise to leave. You may be infringing on its territory.

All the above recommendations make it seem as though the camping experience must be so highly structured that it loses all its fun. But precautions such as these must be followed closely if the greatest safety is to be enjoyed.

Consult with rangers in the area you are entering. They are usually aware of bear activity and will be able to give good suggestions and also indicate areas that are too dangerous to enter. In grizzly country, signs are often posted on trails where bear activity suggests danger. Obey them!

BASIC RULES FOR FINDING DIRECTION

Earlier in this book it was recommended that the outdoor traveler know how to use a topographic map and be familiar with the terrain of the area. It is beyond the scope of this book to deal with map reading and compass work. However, anyone traveling outdoors should be aware of some of the direction indicators found in a natural area.

LAY OF THE LAND

Often ridges have a trend in a particular direction. This is readily apparent from examination of a map of the area. This knowledge can be of great help when disoriented. For example, in Central Pennsylvania the mountains make an arc running roughly southwest to northeast. This knowledge coupled with observation of the sun will assist greatly in route planning.

In snowy terrain the prevailing winds may sculpture the snow in regular ridges called sastrugi (Figure 14-14). These not only occur in arctic regions but also in mountain areas. Keeping a particular orientation with reference to such sastrugi will allow a hiker to travel in a more constant direction. In desert country, sand dunes and ridges may also take on a regular pattern related to prevailing winds (Figure 14-15).

When traveling in the outdoors, too frequently people fail to look behind. Then, when the return begins, the scene is unfamiliar. They have turned 180 degrees and are suddenly disoriented. This is not a problem if they are following a trail. However, it can be troublesome in cross-country travel when all landmarks are no longer familiar.

The solution is an easy one. From time to time turn around and observe the country to the rear so that it will not look like a puzzle on the return leg of the trip. Carefully examine the countryside. Streams as well as hills and ridges tend to trend in certain directions. This knowledge will also provide useful information in traveling.

Figure 14-14 Sastrugi. (Courtesy of Cecil W. Goodwin)

Figure 14-15   Sand dunes. (Courtesy of Peirce F. Lewis Ph.D.)

Study the map of the area before the trip. A significant portion of the pleasure of the experience can be derived from the planning process. Note where there are roads, trails, and habitation. Become familiar with major terrain features even before you arrive.

After arriving, orient yourself. Determine, based on the terrain features, where the cardinal compass points lie. This will build confidence.

FINDING NORTH

Using a Watch

As watches become predominantly digital, this useful tool is disappearing. But a watch with a traditional dial may be used to find true north. First, point the hour hand at the sun. An easy way to do this is to hold up a sliver or other thin object, so that it casts a shadow. Run the shadow down the hour hand. This forms the first side of an angle. Then draw an imaginary line from the center of the watch to noon. This is the second side of the angle. Now bisect this angle. Notice that the three lines form an arrowhead shape pointing toward the north (Figure 14-16). To use a digital watch, place an upright stick in the ground to cast a shadow. Then draw a *picture* of a traditional watch face on

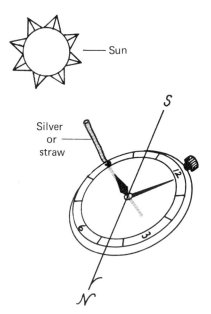

Figure 14-16 Using a watch to find north. A digital watch may be used by drawing the correct positions of the hands on the ground or a piece of paper. (Jan Kolena Cole)

284   SPECIAL CONSIDERATIONS

the ground with the hands oriented to show the correct time. Make the drawing so that the shadow from the stick falls along the hour hand toward the center of the watch drawing. Then follow the instructions for an ordinary watch.

Be aware that this method may be in error as much as 16 degrees if Daylight Saving Time is not corrected for. The watch should be reading Standard Time. If you are on Daylight Saving Time, set the watch *back* an hour.

Shadow Stick

Place a straight stick vertically in the ground so that it will cast the sun's shadow. Mark the end of the shadow. Waiting at least 20 minutes, mark the end of the shadow again. Standing with the toes on the marks and the vertical

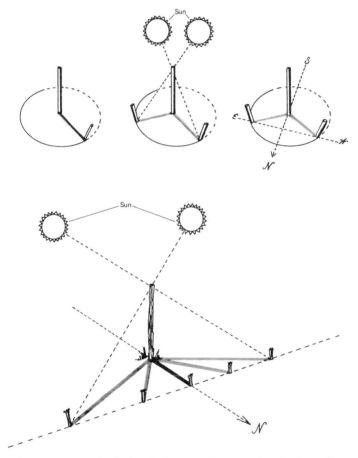

Figure 14-17   Two methods for finding north using the shadow of a vertical stick. Redrawn by Jan Kolena Cole from Survival with Style by permission of Bradford Angier.

stick in front of the observer, you will be facing roughly south if above 23.4 degrees N. latitude and roughly north if below 23.4 degrees S. latitude. In other words, the shadow will be on the north side of the stick in the northern areas and the south side of the stick in the southern. Because of seasonal changes, a line drawn through the end points of the shadows from morning to evening will only be straight at the time of the equinox. At other times of the seasons, it will tend to be curved. But, in any case, the shortest shadow will always be a good indication of true north-south direction (Figure 14-17).

At Night

In both the Northern and Southern hemispheres, various constellations will provide good information on bearings. Orion is visible over most of the globe at certain seasons. Wherever it can be seen, it rises due east and sets due west. To be most accurate, the right-hand star in Orion's belt is exactly on the celestial equator. So it will be exactly east when it rises and exactly west when it sets (Figure 14-18).

In the Northern Hemisphere, Polaris, the Pole Star or North Star, is close enough to north to serve well. Follow the pointer stars in the bowl of the Big Dipper (Ursa Major) to find Polaris in the tail of the Little Dipper (Ursa Minor; Figure 14-19).

In the Southern Hemisphere, there is no handy star over the pole. The Southern Cross is used there. The point in the heavens corresponding to true south is located in an area free of stars which is called the Coal Sack. It is so dark that it appears to be even blacker than the rest of the night sky (Figure 14-20).

Hikers, climbers, and others often spend their nights under a sky that is too often a complete mystery. Become aware and familiar with it. The constellations can be reassuring companions when lost or disoriented.

SNAKEBITE

Over the years, few subjects have received so much discussion. Much misinformation exists not only about the bites of venomous snakes, but about the animals themselves.

Snakes do not seek prey as large as humans. They will avoid humans whenever possible. Most bites occur when a snake is stepped on, startled when it cannot retreat, or feels compromised in some other way. Instances in which snakes have apparently "chased" people are probably attributable to curiosity or error on the part of the snake.

Although some snakes are very dangerous, with extremely toxic venom, there is not a snake on the earth so poisonous that its bite cannot be treated. This even applies to the Krait, the Cobra, and the Tiger Snake, to name three with greatly exaggerated reputations.

In areas where venomous snakes are found, avoid walking in grass or other

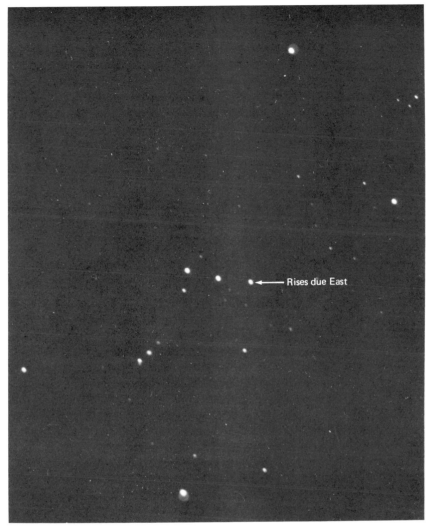

Rises due East

Figure 14-18   The constellation of Orion and a method of finding north.
(Courtesy of Von Del Chamberlain)

areas where the path is not visible. Snakes are often nocturnal in their activity. This is especially true in the tropics. Try to restrict all movement to daytime hours and always wear protective footgear. Snakes are often attracted to areas where rodents are found. Keeping the area free of refuse will reduce the number of rodents. And, finally, do not put hands or feet into places you cannot see.

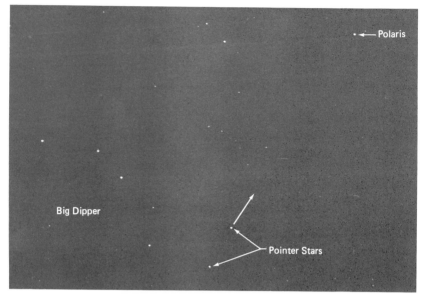

Figure 14-19   How to find north using Polaris. (Courtesy of U.S. Air Force)

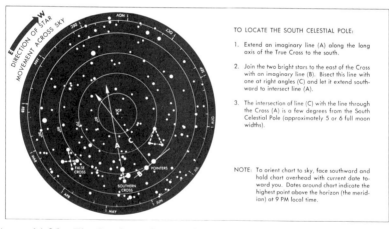

TO LOCATE THE SOUTH CELESTIAL POLE:

1. Extend an imaginary line (A) along the long axis of the True Cross to the south.

2. Join the two bright stars to the east of the Cross with an imaginary line (B). Bisect this line with one at right angles (C) and let it extend southward to intersect line (A).

3. The intersection of line (C) with the line through the Cross (A) is a few degrees from the South Celestial Pole (approximately 5 or 6 full moon widths).

NOTE: To orient chart to sky, face southward and hold chart overhead with current date toward you. Dates around chart indicate the highest point above the horizon (the meridian) at 9 PM local time.

Figure 14-20   The Southern Cross. (Courtesy of U.S. Air Force)

288   SPECIAL CONSIDERATIONS

Snakes may be grouped into four major categories.

1. *Aglypha.* Those without venom.
2. *Opisthoglypha.* Venomous snakes with 1 to 3 teeth at the rear of the upper jaw that are enlarged, fixed, and with grooves on the front edge for the conduction of a relatively mild venom. An example of this type of snake is the African Boomslang.
3. *Proteroglypha.* Having fangs that are small to medium sized, fixed, and deeply grooved in the front of the mouth. Two families in this group are Elapidae (Cobras, Kraits, Mambas, and Coral Snakes) and Hydrophidae (Sea Snakes). Their venom is usually extremely potent and neurotoxic.
4. *Solenoglypha.* These snakes have long, retractable fangs in the front of the mouth that are tubular. Two families in this group are Viperidae (vipers and adders) and Crotalidae (rattlesnakes, Fer-de-Lance, among others).

Two things must be determined before treatment can be accurately prescribed. First, whether the snake is venomous. Second, what degree of envenomization exists.

A nonpoisonous snake will elicit no symptoms. The bite site may show a series of tiny puncture wounds and these may bleed freely. There may be bruising of the tissue. But essentially no swelling will occur, and numbness or severe pain will be absent. Obviously, no treatment beyond that of cleaning the bite site will be required.

A poisonous snake, even if the bite was on target, has several options regarding venom release. (One investigator after sustaining a solid bite from a Fer-de-Lance clearly marked by two definite fang entry wounds developed no symptoms. The snake had not injected venom. Either the snake had no interest in releasing venom or a well-developed sense of humor.) At any rate, the snake may envenomate a wound heavily, moderately, or lightly. Or, it may not produce any venom at all. The severity of the situation is directly related to this, as well as where the bite is on the body. Generally, bites anywhere on the head are very serious, with those on the trunk next in seriousness. Bites on the extremeties are far easier to treat.

In North America, most bites from poisonous snakes would not be fatal even without treatment. However, the secondary problems, even from the milder snakes such as the Massasauga Rattler, are so severe that they must not be minimized. Swelling may become enormous, with the confined tissue so restricted by the skin that circulation is impaired. Slits may have to be cut in the skin to release swelling. Gross discoloration and intense pain are common along with generalized symptoms. Infection, gangrene, and massive tissue destruction from the venom itself may cause permanent disability (Figure 14-21).

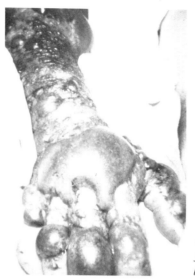

Figure 14-21   Timber rattlesnake bite after four days. (From Snake Venom Poisoning *by F. E. Russell M.D.)*

VENOM TRANSPORT AND ACTION

Venom is transported through cell walls by direct absorption as well as by the lymphatic and general circulatory systems.

Lymph flows in a manner distinctly different from blood. Rather than being moved along in surges by the beat of the heart, it is transported largely by contraction of the muscles. In other words, it is more or less squeezed along. When muscle action is halted, the lymph virtually ceases to move.

The action of the venom depends on the type. While venoms cause a variety of conditions, they are categorized according to their prime site of action in the body. Thus, the venom of the *neurotoxic* snakes such as the Cobra or Coral primarily affects nervous tissue and causes little pain. Its detrimental action is usually caused by interference with the heart beat and respiration.

The venom of the vipers and rattlesnakes, however, attacks the red cells of the blood and dissolves protein. Thus, it is referred to as *hemotoxic* (or hemolytic) and *proteolytic*. Because of its effect on the body, it produces great pain, swelling, and tissue damage. Tissue destruction permits blood and other fluids to infiltrate the damaged area and largely accounts for the discoloration present.

TREATMENT

For years the *cut and suction* method has been prescribed. However, there now is a great deal of debate over its usefulness.

For a time cryotherapy was urged. Originally recommended for the treatment of Bark Scorpion stings, it urged chilling of the bite with cracked ice and water for periods up to 12 or more hours. The theory was that the chemical action of the venom would be greatly slowed by the cooling process and circulation reduced as well. It was hoped that the body could then carry off the venom gradually and detoxify it. However, it was found that this treatment greatly increased tissue damage with many amputations resulting.

Now there seem to be two schools of thought. One suggests that under no circumstances should the bite site be incised. The other states that up to 50 percent of the venom may be removed by the cut-suction procedure if done within 3 minutes of the bite. Studies indicate that most of the venom is removed within the first 15 minutes and not much after 30 minutes. For this reason, the proponents of this school recommend that within the first 30 minutes cutting and sucking be used.

This author is concerned with the fact that cutting may hasten the absorption of the venom. It would appear that incision and suction may expose fresh tissue surfaces and also slice across lymphatics, providing a larger opening for the venom to enter.

Another team has discovered that it is possible to completely excise the pocket (a few drops) of venom if done immediately. However, this is not practical for the average outdoor person. There is far too much danger from accidental severing of major vessels, nerves, and tendons. Perhaps in a "forever situation" where the bite is from a very venomous animal and help is out of the question this might be considered.

In general, treatment for bites of rattlesnakes & their relatives should be managed as follows:

1. Immobilize the victim and place in a prone position. If the bite is on an extremity, splint to prevent movement and to slow transport of the venom through the lymphatics. Keep the victim calm and do not let him move about.

2. Place a broad (2–3 inches) constricting band (ligature) above the bite. This is *not* a tourniquet. It is designed only to limit or restrict lymph flow. It should only be tight enough to firmly dent the tissue. A finger can be easily inserted under the band.

3. Cool the bite site to retard transport and action. But only cool it. Do not use ice; only cool, wet compresses.

4. Cut or not. . . . It is probably a good idea that no cutting be done. But, if it is, the cuts should be no more than 3 mm deep and parallel to the long axis of the limb, to minimize chances of cutting something unintended. This should only be done within the first 15 or so minutes after the bite.

5. Quickly take the victim to a hospital.

WHAT ABOUT ANTIVENIN?

Specific antivenins are available for many snakes. Some are broad spectrum. An example would be *Crotalidae* polyvalent, an antivenin that is effective against the venom of this entire rattlesnake group.

The difficulty is that some people are very allergic to the antivenin. Most antivenin is manufactured by injecting horses with venom. The horse serum can be a serious problem. Even a very dilute amount may cause anaphylactic shock in a sensitive person, resulting in almost immediate circulatory, heart, and respiratory difficulty and perhaps even death. Its onset is often so rapid that the person affected will literally be collapsing before the needle can be withdrawn.

Antivenin kits contain a diluted ampule of horse serum for sensitivity testing. It is either injected subdermally or a drop is placed into the conjunctival space of the eye. The difficulty is that, in very sensitive people, this may also cause anaphylaxis. Unless a well-equipped field hospital is available, anaphylaxis is not treatable. To compound the problems, antivenin is (1) quite expensive, (2) best administered intravenously, and (3) often required in doses up to a dozen units. All the above considerations dictate against the average hiker carrying it.

ETHNIC CONTACT

Although readers whose travel is limited to the confines of their own community, county, state, or country may find it difficult to believe, failure of an outsider to handle contact with another culture correctly may be as dangerous as any other life-threatening condition in the environment.

There are a number of peoples around the world whose contact with outsiders is very limited. Yet, transglobal flights take us over their heads daily. Effective cross-cultural communication is vital if a forced stay in another's environment occurs. Frankly, similar principles applied within our own country might go a long way to easing cultural tensions.

Too often we tend to regard those customs different from ours as strange, barbaric, or even dangerous. We know that they couldn't possibly be an equal or they would be able to speak English! (And often to help with this deficiency, we resort to yelling and speaking slowly. Somehow we expect that either they can't hear or aren't intelligent enough to comprehend.)

If the university student is any example, manners and social etiquette are dying in this country. Students often demonstrate, even under formal conditions, that they know nothing about deportment. One student of survival, as we discussed the fact that a group from another culture might deeply resent a social error and seek to retaliate, responded with disbelief. How could anyone take things so seriously that a person's life could be in danger through ignorance of the particular culture's social graces?

292

RULES FOR CROSS-CULTURAL INVOLVEMENT

Smile. A smile can only be construed as feeble mindedness or friendliness. Neither is threatening. Demonstrate your desire to be friendly and that you are not hostile. But do not be too forward. Your new friends must be allowed to touch you and examine your clothing, even if with some humor at your expense. But you must not reciprocate. Keep your hands to yourself.

This is especially true of children. There is a great temptation to touch or pat children. However, some groups feel this is a spiritual threat to the young person and may become convinced that you are too dangerous to have around.

Keep your eyes off the women. And if anyone fails to maintain eye contact with you, do not force it. There may be a very good reason for it.

Wait for people to approach you. But, if you do approach, do so slowly with your hands in plain view. Smile some more. If you have a weapon, keep it out of sight. This is not the time for them to think you are threatening them.

Show an interest in their handicrafts, tools, and weapons. But, do not touch unless invited to. A weapon may lose its power if handled by an outsider. This could cost you your life.

Be a good sport. If you are the butt of a joke, laugh along with them. Never take yourself too seriously. (Nobody else does.)

However, do not laugh at them or talk in your native language to people in your group in such manner as to develop suspicion that you are either plotting or demeaning them.

If you know some tricks, join in the merriment by demonstrating. But do not do things that are likely to leave a leader or shaman looking bad.

Do not enter a building without being invited. Stand outside and speak quietly or clap your hands.

As a general rule, you will be expected to eat or drink anything that is given you. To refuse will certainly jeopardize your hosts' cooperation and may endanger your life. This is a difficult area since to eat or drink the native fare may also endanger your health. If you cannot or will not, then try to indicate that you are too full.

In essence, watch your hosts. Take your lead from them. Let them offer. Never initiate action without carefully considering all ramifications.

And, be extremely patient. Many cultures do not adhere to the doctrine of rush, rush, rush. There is really no hurry.

15

SURVIVAL
KITS

Previous chapters have emphasized methods to prevent or reduce the seriousness of outdoor emergencies. Techniques have been introduced that will enable you to secure fire, shelter, water, signals, and food under such conditions. Often the methods involved improvisation using materials obtained in the outdoor environment. Certainly these procedures will work. But it is far easier to build a fire, purify water, and signal for help if certain items of equipment are taken with you when you go on an outdoor trip. For example, fire can be made using a bow drill, but matches are much, much simpler to use. So now is the time to plan for your personal emergency. Develop a kit of items that will help you secure the "keys to survival." Some of the guidelines and types of equipment have been mentioned earlier in this book. Now details will be given to help you wisely select those things most likely to accomplish the tasks at hand, reduce bulk, and tolerate long storage.

If a survival kit is to be useful, it must be in your possession. You cannot leave it at home and expect its contents to be of much help. Furthermore, everything originally put in must still be there when an emergency dictates a need for their use. Reference to the first two chapters of this book will refresh your memory on how people tend to minimize the possibility of ever really being in an outdoor emergency. This attitude can either cause outdoor people to fail to construct kits or to fail to take along necessary survival equipment. You must realize, once again, that it does not matter how many times the emergency happens to someone else. When it happens to you, it is imperative that you have the ability and equipment to cope. Start *now* to build or enhance your personal survival kit.

Another failing which creates problems is the tendency to "borrow" items

294

from the kit for purposes other than emergencies. On a picnic the matches have been left at home, so the ones from the survival kit are used. After all, what's a match or two? But if this happens often enough, there will not be any left when you need them under critical conditions. Or the match container is simply thrust into a pants pocket and never finds its way back into the kit. DO NOT use emergency equipment for anything but emergencies. Clearly mark or otherwise identify things carried for this special purpose and control the temptation to use them for anything else. Of course, items such as a knife or compass which are routinely carried and used may be exempt from this warning. Just be sure that they are indeed always carried.

HOW SHOULD THE KIT BE PACKED?

A great variety of containers may be used (Figure 15-1). Small nylon belt packs, fanny packs, and plastic boxes of various sizes are obtainable from many sources.

The purpose of the kit, its contents, and its size will tend to control how it is packed and carried. Kits for automobiles may be small enough to fit in the glove compartment, above the visor, or under the seat. For the person pinned in a crushed car after a single vehicle accident, out of view and possibly in thick trees or brush, it may be critical that they be able to reach something with which to signal without leaving their position. In such a case a signal kit including flares, smoke signals, and flashlight might best be mounted with Velcro above the visor (Figure 15-2). However aerial flares may pose two problems. Gasoline leaking from the damaged car can easily be ignited by any type of spark from such a signal. Also local or state ordinances may prohibit carry-

Figure 15-1   Three types of containers for a survival kit. The belted unit is a fanny pack. A belt pack is in the center foreground, and two types of plastic boxes are shown at the left and right of the photograph. (Paul H. Risk)

Figure 15-2   Automobile visor with emergency items held by Velcro. The mirror is removable. Aerial flares are at each end of the mirror, and a small flashlight is below. (Paul H. Risk)

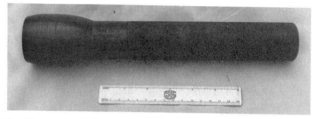

Figure 15-3   Heavy-duty aluminum flashlight. Practically indestructable, it may be used as a club if necessary. (Paul H. Risk)

ing a flare-projecting device in the passenger area of a vehicle. If concentrated enough, fuel vapor can even be ignited by the spark produced by the operation of an ordinary flashlight. Explosion-proof lights are available and are highly recommended for use in automobiles (Figure 15-3).

Kits for backpacking must fit into a pack or its side pockets. Those for airline travel probably should fit into a suit coat pocket and thus be flat and compact overall. The list of variables is endless, and you will have to determine what best suits your needs.

ONLY IN SPECIAL CONTAINERS?

While special containers for survival kits are helpful in localizing equipment, keeping it clean, and making it available, there may also be some problems. In many instances emergencies cause the victim to become separated from kits. Every canoeist has had the experience of losing something when the canoe flips over. Either the item was not fastened into the boat and is lost, or the canoe is carried away. If rapid evacuation from an automobile or aircraft becomes nec-

296

essary, kits in your luggage or the trunk of the car may be useless. It is therefore recommended that you always carry at least basic items such as matches, a knife, a whistle, signals, and water-purification tablets in your pockets. Also, since pockets may be ripped, it is even wiser to spread such things throughout several pockets. Likewise, a small kit attached to your belt is a good idea and can contain more things than you may want in your pockets.

But bear in mind that the mere possession of survival equipment does not guarantee safety. There is sometimes a tendency for the novice outdoor person to buy things in the belief that these provide an almost magical protection. Prevention is still the best medicine. And you must know how to use your equipment to the best advantage. Finally, the skills presented in the rest of this book must be mastered. Don't be lulled into a false sense of security by a well-packed kit.

WHAT EQUIPMENT?

A survival kit is designed basically to assist in providing the five "keys to survival": fire, shelter, signals, water, and food. Other considerations which may be involved when designing more elaborate kits include light sources, tools, medical and first aid items, weapons, direction-finding equipment such as compasses, and many things that can best be categorized as miscellaneous. Examples are given for each group, followed by descriptions of several types of kits.

FIRE

Matches (strike anywhere type)
Match container (waterproof)
Cigarette lighter (butane)
Metal Match® (or other spark-producing device)
Fire Sticks®
Fire Ribbon®
Fire Wick®
Fire Patches
Candles
Steel wool (fine)
Stove (backpacking)
Magnifying glass

> **Note:** Butane cigarette lighters have limited use or are altogether useless in cold weather. The fuel will not vaporize. However, after they are warmed by placing them in your pocket, they should be fine. But they are not to

Figure 15-4 Fire starters. Fire Sticks®, Fire Ribbon®, and Fire Wick® are available commercially. The small package below the Fire Ribbon® contains wax-soaked gun patches. (Paul H. Risk)

be carried on aircraft since they may leak or burst under reduced air pressure. This danger is enhanced at high altitudes during sudden cabin depressurization.

Fire Sticks®, Fire Ribbon®, Fire Wick®, and Fire Patches are trade names for products using wood dust, fibers, cloth, or other materials impregnated with flammable liquid or wax (Figure 15-4).

SHELTER

Tube tent
Plastic leaf or garbage bags
Plastic sheet
Emergency Blanket®
Sportsman's Blanket®

> **Note:** Leaf bags or garbage bags make excellent emergency rain protection.

Figure 15-5 shows how a garbage bag may be worn after cutting out holes for head and arms. Another bag could also be pulled over the feet and legs while the survivor sat out the storm. Leaf bags are longer than garbage bags and may be cut to serve as a hood as well. Emergency Blanket® and Sportsman's Blanket® are trade names for aluminized sheets that may be used as a wraparound cover or for an improvised, small, A-frame shelter (Figure 15-6).

SURVIVAL KITS

Figure 15-5 Garbage bag worn as emergency rain protection. (Paul H. Risk)

Figure 15-6a   Aluminized Sportsman's Blanket® used as an A-frame shelter. (Paul H. Risk)

Figure 15-6b   Aluminized Sportsman's Blanket® used as an emergency wrap-around. Be sure to allow as much ventilation as possible to reduce condensation on the inner surface of the blanket. (Paul H. Risk)

WHAT EQUIPMENT?   **299**

Neither they nor the garbage and leaf bags breathe, and perspiration will tend to build up making the user clammy and damp. Nevertheless, you are better off a bit clammy than exposed to the heat draining effects of rain running over your body. If space can be left between the sheet of plastic or aluminized material and your skin, moisture will escape more easily. The garbage bags and Emergency Blanket® are for a single use, since they are rather fragile and easily damaged. Both are very compact and may be carried in a pocket.

SIGNALS

Aerial flares
Orange smoke
Dye marker
Signal panels
Strobes
Mirrors
Whistle
Railroad flares
Radio

WATER

Iodine water purification tablets
Tincture of iodine
Halazone tablets
Clorox (in small plastic drop bottle)
Purex (in small plastic drop bottle)
Filter (approved type)
Plastic sheeting (to construct stills)
Desalinating device
Plastic bags (for water containers)

FOOD

The list of food and food-related products that might be included in a survival kit is endless. Since food is of very limited importance in most situations, there is generally no reason to carry an extensive variety. Things that may be useful in improving attitude or providing increases in energy might be considered. Individual serving packets are often easier to pack than bulk quantities. Here are some possible items to take along.

300

Sugar cubes
Bouillon cubes or granules
Tea
Coffee
Instant chocolate drink
Kool-Aid or Tang
Salt and pepper
Seasoned salt
Spices
Tropical chocolate bars
Dextrose tablets
Hard candy
Special high-energy snack bars

> **Note:** If you wonder why spices and other flavoring agents such as salt and sugar are emphasized, you simply have not yet had to eat some of the natural fare found in the field. Salt can be invaluable in changing survival food into something palatable. You would be amazed how much better insect larvae taste with a bit of salt! Bouillon can greatly improve the taste of stews and soups. Candy, dextrose tablets, and high-energy snack bars will usually not be carried in sufficient quantity to provide much sustained energy, but their quick lift can be a big help.
>
> Coffee, tea, and chocolate contain caffeine and may produce a burst of energy or an improvement in attitude under emergency conditions.

Fishing and snaring may often be important in extended survival conditions. So the following items may also be needed.

Fish line (braided)
Fish hooks (various sizes)
Flies
Leader (wire and nylon)
Spinners
Sinkers
Plastic worms
Small floats
Snare wire

> **Note:** Monofilament line is virtually impossible to handle without a reel, so be sure to get braided nylon. The most basic fishing kit would include only line, hooks, and sinkers and would be suitable for most emergency situations. Snare wire may be lightweight braided, or #24 single strand.

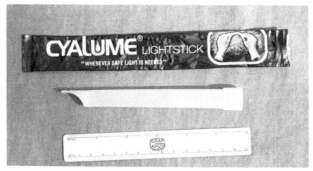

Figure 15-7   Chemical light stick. (Paul H. Risk)

Light Sources
Light sticks
Candles
Candle lantern
Flashlight with extra bulb

Light sticks are plastic tubes containing two chemicals that are mixed by bending the outer plastic tube, thus breaking an inner glass vial. They emit a greenish-yellow light for periods of 30 minutes to several hours. They are waterproof, nontoxic, and explosion proof. Their intensity and duration are controlled by temperature. When it is warmer, they tend to be brighter but last a shorter time. At colder temperatures, they produce less light but last longer (Figure 15-7). Flashlights selected should, when possible, have switches that are not easily turned on in the kit, or the switch should be taped to prevent this. Some people keep the batteries separate until needed to prevent accidental rundown. Tests conducted by the author indicate that Eveready Energizer® batteries last longer under continuous use compared to others. Nevertheless, if other types are used, alkaline or lithium batteries are recommended because of their durable qualities. Consideration should also be given to flashlights that are sealed to prevent ignition of flammable or explosive vapors. As mentioned earlier in this chapter, they are more expensive but compare very favorably when the cost of prolonged treatment for extensive burns is considered! Since batteries have limited shelf life, they should be checked periodically with a battery condition meter and replaced when necessary.

Tools and Weapons
These two categories have been combined with the idea that what may be a tool under one circumstance becomes a weapon in another. In addition, various devices which are only weapons will be mentioned.

302

Flexible wire saw
Vice grip pliers
Slip joint pliers
Screwdriver assortment
Hack saw (miniature)
Hammer
Machete (14 inch)
Sheath knife
Pocket knife (folding)
Sewing kit
    Thread (several sizes)
    Needles (several sizes)
Pistol
Rifle
Shotgun
Ammunition (include shotshells for pistol and rifle)
Sharpening steel, stone, or ceramic

Medical and First Aid

Depending on whether the kit is intended as a basic first aid kit or for an expedition, backup medical and first aid items may make up a large or small portion. However, a great deal of knowledge of appropriate treatment and the effects of drugs is necessary when dealing with pain killers, antibiotics, and other related substances. Also, there are many different substances that can accomplish similar goals, so only categories have been provided rather than specific drugs. If you are planning an extensive kit, consult medical people. Many of the substances will require prescriptions.

Analgesic tablets (aspirin, Tylenol, etc.)
Motion sickness drug (Dramamine, Marezine, etc.)
Diarrhea medication
Antacid
Antihistamine (for hay fever and other allergic reactions)
Antibiotic (broad spectrum)
Stimulant
Pain medication
Muscle relaxant
Sting Kill®
Oil of cloves
Sunscreen cream
Assorted bandage compresses
Kling® bandage

Elastic bandage
Thermometer (rectal)
Scissors
Razor blade
Tweezers
Suture material
Suture needles
Suture forceps

Miscellaneous

Insect repellant (with high percentage of n,n diethyl-meta-toluamide)
Parachute suspension cord (with inner cores; see Figure 15-8)
Heavy-duty aluminum foil
Safety pins (assorted sizes)
Duct or heavy plastic tape
Dental floss
Mosquito head net
Notebook
Pencil
Travelers checks
Identification
Coins for telephone
Survival manual (pocket-sized)
Military-type can opener

> **Note:** Parachute suspension cord, as shown in Figure 15-8, has discrete
> inner cores rather than random fibers. These inner core lines, which may
> have a breaking strength of 35 to 50 pounds, may be pulled out for use in

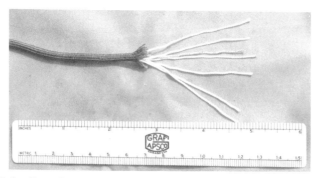

Figure 15-8   Parachute suspension cord or the recommended type of cord.
Note the seven core lines inside the braided sheath. (Paul H. Risk)

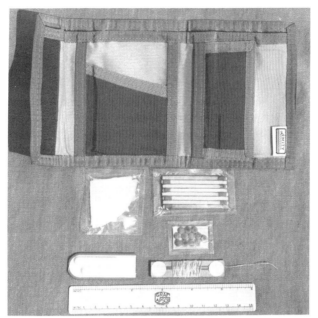

Figure 15-9 Type I pocket kit. Clockwise from the left side of the ruler: whistle, fire patches, nylon wallet container, matches, water purification tablets, needles, and dental floss. (Paul H. Risk)

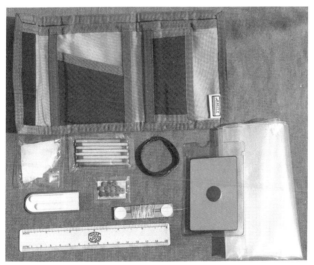

Figure 15-10 Type II pocket kit. Besides the items contained in the Type I kit, there are: wire, signal mirror, and plastic bags. (Paul H. Risk)

emergency. If suspension line is used for boot laces, the braided sheath still remains for use as laces after the cores are withdrawn.

SURVIVAL KIT EXAMPLES

Type I Pocket Kit

This kit (Figure 15-9) represents the utmost in simplicity. The items may either be carried in the pockets or in a small nylon wallet with Velcro closure. Note that a pocketknife is not shown in any kit. It should *always* be carried in your pants pockets or purse.

Type II Pocket Kit

The Type II kit (Figure 15-10) represents an expansion of Type I. While a number of additional items have been added, they are either flat or compressible and may still be carried comfortably in a nylon wallet which is placed in an inner suit coat pocket. In both the Type I and Type II kits, some things are heat sealed in plastic. This may be done with any of the commercially available devices made to seal food in boilable bags such as the Dazey SEAL-a-MEAL®.

Belt Pack Kit

This extremely compact kit contains many items (see Figures 15-11, 15-12, 15-13, and 15-14). It represents a rather extensive kit and may be assembled from most sporting goods stores. Small items are in individual plastic boxes. This keeps items separate and readily available in an emergency. Small boxes of this type may also be used to assemble pocket-sized kits complete in themselves.

Fanny Pack Kit

Such a pack is easy to carry and comfortable to wear (Figure 15-15). Other items beyond those of a survival nature may be carried as well. Although not waterproof under conditions of immersion, the fanny pack material is impervious to rain. Any leakage that may occur would spill through the zipper.

Storm Kit®

The Storm Kit® is commercially available from various sources (Figure 15-16). Compact and light, the design is ideal for tossing in the glove compartment or into a pack. The pipe tobacco style container will serve as an emergency can or a water decanter.

306

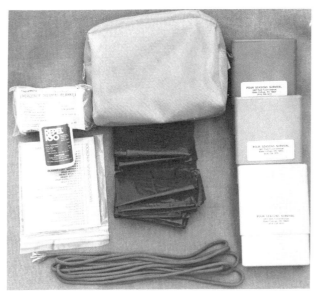

Figure 15-11 Belt pack kit. Parachute cord, two garbage bags, a survival manual, insect repellant, an Emergency Blanket®, and three other modules in plastic boxes are all contained in the nylon belt pack in the top center of the picture. (Paul H. Risk)

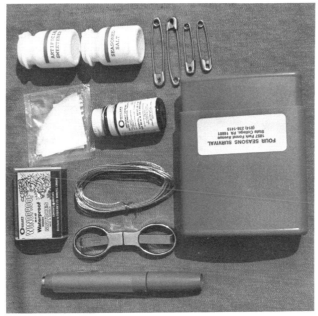

Figure 15-12 Belt pack module A: penlight, collapsable scissors, windproof/waterproof matches, wire, fire patches, water purification tablets with dental floss wound around the neck, artificial sweetener, seasoned salt, and four safety pins. (Paul H. Risk)

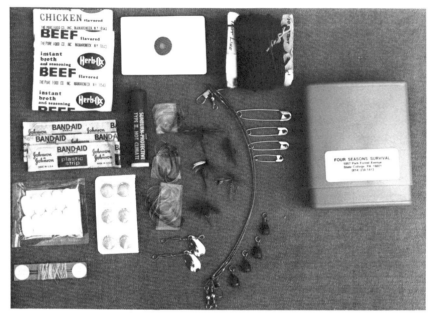

Figure 15-13   Belt pack module B: chicken and beef broth, bandages, aspirin, antihistamine, needles with thread, sinkers, steel leader, spinners, fish hooks with nylon leader, several flies, lip balm, signal mirror, braided fish line, and safety pins. (Paul H. Risk)

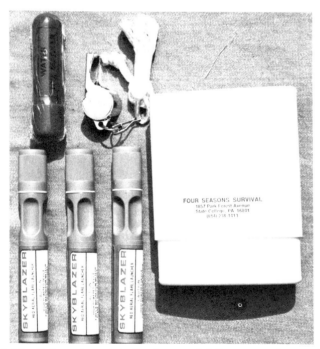

Figure 15-14   Belt pack module C: three aerial flares, sea dye marker, and a police whistle. (Paul H. Risk)

Figure 15-15   Fanny pack. From left to right, items are arranged roughly in rows: gill net, plastic water bag with purification tablets, parachute cord, garbage bags (2) signal mirror, steel wool (2), compass, toilet paper, aspirin, bandages, antihistamine tablets, aerial flares (3), sea dye marker, Emergency Blanket®, insect repellant, thermometer with case, folding scissors, wire, plastic tape, needles and thread, candles (2), fire patches, match container, flashlight, smoke signal, sharpening steel, artificial sweetener, seasoned salt, herb seasoning, eating utensils, whistle, Metal Match®. (Paul H. Risk)

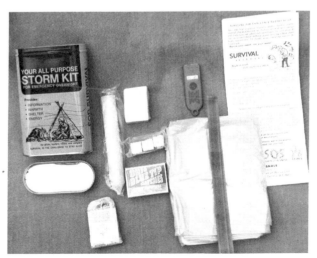

Figure 15-16   Storm Kit®, containing signal mirror (in lid), salt, tea, candle, matches, bouillon, sugar cubes, whistle, emergency tube tent, and survival instructions. (Paul H. Risk)

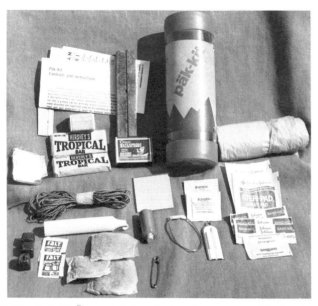

Figure 15-17 Pak-Kit®, containing instructions, razor blade, dextrose tablets, tropical chocolate, aluminum foil, nylon cord, bouillon, salt, tea, Fire Sticks®, matches, mirror, duct tape, wire, safety pin, whistle, analgesic tablets, bandages, gauze pads, and emergency plastic tube tent. (Paul H. Risk)

Pak-Kit®

This commercial kit can give you some idea of the number of items that can be placed in a relatively small container (Figure 15-17). Once you take them out, they may never fit back in! But the kit is an excellent one.

This chapter has been designed to provide you with some ideas on what may be included in emergency survival kits. Certainly the ideas presented here are not the only suitable ones. Use your imagination combined with a knowledge of your personal needs, and assemble your own custom kit.

RECOMMENDED READING

GENERAL SURVIVAL

BOOKS

Acerrano, Anthony J. *The Outdoorsman's Emergency Manual*. Winchester, 1976.

Allen, William H. *Analysis of Survival Equipment*. Arctic, Desert, Tropic Information Center, Maxwell AFB, No. G-105.

Anderson, Eric G. *Plane Safety and Survival*. Aero Publishers, Inc., 1978.

Angier, Bradford. *How to Stay Alive in The Woods*. Collier Books, 1970.

———. *Survival with Style*. Scribner's, 1972.

———. *Wilderness Cookery*. Stackpole Co., 1963.

Beard, Daniel Carter. *Wisdom of the Woods*. J. B. Lippincott, 1926.

Berglund, Berndt. *Wilderness Survival*. Scribner's, 1974.

Best, Herbert. *Parachute to Survival*. John Day, 1964.

Boy Scouts of America. *Fieldbook for Boys and Men*. BSA, 1967.

Brower, David Ross, ed. *The Sierra Club Wilderness Handbook*. Ballantine, 1967.

Brower, David. *Manual of Ski Mountaineering*. Sierra Club, 1962.

Bruce, Ronald, ed. *The Survival Handbook*. Award Books, 1971.

Burt, Calvin P., R. L. Dawson, and F. G. Heyl. *Survival in the Wilderness*. Life Support Technology, Inc., 1969.

Clark, Eric. *Everybody's Guide to Survival*. Collins, 1969.

Colby, Carroll B. *Survival-Training in our Armed Services*. Coward-McCann, 1965.

———, and Bradford Angier. *The Art and Science of Talking to the Woods*. Stackpole Co., 1970.

Craighead, Frank C., Jr. *Track of the Grizzly*. Sierra Club, 1979.

———, and John J. Craighead. *How to Survive on Land and Sea: Individual Survival*. U.S. Naval Institute, 1958.

Dakan, Norman E. *Escape, Evasion, Rescue, and Survival*. USAF, Pacific Air Forces, 1957.

Dietz, Lew. *Touch of Wildness*. Holt, Rinehart and Winston, 1970.

East, Ben. "Survival: 23 True Sportsmen's Adventures." *Outdoor Life*, Dutton, 1967.

Easton, Roger, and C. B. Harston. *Outdoor Survival—Washington 4-H Natural Resources Project*. Cooperative Extension Service. Washington State University, 1968.

Edholm, O. G., and A. L. Bacharach. *The Physiology of Human Survival*. Academic Press, 1965.

Fear, Gene. *Surviving the Unexpected Wilderness Emergency*. Survival Education Council, Tacoma Unit, 1972.

Gatty, Harold. *Nature is Your Guide—How to Find Your Way on Land and Sea by Observing Nature*. Dutton, 1958.

Graininger, Donald Howard. *Don't Die in the Bundu*. Timmins, 1969.

Graves, Richard H. *Food and Water in the Bush—How to Live off the Land*. J. M. Graves, 1952.

Greenbank, Anthony. *The Book of Survival*. Harper & Row, 1967.

Hafen, Brent Q., Keith J. Karren, and Keith R. Hooker. *Surviving Health Emergencies and Disasters*. Emergency Medical Services Associates, 1979.

Halstead, Bruce W. *Dangerous Marine Animals*. Cornell Maritime, 1959.

Harding, A. R., ed. *Deadfalls and Snares*. A. R. Harding Publisher, 1935.

Heizer, R. F., and M. A. Whipple. *The California Indians*. The University of California Press, 1951.

Hersey, John R. *Here to Stay*. Knopf, 1963.

Hood, Mary V. *Outdoor Hazards—Real and Fancied: A Guide to Out-of-Doors Safety for Campers, Hikers, Hunters, Fishermen, and Travelers in the United States*. Macmillan, 1955.

Hutton, Clayton. *Official Secret—The Remarkable Story of Escape Aids, Their Invention, Production, and Sequel*. Crown Publishers, 1961.

RECOMMENDED READING

Jaegar, Ellsworth. *Tracks and Trailcraft*. Macmillan, 1948.

———. *Wildwood Wisdom*. Macmillan, 1961.

Johnson, James R. *Anyone Can Live off the Land*. David McKay, 1961.

Kephart, Horace. *Camping and Woodcraft*. Macmillan, 1921.

Kittredge, R. Y. *Self-Taught Navigation*. Northland, 1970.

Kjellstrom, Bjorn. *Be an Expert with Map and Compass*. American Orienteering Service, 1955.

Krizek, D. T., and E. V. Saunders. *Annotated Bibliography of Basic Survival, Combat Survival, and Counterinsurgency*. Arctic, Desert, Tropic Information Center, No. G-110, 1963.

Kroeber, A. L. *Handbook of the Indians of California*. Bureau of American Ethnology, The Smithsonian Institution, 1925.

Lansing, Alfred. *Endurance*. McGraw-Hill, 1959.

Laubin, R., and G. Laubin. *The Indian Tipi—It's History, Construction, and Use*. University of Oklahoma Press, 1957.

Laurel, Alicia Bay. *Living on the Earth*. Random House, 1971.

Lehman, Charles A. *Emergency Survival*. Medical & Technical Books, Inc., 1979.

Mariner, W. *Mountain Rescue Techniques*. Sierra Club,

Merrill, William K. *Getting Out of Outdoor Trouble—The Lifesaving Handbook on Dealing with Emergencies, for Careful Families, Outdoorsmen, Boaters, Vacationers*. Stackpole Co., 1965.

Merryman, H. T. *Mountain Rescue*. Air Ministry, Dept. of Opsl., 1953.

Millard, W. C. *Evaluation of Pocket Pen Flare*. Arctic Aeromedical Lab, No. 63-3, 1963.

Mitchell, Jim, and Eugene Fear. *Fundamentals of Outdoor Enjoyment*, Survival Education Association, 1977.

Morris, Ailene, ed., and E. Porter Horne. *Visual Search Techniques*. National Academy of Sciences, National Research Council, 1960.

Nesbitt, Paul H., Alonzo W. Pond, and William H. Allen. *The Survival Book*. Funk & Wagnalls, 1968.

Olsen, Larry Dean. *Outdoor Survival Skills*. Division of Continuing Education, Extension Publications, Brigham Young University, 1973.

Ormond, Clyde. *Complete Book of Outdoor Lore*. Harper & Row, 1964.

———. *The Outdoorsman's Handbook*. Dutton, 1970.

Patterson, Craig. *Mountain Wilderness Survival*, And/Or Press., 1979.

Riviere, Bill. *Backcountry Camping*. Doubleday and Co., 1971.

Rodman, Stanley, ed. *Robinson Crusoe, The Raft, and The Rime of the Ancient Mariner*. Comparative Classics Series. Noble, 1965.

Roninger, L. E., ed. *Survival*. Department of the Army Field Manual, F. M. No. 21-76, 1957.

Rowlands, John J. *Spare Cache Lake Country: Life in the North Woods*. W. W. Norton, 1947.

Russell, P. J. *Sea Signalling Simplified*. Fernhill, 1970.

Rutstrum, Calvin. *Wilderness Route Finder*. Macmillan, 1967.

Seton, Ernest Thompson. *The Book of Woodcraft and Indian Lore*. Doubleday and Co., 1929.

Shanks, Bernard. *Wilderness Survival*. Universe Books, 1980.

Shockley, Robert O., and Charles K. Fox. *Survival in the Wilds*. A. S. Barnes, 1970.

Stewart, George. *Ordeal By Hunger*. Houghton-Mifflin, 1960.

Stoffel, Robert. "Skip," *Emergency Preparedness Today*. Dept. of Emergency Services, State of Washington, 1976.

Sullivan, J. J., N. R. Disco, and A. Wong. *Feasibility Study and Conceptural Design for a Personal Thermal Conditioning System*. Technical Report 68-1, Sanders Nuclear Corp., 1967.

Troebst, Cord-Christian. *The Art of Survival*. Doubleday and Co., 1963.

U.S. Dept. of the Air Force. *Helicopter Rescue Sense*. Aviation Training Div., 1954.

———. *Survival, Search, and Rescue*. AFM No. 64-5, 1969.

———. *Survival Training Edition*. AFM No. 64-3, 1969.

———. *Survival Uses of Parachute*. AFM No. 64-15, 1969.

U.S. Dept. of the Army. *Survival, Evasion, and Escape*. FM No. 21-76, 1969.

———. *Survival Radios, Material Test Procedure*. Report No. MTP-6-3-024, 1971.

———. *Survival Sense*. Pamphlet No. 95-10, 1963.

U.S. Dept. of Defense. *Personal and Family Survival*. Office of Civil Defense, Adult Education Course, 1963.

U.S. Government Printing Office. *International Codes and Signals*. No. D203.22:102, 1969.

West Virginia Bureau of Highway Safety Promotion. *Blizzard: Safety and Survival*. 1968.

Whelan, Townsend, and Bradford Angier. *On Your Own in the Wilderness*. Stackpole Co., 1965.

ARTICLES

Chassler, Sey. "School for Survival." *Collier's*, 1951, 128(23):24–25.

Colby, C. B. "Camp Shelters." *Outdoor Life*, 1969, 143(4):16–26.

Conley, Clare. "Kits for Survival." *Field and Stream*, 1968, 72(12):173.

Crimmin, Eileen. "What to do in an Earthquake." *Science Digest*, 1966, 59(4):67–70.

———. "What to do if Your Boat Sinks." *Science Digest*, 1966, 59(6):57–59.

———. "What to do in a Landslide." *Science Digest*, 1966, 60(1):75–77.

———. "What to do in a Forest Fire." *Science Digest*, 1966, 60(3):58–61.

———. "How to Survive an Air Crash." *Science Digest*, 1966, 60(4):44–47.

———. "The Anatomy of Survival." *Science Digest*, 1966, 60(5):57–61.

Crush, Marion A. "Suggestions for Survival Reading: The Noble Savage." *Wilson Library Bulletin*, 1971, 45(9):864–869.

Greenbank, Anthony. "Could You Survive?" *Outdoor Life,* 1969, 143(4):90–93.

Halacy, D. S., Jr. "How to Find Water Anywhere." *Outdoor Life*, 1965, 136:14–15.

Kahn, Frederick H., and Barbara R. Visscher. "A Simple, Safe Method of Water Purification For Backpackers." *Backpacker* #26.

Kirkman, N. F. "Mountain Accidents and Mountain Rescue in Great Britain." *British Medical Journal*, 1966, 1:162–164.

LeMay, Curtis E. "School for Survival." *National Geographic*, 1953, 103(5):565–602.

Lentz, E. C. "Survival Following Controlled Aircraft Crashes." *Aerospace Medicine*, 1964, 35:53–57.

Merryman, H. T. "Tissue Freezing and Local Cold Injury." *Physiological Review*, 1957, 37:233.

Oertle, Lee. "How to Travel Safely in the Wilds." *Popular Science*, 1970, 197(1):82–83.

Phillips, James G. "Hot Tips for Cold Days." *Sports Illustrated*, 1970, 32:48–49.

Pond, Alonzo. "What's Your Survival Quotient?" *Field and Stream*, 1971, 75(11):72–73, 204–206.

Pugh, L. G. C. E. "Accidental Hypothermia in Walkers, Climbers, and Campers." *British Medical Journal*, 1966, 1:123–129.

Rathburn, Jim. "How to Make Your Boat Family-Safe." *Today's Health*, 1961, 39(6):48–51, 76–82.

Risk, Paul H. "Lost Children Can Survive if We Stop Scaring Them to Death." *Michigan Natural Resources*, July/August 1976.

———. "Don't Flunk Survival." *Michigan Natural Resources*, November/December 1974.

———. "Survival is an Attitude." *Michigan Natural Resources*, September/October 1974.

Roninger, L. E., ed. "The Castaways: An Experiment in Survival." *London Weekend Telegraph*, February 11, 1966.

Schneider, William. "Bears or Hikers." *Backpacker*, October/November 1980.

Snook, Pat. "Desperate Vacation." *National Wildlife*, 1968, 6:8–15.

———. "Prescott Kids Go Wild." *National Wildlife*, 1970, 8:4–11.

Starnes, Richard. "Think . . . and Live." *Field and Stream*, 1963, 68(6):12–15, 112, 135.

Troebst, Cord-Christian. "How to Survive . . . Anywhere." *Popular Science*, 1966, 189(2):62–65, 172, 175.

Wahl, Paul. "The Rifle That's Also a Shotgun." *Popular Science*, 1967, 191(4):138–139.

Washburn, Bradford. "Frostbite." *New England Journal of Medicine*, 266:974–989.

Wilkinson, S. "Help! Survival Kit." *Flying*, 1968, 83:45–47.

Williams, Thomas. "Outdoors." *Esquire*, 1965, 64(4):62–68.

Woodbury, Richard. "What Would You do in a Fix Like This." *Life*, 1970, 69(22):85–88.

ARCTIC SURVIVAL

BOOKS

Buckley, John L., and Wilbur L. Libby. *The Distribution in Alaska of Plant and Animal Life Available for Survival*. Arctic Aeromedical Lab, Technical Report No. 58-10, 1959.

Freeman, Thomas Nesbitt. *Manual of Arctic Survival and Useful Eskimo Words*. Canada Dept. of Agriculture, Science Service, No. ME-1, 1950.

Howard, Richard A. *An Analysis of Survival Experiences in the Arctic Areas.* Arctic, Desert, Tropic Information Center, Maxwell AFB, No. A-103, 1953.

Innes-Taylor, Alan, ed. *Arctic Survival Guide.* Scandinavian Airlines System, Stockholm, 1962.

Klaben, Helen, with Beth Day. *Hey, I'm Alive.* McGraw-Hill, 1964.

National Science Foundation. *Survival in Antarctica.* U.S. Government Printing Office, Washington, D.C., 1979.

Nelson, Richard K. *Literature Review of Eskimo Knowledge of the Sea Ice Environment.* Arctic Aeromedical Lab, USAF, AAL-TR-65-7, 1966.

Riewe, Roderick R. "A Lesson on Winter Survival From the Inuit," *Manitoba Nature,* Winter 1975.

Rogers, T. A., J. A. Setcliff, and Alan C. Buck. *Ameliorative Measures in Fasting, Subarctic Survival Situations.* Pacific Biomedical Research Center, University of Hawaii, AF pamphlet 65-10, 1965.

Royal Canadian Air Force Training School. *Down But Not Out.* R. Duhamel, Queen's Printer, 1975.

U.S. Dept. of the Air Force. *Development of an Arctic Survival Shelter.* Arctic Aeromedical Lab, AAL-TR-67-7, 1966.

U.S. Hydrographic Office. *Meteorological and Oceanographic Factors Relating to Antarctic Air-Sea Rescue Operations and Human Survival.* 1957.

Veghte, J. H., F. E. White, and R. C. Studley. *Simulated Survival Trek from Confluence of Anaktuvuk and Colville Rivers to Arctic Coast.* USAF, No. 62-15, 1963.

ARTICLES

Banks, W. J. "School for Survival." *Rotarian,* 1953, 82(1):20–21.

Crane, Leon. "I was Lost 84 Days in the Arctic." *The American Magazine,* 1944, 138(2):32–33, 96–104.

Custer, Ben Scott. "Down in the Arctic." *Collier's,* 1949, 123(5):28–36.

Elliott, Lawrence. "Ordeal on Mendenhall Glacier." *Reader's Digest,* 1963, 82(489):54–60.

———. "The Man Who Refused to Die." *Reader's Digest,* 1967, 91(547):73–80.

Howard, Richard A. "Survival in the Arctic." *Science Digest,* 1957, 42(4):56–61.

Hunt, Caspar. "A School for Survival in the Arctic." *Travel,* 1948, 91(5):18–21, 34.

Karow, Armand, M., Jr., and Watts R. Webb. "Tissue Freezing: A Theory for Injury and Survival." *Cryobiology,* 1965, 2(3):99–108.

Lansing, Alfred. "Endurance: Shackleton's Incredible Voyage." *Reader's Digest,* 1959, 74(443):238–264.

Rogers, T. A., et al. "Minimal Rations for Arctic Survival." *Aerospace Medicine,* 1968, 39:595–597.

Stover, Charles W. "I Was Marooned on an Arctic Icecap." *Collier's,* 1952, 130(24):99–108.

———. "Survival in Arctic Waters." *British Medical Journal,* 1968, 1:399–400.

DESERT SURVIVAL
BOOKS

Adolph, E. F. *Physiology of Man in the Desert.* Wiley-Interscience, 1947.

Dodge, Natt N. *Poisonous Dwellers of the Desert.* Southwestern Monuments Assoc., 8th edition, 1961.

George, Uwe. *In the Deserts of This Earth.* Harcourt Brace Jovanovich, 1977.

Howard, Richard A. *Sun, Sand, and Survival: An Analysis of Survival Experiences in Desert Areas.* Arctic, Desert, Tropic Information Center, Maxwell AFB, No. D-102, 1953.

Jaeger, Edmund C. *The North American Deserts.* Stanford University Press, 1957.

Kraus, Joe. *Alive in the Desert,* Sycamore Island Books, 1978.

Larson, Peggy. *The Deserts of the Southwest.* Sierra Club, 1977.

Pond, Alonzo. *Afoot in the Desert: A Contribution to Basic Survival.* Arctic, Desert, Tropic Information Center, Maxwell AFB, No. D-100, 1956.

———. *The Desert World.* Thomas Nelson and Sons, 1962.

Roninger, L. E., ed. *Desert Survival.* Maricopa County Civil Defense and Disaster Organization, 1967.

Story, R. *Some Plants Used by the Bushmen in Obtaining Food and Water.* Dept. of Agriculture, Division of Botany, Pretoria, 1958.

Strauss, Maurice B. *Body Water in Man: The Acquisition and Maintenance of the Body Fluids.* Little, Brown, 1957.

Trench, Charles C. *The Desert's Dusty Face.* William Morrow and Co., 1966.

U.S. Dept. of Agriculture. *Solar Still for Survival Water.* Agricultural Research Service, No. PA-187, 1965.

Wolf, A. V. *Thirst: The Physiology of the Urge to Drink and Problems of Water Lack*. Thomas, 1958.

ARTICLES

Anderson, Ken. "How to Survive in the Desert." *Popular Mechanics*. August 1971.

Billingham, J. "Snail Haemolymph—An Aid to Survival in the Desert." *Lancet*, 1961, 1:903–906.

Gibbons, Euell. "Wilderness Survival Challenge in Arizona." *Organic Gardening and Farming*, 1971, 18:121–122.

Halacy, D. S., Jr. "New Survival Technique: Get Water Anywhere." *Outdoor Life*, 1965, 136(2):14–15.

Jackson, R. D., et al. "Solar Distillation of Water from Soil and Plant Materials: A Simple Desert Survival Technique." *Science*, 1965, 149:1377–1379.

Science News Letter. "Desert Snail's Juice Can Save Stranded Men." 1960, 78(14):217.

Wylie, Evan. "Ordeal in the Desert." *Readers Digest*, 1959, 75(451):61–66.

EDIBLE AND POISONOUS PLANTS
BOOKS

Angier, Bradford. *Field Guide to Edible Wild Plants*. Stackpole Co., 1974.

———. *Free for the Eating*. Stackpole Co., 1966.

———. *Living Off the Country*. Stackpole Co., 1956.

———. *Feasting Free on Wild Edibles*. Stackpole Co., 1969.

Balls, Edward K. *Early Uses of California Plants*. University of California Press, California Natural History Guides, No. 10, 1962.

Bartelli, Ingrid. *May is Morel Month in Michigan*. Extension Bulletin E-614, Cooperative Extension Service, Michigan State University, 1966.

———. *Best of the Boletes*. Extension Bulletin E-926, Cooperative Extension Service, Michigan State University, 1976.

———. *Mushrooms Grow On Stumps*. Extension Bulletin E-924, Cooperative Extension Service, Michigan State University, 1976.

———. *Wood Waste Makes Wonderful Mushrooms*. Extension Bulletin E-925, Cooperative Extension Service, Michigan State University, 1976.

Berglund, B., and C. Bolsby. *The Edible Wild*. Scribner's, 1971.

Billington, Cecil. *Shrubs of Michigan.* Cranbrook Institute of Science, 1968.

Bock, Alan W. *Living Off the Land.* Nash Publications, 1971.

Coon, N. *Using Wayside Plants.* Hearthside, 1969.

Crowhurst, Adrienne. *The Weed Cookbook.* Lancer Books, Inc., 1972.

Dickey, Esther. *Passport to Survival—Four Foods and More to Use and Store.* Bookcraft, 1969.

Fernald, Merrit L., and Charles A. Kinsey, revised by Reed C. Rollins. *Edible Wild Plants of Eastern North America.* Harper Brothers, 1958.

Gaertner, E. *Harvest Without Planting,* Erika E. Gaertner, Publisher, 1967.

Gibbons, Euell. *Stalking the Wild Asparagus.* David McKay, Inc., 1962.

———. *Stalking the Good Life: My Love Affair with Nature.* David McKay, Inc., 1971.

Gillespie, William H. *A Compilation of Edible Wild Plants of West Virginia.* New York Scholar's Library, 1959.

Graves, Richard. *Bushcraft.* Schocken Books, 1972.

Groves, Walter, J. *Edible and Poisonous Mushrooms of Canada.* Canada Dept. of Agriculture, Pub. 1112, 1962.

Hall, Alan. *The Wild Food Trail Guide.* Holt, Rinehart and Winston, 1973.

Hardin, James W., and Jay M. Arena. *Human Poisoning from Native and Cultivated Plants.* National Recreation and Parks Association, 1974.

Harrington, H. D. *Edible Native Plants of the Rocky Mountains.* University of New Mexico Press, 1967.

Hatfield, Audrey Wynne. *Pleasures of Wild Plants.* Tapplinger Publishing Co., 1966.

Hedrick, U. P., ed. *Sturtevant's Notes on Edible Plants.* New York State Dept. of Agriculture, 27th Annual Report, Vol. 2, Part 11, 1919.

Heizer, R. F., and M. A. Whipple. *The California Indians.* University of California Press, 1951.

Hutchinson, Raymond C. *Food for Survival After a Disaster.* Melbourne University Press, 1959.

Jaegar, Ellsworth. *Wildwood Wisdom.* Macmillan, 1961.

Johnson, Ralph. *Anyone Can Live Off the Land.* David McKay, Inc., 1961.

Keeler, Harriet. *Our Northern Shrubs and How to Identify Them.* Dover Publications, 1969.

Kingsbury, John M. *Poisonous Plants of the United States and Canada.* Prentice-Hall, 1964.

Kroeber, A. L. *Handbook of the Indians of California*. Bureau of American Ethnology, Smithsonian Institution, 1925.

Life-Support Technology, Inc. *Foods in the Wilderness*. 1963.

Medsger, Oliver Perry. *Edible Wild Plants*. Macmillan, 1939 (12th printing 1962).

Morton, Julia F. *Wild Plants for Survival in South Florida*. Hurricane House, 1962.

Office of the Quartermaster General. *Conference on Survival and Emergency Rations*. Quartermaster Food and Container Institute for the Armed Forces, 1947.

Otis, Charles H. *Michigan Trees*. University of Michigan Press, 1968.

Peterson, Lee. *Field Guide to Edible Wild Plants*, Peterson Field Guide Series, Houghton Mifflin, 1977.

Portola Institute and Random House. *The Last Whole Earth Catalog: Access to Tools*. 1971.

Sargent, Frederick, et al. *The Physiological Basis for Various Constituents in Survival Rations*. Air Research and Development Command, Wright-Patterson AFB, 1954.

Smith, A. H. *The Mushroom Hunter's Field Guide*. University of Michigan Press, 1963.

Smith, Helen V. *Michigan Wildflowers*. Cranbrook Institute of Science, 1966.

Sweet, Muriel. *Common Edible and Useful Plants of the West*. Naturegraph Co., 1962.

Szcawinski, Adam F., and George Hardy. *Guide to Common Edible Plants of British Columbia*. British Columbia Provincial Museum, Dept. of Recreation and Conservation, Handbook No. 20, 1967.

U.S. Dept. of Agriculture. *Family Food Stockpile for Survival*. Office of Civil and Defense Mobilization, Home and Garden Bulletin, No. 77, 1969.

U.S. Dept. of the Air Force. *Survival Manual*. AFM 64-3, 1961.

U.S. Naval Institute. *How to Survive on Land and Sea*. 2nd edition, 1965.

Verill, A. H. *Foods America Gave the World*. L. C. Page and Co., 1937.

Wiener, Michael A. *Earth Medicine—Earth Foods, Plant Remedies, Drugs, and Natural Foods of the North American Indians*. Collier Books, 1972.

ARTICLES

Alston, Elizabeth. "Eating Off the Land—Salad That's Free for the Picking." *Look*, 1969, 33(22):64–65.

Browe, J. H. "Nutritional Quality of Survival Biscuits and Crackers." *American Journal of Clinical Nutrition*, 1964, 14:180.

Colby, C. B. "Living Off the Land." *Outdoor Life*, 1961, 127:124–126.

Gibbons, Euell. "Wilderness Survival." *Organic Gardening and Farming*, 1968, 15(10):64–68.

————. "Camping the Wild Way." *National Wildlife*, 1969, 7(3):35–38.

————. "Playing Indian." *Organic Gardening and Farming*, 1969, 16:88–91.

Howard, Richard A. "What Men Will Eat to Keep Alive." *Science Digest*, 1957, 41(4):109–116.

Johnson, R. E. "Water and Osmotic Economy on Survival Rations." *Journal of the American Dietetic Association*, 1964, 45:124–129.

Morrow, R. C. "Food for Survival." *Canadian Journal of Public Health*, 1963, 54:426–430.

Science News Letter. "All-Purpose Survival Ration for Air Force." 1956, 70(15):231.

Mother Earth News, see issues of The Underground Press Syndicate, 1970.

EXPERIENCES

BOOKS

Bickel, Lennard. *Mawson's Will*. Avon, 1977.

Byrd, Richard E. *Alone*. Putnam, 1938.

Elder, Lauren, with Shirley Streshinsky. *And I Alone Survived*. E. P. Dutton, 1978.

Lansing, Alfred. *Endurance*. Avon, 1960.

Read, Piers Paul. *Alive: The Story of The Andes Survivors*. Lippincott, 1974.

Robertson, Douglas. *Survive the Savage Sea*, Bantam Books, 1974.

Stewart, George R. *Ordeal by Hunger: The Classic Story of the Donner Party*. Pocket Books, 1971.

Todd, A. L. *Abandoned*. McGraw-Hill, 1961.

Troebst, Cord Christian. *The Art of Survival*. Doubleday, 1965.

Whittaker, Lt. James C. *We Thought We Heard the Angels Sing*, Pocket Books, 1970.

ARTICLES

Beauregard, Guy. "Ordeal by Death." *Outdoor Life,* 1968, 142(1):28–31, 84–86.

Doucette, Earle. "Terror in the Woods." *Coronet,* 1950, 29(1):134–137.

Fredrickson, Olive. "Nightmare Spring." *Outdoor Life,* July 1969.

Garde, Warren. "Lost in Icy Hell." *Outdoor Life,* 1971, 147(2):54–55.

Gibson, Walter. "Death in the Lifeboat." *Readers Digest,* 1950, 56(6):1–6.

Klaben, Helen, as told to Dora Jane Hamblin and Wilbur Jarvis. "Girl Behind the Frozen Scream." *Life,* 1963, 54(4):68B–73ff.

McCarty, Owen. "Dead Men's Diary." *Saturday Evening Post,* 1947, 219(5):15–17.

Moon, Dale. "Ordeal on Mt. Hood." *National Wildlife,* June/July 1971.

Mulling, Robert J., as told to Ben East, "Lost for Forty Days." *Outdoor Life,* 1954, 113(5):36–37.

Neary, John. "The Lost Men of Muldoon Canyon." *Life,* March 19, 1971.

Ridgeway, John. "We Rowed Across the North Atlantic." *Saturday Evening Post,* November 5, 1966.

Stenmark, E. "Eight Days Buried in an Avalanche." *Readers Digest,* 70:80–84.

Tiira, Ensio. "Raft of Despair." *Coronet,* 1955, 38(9):151–170.

Wylie, E. "Ordeal in the Desert." *Readers Digest,* 1959, 75(11):61–66.

MEDICAL ASPECTS OF SURVIVAL

BOOKS

Arnold, Robert E., M. D. *What to Do About Bites and Stings of Venomous Animals.* Collier Books, New York, 1973.

Benjamin, Bry, and Annette Francis Benjamin. *In Case of Emergency: What to Do Until the Doctor Arrives.* Doubleday and Co., 1965.

Carleson, L. D. *Maintaining Thermal Balance in Man.* University of Kentucky Press, 1963.

Clarke, C., M. Ward, and E. Williams, eds. *Mountain Medicine and Physiology.* London: The Alpine Club, 1975.

Edholm, O. G., and A. L. Bacharach. *Exploration Medicine.* John Wright and Sons, Ltd., 1965.

———. *The Physiology of Human Survival.* Academic Press, 1965.

Hackett, Peter, M. D. *Mountain Sickness—Prevention, Recognition and Treatment.* Mountain Travel, 1978.

Harnett, R. M., F. R. Sias, and S. R. Pruitt. *Resuscitation from Hypothermia. A Literature Review.* Clemson University, 1979. (Available as Coast Guard Report –CG-D-26-79.)

Hubbard, Ron. *Science of Survival—Predictions of Human Behavior.* American Saint Hill Organization, 1951.

Kodet, E. Russell, M. D., and Bradford Angier. Being Your Own Wilderness Doctor. Stackpole Co., 1968.

Lathrop, Theodore G., M. D. *Hypothermia, Killer of the Unprepared.* The Mazamas, 1970.

MacQueen, James. *Further Problems in Individual and Group Survival.* University of California at Los Angeles, U.S. Office of Technical Services, 1962.

Nemiroff, M. S., G. R. Salts, and J. G. Weg. *Survival of Cold Water Near Drowning; Protective Effect of Diving Reflex.* American Thoracia Society, Annual Meeting, San Francisco, May 17, 1977.

Resnik, H. L. P., and Harvey L. Ruben, eds. *Emergency Psychiatric Care: The Management of Mental Health Crisis.* Charles Press Publishing, 1975.

Russell, F. E. *Snake Venom Poisoning.* J. B. Lippincott Co., 1980.

Torrance, Ellis Paul. *Psychological Aspects of Survival—A Study of Survival Behavior.* Human Factors Operations Labs, Air Research and Development Command, Bolling AFB, 1954. Supplement: *Teaching the Psychological Aspects of Survival,* 1954.

U.S. Dept. of Transportation. *Cold Water Drowning—A New Lease on Life.* Pamphlet CG-513, USCG Headquarters, Washington, D.C., 1978.

Ward, Michael, M. D. "Frostbite," *Mountain Medicine and Physiology.* R. & C. Moore and Company, 1970.

Washburn, B. *Frostbite.* Boston Museum of Science, 1975.

Wilkerson, J. A., M. D. *Medicine for Mountaineering,* 2d ed. The Mountaineers, 1973.

Winter First Aid Manual. National Ski Patrol System, Inc., 2901 Sheridan Boulevard, Denver, Colorado, 1974.

ARTICLES

Ahern, T. R., et al. "Reactions of Large Groups Experimentally Confined in an Austere Environment." *Perceptual and Motor Skills,* 1969, 29:611–620.

Andrew, P. J. "Treating Accidental Hypothermia." *British Medical Journal,* December 9, 1978.

Athanasiou, Robert. "Keeping Your Eyes on the Trail." *Backpacker,* October/November 1981.

Bangs, Cameron, M. D. "Do's and Dont's of Immediate Treatment." *RN,* November 1979.

Baughman, Diane, R. N. "The Frozen Patient: Handle With Care." *RN,* November 1979.

Cahill, G. F., Jr., et al. "Starvation and Survival." *Transactions of the American Clinical and Climatological Association,* 1968, 79:13–20.

Chinard, F. P. "Accidental Hypothermia—A Brief Review,." *Journal of the Medical Society of New Jersey,* 1978, 75(9):610–614.

Clifford, E., et al. "Self-Concepts Before and After Survival Training." *British Journal of Social and Clinical Psychology,* 1967, 6:241–248.

Drummond, A. H., Jr. "Hypothermia—The Chill That Kills." *Motor Boating & Sailing,* February 1977.

Fitzgerald, F. T., et al. "Accidental Hypothermia: A Report of 22 Cases and Review of the Literature." *International Medicine,* 1982, 27:128–150.

Gallagher, J. Q. "Survival—Physiologic and Psychologic Aspects." *Rocky Mountain Medical Journal,* 1969, 66:23–26.

Glass, Thomas G., Jr., M. D. "Early Debridement in Pit Viper Bites." *Journal of the American Medical Association,* 1976, 235(23):2513–2516.

Gunderson, E. K. Eric. "Emotional Health in Extreme and Normal Environments." *Proceedings of the International Congress on Occupational Health,* 1966:631–634. (Available as Navy Medical Neuropsychiatric Research Unit, San Diego, Report No. 66-23.)

Hammers, J. A., et al. "Environmentally Confined Groups on Semi-Starvation Diets." *Psychological Reports,* 1965, 16:1291–1292.

Hampton, W. R. "Hypothermia in Winter and High Altitude Sports." *Connecticut Medicine,* 1981, 45(10):633–636.

Hayward, John S., John D. Eckerson, and Martin L. Collis. "Effect of Behavioral Variables on Cooling Rate of Man in Cold Water." *Journal of Applied Physiology,* 1975, 38(6):1073–1077.

Houston, C., M. D. "Altitude Illness—1976 Version." *American Alpine Journal,* 1976, 20(2).

Hunt, Glenn R., M. D. "Bites and Stings of Uncommon Arthropods. 1.Spiders." *Post Graduate Medicine,* 1981, 70(2):91–102.

———. "Bites and Stings of Uncommon Arthropods. 2. Reduviids, Fire Ants,

Puss Caterpillars, and Scorpions." *Post Graduate Medicine*, 1981, 70(2)107–114.

Lloyd, E. L. "Treatment of Accidental Hypothermia." *British Medical Journal*, 1(6160):413–414.

Marcus, P. "Laboratory Comparison of Techniques for Rewarming Hypothermia Casualties." *Aviation, Space, and Environmental Medicine*, 1978, 49(5):592–597.

Martyn, J. W., "Diagnosing and Treating Hypothermia." *Canadian Medical Association Journal*, 1981, 125(10):1089–1096.

"Medical Aspects of Mountain Climbing." *The Physician and Sportsmedicine*, March 1977.

Milner, John E. "Hypothermia." *Annals of Internal Medicine*, 1978, 89(4).

Monkerud, Donald. "Beware of Mountain Sickness." *Nordic World*, 1978, 6(1).

Mountain Medicine Symposium. "Summary of Treatment of the Cold Injured Patient." Seattle, 1976.

Mountain Medicine Symposium. Proceedings. The Yosemite Institute, 1976.

Neel, S. "Military Survival Medicine." *Military Medicine*, 127:579–582, 737–790, 827–832.

Nemiroff, M. "Cold Water Near-Drowning." *Journal of Physical Education and Recreation*, 1979, 50(8):76–77.

Nemiroff, M. S., G. R. Salts, and J. G. Weg. "Reprieve from Drowning." *Scientific American Magazine*, August 1977.

Noto, James V. "Psychological First Aid." *Emergency*, 1978, 10(11):63–65.

Nutrition Reviews. "The Influence of Body Composition on Survival Under Stress." 1960, 18:125–126.

Popefe, et al. "Some Psychiatric Aspects of an Arctic Survival Experiment." *Journal of Nervous and Mental Disease*, 1968, 146:433–445.

Russell, Findlay E., M. D., Richard W. Carlson, M. D. Ph.D., Jack Wainschel, M. D., and Arthur H. Osborne, M. D. "Snake Venom Poisoning in the United States." *Journal of the American Medical Association*, July 28, 1975, 233(4): 341–344.

Simon, Toby L. M. D., and Thomas G. Grace, M. D. "Envenomation Coagulopathy in Wounds From Pit Vipers." *The New England Journal of Medicine*, 1981, 305(8):443–447.

Smutek, Ray, ed. *Mountain Medicine 1. Off Belay* Reprint Series, Renton, Washington, *Off Belay* magazine, 1979.

Stewart, J. Clayton. "Growing Weak by Degrees." *Sports Illustrated*, March 10, 1975.

Sumner, David. "The Snakebite Controversy." *Backpacker*, June/July 1979.

Turner, Edward T. "How to Treat Snakebites." *Parks & Recreation*, April 1979.

Watt, Charles H., Jr., M. D. "Poisonous Snakebite Treatment in the United States." *Journal of the American Medical Association*, 1978, 240(7):654–656.

MOUNTAIN AND COLD WEATHER SURVIVAL
BOOKS

Auliciems, Andris, Christopher R. De Freitas, and F. Kenneth Hare. Winter *Clothing Requirements for Canada*, Climatological Studies No. 22, Environment Canada, Information Canada, Ottawa, 1973.

Bridge, R. *The Complete Snow Camper's Guide*. Scribner's, 1973.

Coffey, M. F. *Aids to Working in the Cold*. Defence Research Board, Dept. of National Defense, Canada, Information Canada, Ottawa, 1975.

Edholm, O. G., and A. C. Bacharach. *Exposure*. British Mountaineering Council, No. 380, 1964.

Goode, Merlin. *Winter Outdoor Living*. Brighton Publishing Co., 1978.

London, Jack. *Short Stories*. Funk and Wagnalls, 1968.

Martinelli, M., Jr. *Snow Avalanche Sites*. Agriculture Information Bulletin 360, U.S. Government Printing Office, Washington, D.C., 1974.

McLaren, F. Douglas, et al. *Mountain Search and Rescue Operations*. Grand Teton Natural History Association, 1969.

Merryman, H. T. *Mountain Rescue*. Air Ministry, 1953.

Montana State University. *Winter Survival*. Cooperative Extension Service, 1970.

Palmer, E. Laurence. *Survival in Winter*. Cooperative Extension Service, Cornell University, 1952.

Perla, Ronald I., and M. Martinelli, Jr. *Avalanche Handbook*. U.S. Department of Agriculture, Forest Service, Agriculture Handbook 489, July 1976.

Roninger, L. E., ed. *Mountain Operations*. U.S. Dept. of the Army, FM 31–72, 1964.

Royal Canadian Air Force Training School. *Down But Not Out*. R. Duhamel, Queen's Printer, 1975.

Rutstrum, Calvin. *Paradise Below Zero.* Macmillan, 1968.

U.S. Dept. of the Army. *Basic Cold Weather Manual.* FM 31–70, 1968.

———. *Cold Weather Clothing and Sleeping Equipment.* TM 10–275, 1964.

ARTICLES

Blodget, R. "Survival in the North." *Flying,* 1967, 80:40–41.

Bryant, Mark. "Piles of Winter Warmth." *Backpacker,* October/November 1981.

Carlisle, Norman. "The Man Who Wouldn't Die." *Coronet,* 1952, 32(4):148–154.

Davis, Bruce. "Our Days of Horror." *Saturday Evening Post,* 1958, 231(2):40–41, 125–128.

Fisher, Robert, and Ben East. "I Made My Death Bed." *Outdoor Life,* 1965, 135(4):60–61, 161–169.

Grieve, R. R. "Polyethylene Bags in Mountain Rescue Operations." *Practitioner,* 1969, 203:203–205.

Haddon, E. P. "Clues and Clothing for Snow Survival." *Popular Mechanics,* 1969, 132(5):104–107, 211.

Hamblin, Dora Jane, and Wilbur Jarvis. "Girl Behind a Frozen Scream." *Life,* 1963, 54(15):68B–79.

Hansen, John V. E. "Clothing for Cold Climes." *Natural History,* 1981, 90(6):90–92.

Jensen, Clyde E. "Don't Panic." *Field and Stream,* 1963, 68(6):30–32, 93–97.

Kirkman, N. F. "Mountain Accidents and Mountain Rescue in Great Britain." *British Medical Journal,* 1966, 1:162–164.

Kowalski, J. M. "Cold Weather Survival." *Illinois Medical Journal,* 1962, 121:46.

Littell, Robert. "Eight Days Buried in an Avalanche." *Reader's Digest,* 1957, 70(420):80–84.

Martin, Harold. "Please Hurry, Someone." *Saturday Evening Post,* 1968, 241(1):30–39.

Neary, John. "The Lost Men of Muldoon Canyon." *Life,* 1971, 70(10):50D–61.

Nelson, Morlan W. "Cold-Weather Survival." *Popular Science,* November 1971.

Petalan, Jack. "How to Live With Cold." *Alaska,* October 1970.

Phillips, James G. "Hot Tips for Cold Days." *Sports Illustrated*, January 26, 1970.

Phillips, Joseph. "The Woman Who Wouldn't Give Up." *Reader's Digest*, 1958, 72(431):27–31.

Popular Science. "How to Survive a Blizzard Using Your Car and Your Head." 182(2):182.

Richardson, D. K. "Cold is a Killer." *Nursing Times*, 1970, 66:1234–1236.

Riewe, Rick. "Winter Camping—A Viable Alternative." *Manitoba Nature*, Winter 1974.

Robinson, Douglas. "Polyproliferation." *Backpacker*, October/November 1981.

Rosbert, C. J. "Only God Knew the Way." *Saturday Evening Post*, 1944, 216(33):12–13, 73–77.

Sherin, Ray. "Cold as Death." *Outdoor Life*, 1955, 116(4):56–57, 122–126.

Smutek, Ray. "Portrait of an Avalanche Survivor." *Off Belay*, 1977, 36(12):8–12.

Tabor, James. "Layering: The Inside Story." *Backpacker*, August/September 1981.

Tucker, Gerald J. "13 Days in a Blizzard." *Outdoor Life*, 1964, 133(1):20–23, 104–107.

Washburn, Bradford. "Frostbite." *New England Journal of Medicine*, 266:974–989.

Whiteside, Thomas. "The Couple Who Wouldn't Die." *Saturday Evening Post*, 1963, 236(24):56–65.

Williams, Knox. "Portrait of an Avalanche Victim." *Off Belay*, 1977, 36(12):5–7.

SEA SURVIVAL
BOOKS

Bombard, Alain (translated by Brian Connell). *The Bombard Story*. A. Deutsch, 1953.

Carse, Robert. *The Castaways—A Narrative History of Some Survivors from the Dangers of the Sea*. Rand McNally, 1966.

Cooke, Kenneth. *What Cares the Sea?* McGraw-Hill, 1960.

Engle, Eloise Katherine. *Escape from the Air and from the Sea*. Day, 1963.

Gibson, Walter. *The Boat*. Houghton-Mifflin, 1953.

Gilbert, Perry W., ed. *Sharks and Survival*. D. C. Heath and Co., 1963.

Halstead, Bruce. *Dangerous Marine Animals.* Cornell Maritime, 1959.

Heyerdahl, Thor. *Kon-Tiki: Across the Pacific by Raft.* Rand McNally, 1950.

Howard, Richard A. *999 Survived—An Analysis of Survival Experiences in the Southwest Pacific.* Arctic, Desert, Tropic Information Center, Maxwell AFB, No. T-100, 1953.

Lee, Eric, and Kenneth Lee. *Safety and Survival at Sea.* Norton, 1971.

Llano, George Albert. *Airmen Against the Sea—An Analysis of Sea Survival Experiences.* Arctic, Desert, Tropic Information Center, Maxwell AFB, No. G-104, 1955.

Nicholl, George W. R. *Survival at Sea: The Development, Operation, and Design of Inflatable Marine Lifesaving Equipment.* J. de Graff, 1960.

Noyce, Wilfrid. *They Survived—A Study of the Will to Live.* Dutton, 1963.

Richards, Phillip, and John J. Banigan. *How to Abandon Ship.* Cornell Maritime, 1943.

Robertson, Dougal. *Sea Survival: A Manual.* Praeger, 1975.

Russell, Findlay E., M.D. *Poisonous Marine Animals,* Academic Press, 1965.

Seasholes, Henry Craig. *Adrift in the South Pacific, or Six Nights in the Coral Sea.* W. H. Baker Co., 1950.

Survival in Antarctica. National Science Foundation, U.S. Government Printing Office, Washington, D.C., 1979.

Tiira, Ensio. *Raft of Despair.* Hutchinson, 1954.

U.S. Coast Guard. *Aircraft Emergency Procedures Over Water.* USGPO, 1956.

U.S. Dept. of the Air Force. *North Pacific Survival Manual.* Arctic, Desert, Tropic Information Center, Maxwell AFB, No. A-101, 1950.

———. *Pilot Rescue Facts: You Can Save Pilot.* Aviation Training Division. No. 408-B-1, 1962.

———. *Edible and Hazardous Marine Life.* Information Bulletin No. 13, Air Training Command, 3636th Combat Crew Training Wing, Environmental Information Division, Maxwell Air Force Base, Alabama, 1976.

———. *Toxic Fish and Mollusks.* Information Bulletin No. 12, Air Training Command, 3636th Combat Crew Training Wing, Environmental Information Division, Maxwell Air Force Base, Alabama, 1975.

Wade, Wyn Craig. *The Titanic: End of a Dream.* Rawson, Wade, 1979.

ARTICLES

Air-Sea Rescue Bulletin, see issues of June 1944–October 1946, Washington.

Air-Sea Safety, see issues of November 1946–April 1947, Washington Search and Rescue Publishing Corp.

Alexander, Holmes. "Fishers of Men." *Saturday Evening Post,* 1945, 217(29):34, 46–51.

Allen, William H. "Thirst." *Natural History,* 1956, 65(10):513–518, 555–556.

Bails, E. K. "Dangers of Drinking Sea Water." *World Health Organization Chronicle,* 1962, 16:343.

British Medical Journal. "Survival in Cold Water." 1969, 1:459.

Brown, Kevin. "How to Survive at Sea." *Popular Mechanics,* 1963, 120(5):112–117, 206–212.

Hall, J. F., et al. "Thermal Protection in Life Raft Exposures." *Aerospace Medicine,* 1969, 40:31–35.

Harby, Samuel F. "They Survived at Sea." *National Geographic,* 1945, 87(5):617–640.

Heyn, Alan. "One Who Survived: The Narrative of Alan Heyn." *American Heritage,* 1956, 7(4):64–73.

Kieran, John. "Lost . . . and Found." *Collier's,* 1943, 112(26):18–19, 43.

Kierst, W., et al. "Investigations on Survival Rations for Castaways After Shipwreck." *Bulletin of the Institute of Marine Medicine in Gdansk,* 1966, 17:425–432.

Life. "On a Raft with Only Food from the Sea." 1953, 34(20):115–122.

Lindemann, Hannes. "Alone at Sea for 72 Days." *Life,* 1957, 43(4):92–108.

Llano, George A. "Survival from Sharks." *Science Digest,* 1957, 41(1):7–11.

Locke, Esther. "Night of Terror." *The American Magazine,* 1955, 160(1):22–23, 94–97.

Maude, H. E. "Beachcombers and Castaways." *Polynesian Social Journal,* 1964, 73:287–293.

McFadden, E. B., et al. "Development of a Tritium Self-Luminous Life Raft Light Source." *Aerospace Medicine,* 1965, 36:548–551.

Pittman, J. C., et al. "Physiologic Evaluation of Sea Survival Equipment." *Aerospace Medicine,* 1969, 40:378–381.

Ridgeway, John. "We Rowed Across the North Atlantic." *Saturday Evening Post,* November 5, 1966.

Rogers, E. L. "A Saga of Survival." *Field and Stream,* 1969, 74(2):78–79, 118–121.

Schwartz, Robert L. "The Terrible End of the U.S.S. Juneau." *Saturday Evening Post,* 1950, 222(35):22–23, 47–64.

Science News Letter. "Shiver to Keep Warm." 1957, 71(25):386.

Sierks, Ted. "Don't Give Up, You Weakling." *Life,* 1951, 31(6):59–62.

Tiira, Ensio. "Raft of Despair." *Coronet,* 1955, 38(5):151–170.

Whipple, A. B. C. "Three-Month Ordeal in Open Boats." *Life,* 1952, 33(19):144–156.

TROPICAL AND JUNGLE SURVIVAL
BOOKS

Aubert de la Rue, Edgar, Francois Bourliere, and Jean-Paul Harroy. *The Tropics.* Harrap, 1957.

Balls, Edward K. *British Jungle Survival.* Air Ministry, Pub. 214.

Calverly, Eleanor T. *How to be Healthy in Hot Climates.* Thomas Y. Crowell Co., 1953.

Hildreth, Brian. *How to Survive in the Bush, on the Coast, in the Mountains of New Zealand.* Government Printing, 1970.

U.S. Dept. of the Air Force. *Living Off the American Tropics.* Arctic, Desert, Tropic Information Center, Maxwell AFB, Informational Bulletin No. 10, AFM 64-10, 1944.

ARTICLES

Crimmin, Eileen. "What to do in a Hurricane." *Science Digest,* 1966, 60(2):80–82.

Emory, Kenneth. "Every Man His Own Robinson Crusoe." *Natural History,* 1943, 52(5):8–15.

Gannon, Robert. "I Survived a Jungle Survival Test—Could You?" *Popular Science,* 1965, 187(2):62–65, 182.

Jenkins, Will F. "Survival." *Collier's,* 1940, 105(19):13, 39–42.

Life. "How to Survive in the Southwest Pacific." 1944, 17(19):74–76.

Maxwell, M. S. "Survival in the Tropics." *Flying Safety,* 1953, 9(6):2–8.

McKulla, Lawrence R. "32 Coconuts." *Saturday Evening Post,* 1943, 216(1):19, 74.

Popular Mechanics. "They Bring Themselves Back Alive." 1944, 81(4):56–61, 152–154.

———. "How to Beat the Jungle." 1945, 84(3):56–57.

Robb, Inez. "A WAC in Shrangri-La." *Reader's Digest,* 1945, 47(283):1–13.

INDEX

Pages in *italics* indicate illustrations.

334

338